Pornography and Difference

Pornography *and* Difference

Berkeley Kaite

Indiana
University
Press

BLOOMINGTON AND INDIANAPOLIS

The paper used in this publication meets the minimum require-
ments of American National Standard for Information Sciences—
Permanence of Paper for Printed Library Materials, ANSI
Z39.48-1984.

Manufactured in the United States of America

Library of Congress Cataloging-in-Publication Data

Kaite, Berkeley.
    Pornography and difference / Berkeley Kaite.
        p.   cm.
    Includes bibliographical references and index.
    ISBN 0-253-32907-8 (cloth : alk. paper).—ISBN 0-253-20979-X
(pbk. : alk. paper)
        1. Pornography—Psychological aspects. 2. Photography, Erotic—
Psychological aspects. 3. Sex differences (Psychology) 4. Sexual
fantasies. I. Title.
HQ471.K35   1995
363.4'7—dc20   94-49090

1 2 3 4 5   00 99 98 97 96 95

Contents

Introduction

WHAT FOLLOWS IS a translation of the contemporary pornographic photograph. The photographs I looked at, lived with, and dreamt about are found in mainstream, commercially popular soft-core magazines, and in several hard-core titles, most of them available in sex boutiques. I argue that the pornographic moment involves the deployment of the sexual fantasization of desire, which is disrespectful of the "sexual fix," the obsessive will-to-display of culture's sexually repressed material, and the symbolic codification of sexual difference.[1] By this is meant that pornography is indeed a radical play on difference and "otherness," to the extent, however, that normative boundaries of masculinity and femininity are transgressed rather than reinforced. Sexual difference, far from, in this case, the apparently visible and immediately knowable instance which rises and falls on representations of the essential body (and/or its discursive effects), is actually a textual fix. The pornographic engages in the systematic transgression of codes of sexual difference so that sexual difference is a strategic deployment of signs and subject to renegotiation(s). D. N. Rodowick notes how a preoccupation with certain images and narratives is a return to sites of reassurance and an indication that identities, cultural and psychic, are characterized by slippage.[2] Hence one reason for the obsessive and repetitive fascination with pornographic tedium.

Pornographic significance lies in the way it flouts respected categories of difference so that textual bodies "speak" the language of the other. This involves an erotic consort which privileges not the phallus but a language, an exchange, whose elements are borrowed from both the masculine and the feminine in the service of simulated androgyny. This is part of the logic of seduction.

Although pornography is charged with revealing all, with a vulgarity of exposure, I argue, with Jacques Chevalier, that just as the ascetic discourses of denial, renunciation, and servitude are laced with erotic significance,[3] the illicit visual images charged with excessive display are, in a contradictory move, given to their own sacrificial logic. The phallus, I will argue, is subsumed under the maneuvers of the "cut," the vulnerability of difference.

The inquiry into this seductive moment is synchronic in that it suspends the photograph in an analytic space and descends into it. The analysis proceeds through a consideration of the relationship among the elements in the visual narrative. These recurring elements, the conventional symbolic gestures and fetish nominations (and the absence of others), are isolated to investigate their systematic deployment under the sign of "the pornographic." The book is thus divided into two parts, "The Body" and "The Fetish," each with two chapters devoted to the dominant features which appear under those rubrics, i.e., the choreographies of the genitals and the eyes/the looks, and the fetish nominations of the shoe and of jewelry and lingerie.

Implicit in this kind of inquiry, a close reading of the photograph, is attention to the relationship between text and spectator. The photograph's formal rhetorical structure is in consort with its readers, especially in these illicit moments. Certain features—objects, discursive strategies, fetishized exchanges—occur and recur with a vengeance and have a textual effect, replete with repressed associations and displaced and condensed mechanisms. We may say that the pornographic photograph is a "published dream."[4] The illusion of a private "phantasmatic" (the secret, privileged view at the keyhole) is contradicted by acknowledgment of the mass circulation and popularity of various pornographic genres. The first word in the phrase "published dream" is what locates the text as artifact: it is a dream for specific publics, or which specific publics are having. Secondly, it has the structure of a dream sequence. It is a dream which appears, like myths, symbols, rituals, and other artifacts, to be an anonymous utterance (but is symbolically stratified). Its privileging of certain objects and structured exchanges circulate with a tenacity and suggest a historical significance as well as the convergence of meaningful investments in and around certain sites.

To say that the pornographic photograph is a published dream is to suggest a number of things. A dream is a production of seemingly incoherent features. Frequently resistant to narrative closure, it is a particularly dense articulation of often disconnected visual and verbal images, characters whose identities shift, signifiers whose meanings are repressed both in the dream and for the dreamer. Furthermore, through dream analysis the dream as a finished product is dismantled to render itself as rather unfinished, or as a narrative whose meanings are deferred. Various aspects of the dream are disassembled to allow for particular elaborations and linguistic associations which in the telling, or the writing, are much longer than the dream itself. As various layers are scrutinized, things are often not as they first appear, or are the inverse of what they appear; surface "realities" give way to a reservoir of associations and anecdotes which are read from within the text of the dream and are also interpreted to have significance outside it.

The analytic assumption is that there is no obvious transparency of meaning or constellate of meanings in pursuit of a supertext. Each incident, detail, datum, etc., might work against another, and a small, seemingly unpowerful element will dominate and signify beyond a surface description of the dream. These are the "condensations" and "displacements" that circulate in the production and subsequent consumption or reading of a dream.[5] Freud underscores this point: "Dreams are brief, meagre and laconic in comparison with the range and wealth of the dream-thoughts. If a dream is written out it may perhaps fill half a page. The analysis setting out the dream-thoughts underlying it may occupy six, eight or a dozen times as much space."[6]

The observation that female porn models are almost never completely naked refers to the workings of condensation: the interaction of nudity with a fixed repertoire of fetish objects assumes the fusion "into a single action [of] all events of interest which occur simultaneously."[7] Both the accouterments (shoes, lingerie, etc.) and the biological credentials of the model, and more pointedly their relationship to each other—the contexts in which they signify—are the repository of cultural, sexual, linguistic, and psychic significance. "Compression" and "rapprochement force" ("enforced convergence"), also used by Freud, further suggest a schema for entry into the corpus of the dream. The analytic separation of dream content and dream thoughts (along with a discussion of what is "absent" from the dream) also allows for its symptomatic reading, a nuanced treatment of aspects of the dream-text as symptoms of a (perhaps no less coherent) larger structure. In the analyses of the pornographic conventions which constitute the following chapters, visual representations and their linguistic associations are treated as the symptomatic elaboration of unspoken wishes and fears.

"Displacement" is equally tricky. It refers to distortions in dream content which channel psychic intensity into (often) censored wishes, so that the resulting representation appears diffuse, contradictory, or distorted. For example, meanings converge on the high-heel shoe to claim sexiness, fragility, and sometimes the phallic power of the sexual libertine or the prostitute. Within the pornographic genres, the high-heel shoe has special significance. One must ask why the semi-naked (or rather partially invested) female model almost never has a bare foot and instead brandishes the stiletto heel. What are the deferred and rather free-floating signifieds which attach to the shoe and its protuberance in this pornographic moment? Under the familiar rubric of "phallic symbol," the spike-heel shoe as "sign" is exchanged, in devious and transgressive ways, for manifest and concealed signification, so that the fragile and unmistakably culturally feminine heel is at the same time endowed with phallic significance: difference unbound.

I am concerned to locate the tensions and negotiations around the production of pornographic meaning, seduction, and difference in this spectator-text relationship. I treat the sexual story in the pornographic machine as a dream whose narrative elements take us beyond the biological nominations of sexual difference, beyond, as well, the fixed, steady, binary assignments of identity emerging from vocabularies (body, language, clothing) coded as masculine or feminine. That is, the pornographic text is implicitly concerned with the discursive play or performance of subjectivities within an illicit cultural technology. It is composed with a specific public in mind/body: in this case the gendered (as masculine) subject. Who is he? With regard to an artifact which nominates discourses on sexuality, the issue of the production and reproduction of gendered identity (or identities) is of central importance.

Emergent, and by now to a degree clichéd, literatures which problematize subjectivity suggest that the "ideal" sexed subject is in fact a fiction, an unstable one at that, and voyeurism and narcissism often overlap.[8] While the phrase "decentered subjectivity," because of its promiscuous use, risks losing specific applications,[9] one can (and must) isolate the contradictions, the slips of the code, the cracks *in* the code, so that cultural texts may be rewritten, imagined "otherwise," and subverted. Although Freud himself noted that the radical separation of subjects and objects is an impossibility, i.e., that voyeurism and exhibitionism, sadism and masochism, for example, are not flip sides in a linear equation but frequently form an admixture, often critics in the mainstream want to insist on the binary formula "men look and women appear."[10] My reading of what constitutes a logic of seduction is offered as a subversive, rather than oppositional, dialogue with the pornographic text and is influenced by assumptions of instabilities in subject, text, meaning. It also takes up an interest articulated by Laura Mulvey in her famous article from 1975, although not the one for which she is most well known. Mulvey makes the point that "alternative" readings of any symbolic cultural product must still rely on the linguistic apparatus of which it is a part: "The problem [is] how to fight the unconscious structured like a language (formed critically at the moment of arrival of language) while still caught within the language of the patriarchy."[11] Her suggestion, however, is to embark upon the "destruction of pleasure as a radical weapon" through examining the cultural artifact (itself a product of the phallocentric economy) "with the tools it provides." I take this to mean that the subversive option is to dismantle the symbolic imagery on its own terms, from within its own language. This is a turn of the more recent adage of "dismantling the master's house with the master's tools."[12]

Throughout this book I try to maintain a commitment to a linguistic deconstructive technique. Which is to say the following: The task at hand, as with all encounters with the visual image, is to render the picture in literal terms. So, for example, in the chapter containing an analysis and discussion of the shoe as fetish object, particularly its recurrence in contemporary pornographic symbology, I accept the ideological assignment of the shoe with cultural femininity. But I also ask, "What is a heel?" This is done as a strategy to agitate the categories of sexual difference, to indicate, in the words of Marjorie Garber, "category confusion,"[13] and to promote it, to refuse the fixity of connotation and to refuse textual closure, to prize open the text to reveal what it won't say, what it cannot say, to make it mean differently. This strategy finds itself in Mulvey's appeal. Rather than tell new stories about old material (isn't porn recognizable at first sight?), I try to tell stories differently. This is a writing with and through, rather than "about."

The attempt is to employ Gayatri Spivak's Derridean-derived slogan "Use it, don't accuse it."[14] John Ellis illustrates how this deconstructive technique is employed in urban "gorilla feminist" tactics.[15] He cites the practice of slapping stickers which read "This insults women" on top of advertisements in bus shelters or on billboards that are deemed offensive, i.e., thought to "objectify" women, the female body, and to distort essential femininity. Ellis points out that such maneuvers, far from dismantling the representation, oppose and thus leave the offending representation intact. They also leave the viewer/voyeur intact; that is, he is still a voyeur, "voyeur to women speaking to the advertisers."[16] And we know, at least from Foucault, that censorship is a slippery mechanism, that "silence" is equally deceptive in the power matrix, and that willing something away doesn't work (but instead reinforces "will," "power"). Instead, Ellis suggests the subversive strategy of confronting the representation on its own terms, to get it to render (to render it) a different significance, and in the process confuse the fictional boundaries between the representation and the real. His preferred example, designed to address and unsettle both representation and reader, is the rejoinder "Who does this poster think you are?"[17] Indeed, I employ that as one of the embedded, guiding questions throughout the analysis in the chapters here: "Who does this photo think you are?"

Can a reading of a text speak for its reader? This question is posed by Nancy K. Miller, and I want to borrow it for slightly different purposes here.[18] As I try to open the pornographic texts to expose their own critical undoing, I impute an ideal reader of the photograph/magazine, though determined not by "masculinity" but by the vulnerability of difference; vulnerable: Latin *vulnerabilis,* "wounding." I think one can discursively reconstruct a reader/consumer in and for a text, and one can rewrite a text and in the process be rewritten, through complicity with the text. Laura Kipnis, in a discussion of transvestite pornography, writes: "I suggest that in looking at pornography we should not be so distracted by surfaces, and that like art critics, we're alert for meaning, to what we don't yet know, are threatened by, or may have forgotten."[19]

So I return to the (necessary) wound that difference enacts, and I hope this work takes up some problematics which are currently circulating about masculinity and male sexuality. Accordingly, the genres I look at are those which presuppose a male audience, that is, straight soft- and hard-core, and magazines which feature the transsexual/transvestite. In each chapter these are contrasted. I conclude with a discussion of gay pornographic photographs, to test the limits of the "difficulty of difference."

* * *

Thanks to Jacques Chevalier, Caryll Steffens, Ian Taylor, and John Harp.

Pornography and Difference

1 | Pornography and Desire

PORNOGRAPHY IS A regime of representation which, as Ros Coward notes, organizes sexualized meaning in conventional ways, according to a society's interpretations of the pornographic.[1] This is of course a tautology, and yet not an easy one to escape. As Thomas Laqueur notes in his historical study of the location of sex, the body, and sexual difference in the exigencies of discourse, and the inverse phenomenon, the far-reaching poetics of biology: "No historically given set of facts about 'sex' entailed how sexual difference was in fact understood and represented . . . and . . . no set of facts ever entails any particular account of difference."[2] Pornography depicts acts that are sexual, and is about sexual difference; but it is more than just another discourse on both, and is not defined purely by its content or its context. Pornographic magazines, as an economic phenomenon, take their place among the circulation and exchange of commodities designed for profit. Their internal economy is dependent on other productive and reproductive relations, yet not so apparently visible. Precisely how the pornographic artifact works is not easily identifiable.[3] There is a pornography industry and, by extension, commoditized images of sexuality. But "the sexual" is represented in other media, suggesting that there is nothing inherently pornographic.[4] These issues, the problems of mediation and consumption, open onto issues of "exchange" which extend beyond the economic imperative of the cash nexus. Pornographic photographs, like all popular representations, are commodities exchanged as signs, and sign value is heavily invested with symbolic exchange value, not just use value.[5] What is more, they enunciate phantasies which in some way elaborate a logic of seduction and desire.

Pornographic magazines dramatize what in Western society (at least) is a contradiction: the quintessentially private and intimate act is rendered public in its consumption, and at the same time anonymous. This consumption transgresses the normative and the licit; as such, it confronts a reading subject who, at the point of purchase, is already engaged in behaviors and fantasies considered to be "deviant," whether morally, sexually, or legally. But this narrow formulation of social deviancy assumes a "subject" who is in some way at odds with social definitions of acceptable behavior: he is assumed to be in control of his actions, however misguided. How the pornographic photograph works, for and through the reader, and to incite desire, needs to be theorized. These assumptions of the mythic rational, self-determining subject are challenged by the contribution of poststructuralism and psychoanalysis, particularly rereadings of Foucault, Freud, and Lacan, which illustrate the failure of identity and the struggles involved in the never-complete internalization of culture.[6] Pornography as an illicit cultural artifact formally elaborates sexual imagery and sexual difference in specific ways. It engages the sexed subject determined not cognitively, and not firmly ensconced in narratives of radical difference, but determined by transgressive effects.[7] Even in the seemingly most masculinist (or "phallic," in the vernacular sense) representations, identities of subjects and objects, men and women, models and readers, are acquired under threat and characterized by decenteredness, instabilities, and impurities (in the logical, not moral, sense). The eroticization of "tabooed" material recalls and replays contradictory and continually negotiated strategies of sexual (in)difference, voyeurism, fetishized relations, seduction. Pornographic signification involves those strategies, in choreographing the body and the fetish, ultimately to veil and counterveil sexual difference.

Be Human; Be Different

How does this work? Behaviorist approaches (a kind of ego psychology) focus on the act and most often assume that there is a singular, antisocial, hegemonic meaning, unproblematically read off the surface of an image.[8] Humanist feminism often appropriates behaviorist dogma,[9] but is as concerned with the status of the image and the hegemony of a privileged mode of representation: men look and women appear (in a limited repertoire).[10] In both these formulations, questions of mediation are elided in favor of a blanket description of what appears to be "on sight" an elaboration, and exacerbation, of sexual difference. Also ignored within behaviorism and humanist feminism are the mediated effects of photography, the fact that much nudity exists in other media *not* considered pornographic (content alone does not determine a preferred reading), in sexually provocative prose, and a host of other symbolic properties. There is another confusion of contexts (or the collapse of form into content). This confusion occurs when pornographic images, or fragments of images, are chosen to illustrate a point *contra* pornography. In this case, the assumption is that audiences for these reassembled materials (in university classrooms, at Women Against Pornography meetings, etc.) are properly socialized and will know better than to get aroused. Susan Barrowclough notes how the pedantic selection of visual materials in this way positions audience members as voyeurs: an ironic if not parodic point of view in instances designed to critique just such a point of view.[11]

The concern of humanist feminism regarding the misappropriation of some essence of femininity is not restricted to pornographic imagery. In denouncing normative "fixity," the body, identity, subjectivity, sexual difference, and desire are left unproblematized. The "reality" of dominant discourses is assigned to a terrorism of lived sexuality: a description of the "realpolitik" based on norm, stereotype, cliché—a surface reading of representations assumed to anchor sexual difference. These are liberal critiques, radical or not, which assume that identity is constituted and firmly fixed through socialization, the self is fully rational, apparent, and uncontradictory. Hence, "men have this self [which] women must, by definition, lack. . . . To him it is given, by faith and action, from birth. To her it is denied, by faith and action, from birth,"[12] and women are always and inevitably victims, passive objects. At the level of the representation, this assumes an unproblematic masculine/feminine polarity, the symbolic and immediately knowable differentiation along sexual lines.

Behaviorism focuses on the act, particularly the alleged pernicious effects of the pornographic image or artifact on the measurable attitude and behavior of the male consumer. The concern for humanist feminism is the status of the image and its so-called misrepresentation of the "reality" of women. The limitations of both these approaches center on a number of things. First, they unproblematically accept a transparent and singular meaning, which supposedly resides on the surface of the representation. Both approaches employ a representational logic and are thus silent about questions of fantasy, and "reality" as an endlessly mediated process. They are also elitist in assuming that the uneducated and politically unenlightened will read one meaning, and the politically correct (i.e., academics and liberal feminists) another. And finally, following from this, other questions remain unexplored. These are the critical inquiries into the construction of subjectivity in the spectator-text relationship; the construction of the desiring subject, addressed and reconstituted in a sexual discourse; the production of pleasure through the text; and the struggle to symbolically represent sexual difference, desire, and the phallus, in the representation and for a reader. All these are taken up below and in subsequent chapters.

What follows is a brief discussion of accounts of the body, the pornographic ouevre, the "subject," the text, and desire, which fall under the rubric of "poststructuralism." They lead into an excursus on the theoretical orientation which shapes the arguments contained herein.

Feminism, Poststructuralism, and Pornography

Since Foucault's *The History of Sexuality* it is possible to conceive of sexuality as the history of discourses.[13] Foucault's work has premised the idea of the textual body, thereby pronouncing a death sentence on the biological body.[14] His disquisition on sexuality (or sexualities) upset those notions according to which the body itself is the repository of unbridled passions, meanings, and sexual desires—heretofore "repressed"—and that the body always signifies in the same way. The Foucauldian body is no transcendental signifier. To talk of the discursive body, however, suggests that there are shifting associations attached to social and local bodies *and* that our sexual desires are formed for us in discourse, in economies of regulation, confession, technique.[15]

The privileging of discourse over the "body" hence foregrounds the idea of the body as "spoken," articulated within and around a corpus of signification. Foucault demonstrates how the body is subject to historico/medical discipline and how sexual "abnormalities" are pathologized.[16] In the introduction to *Herculine Barbin: Being the Recently Discovered Memoirs of a Nineteenth-Century French Hermaphrodite,* he addresses the status of the hermaphrodite in sexual, legal, and medical terms. The discursive voice of the hermaphrodite, a corporal statement of staunch refusal to be inducted into the "happy family of sexually confirmed individuals,"[17] who wears a biological duality for which language does not exist ("Is it a boy or a girl?"), has changed slightly since the Middle Ages. At that time the granting of a "true sex" to a body with the potential for a plurality of pleasures was the responsibility of the father or godfather (the one who "named" the child), at baptism. The option to change the label, not the biological disposition, was available to the individual upon another initiation rite, marriage. "Biological theories of sexuality, juridical conceptions of the individual, forms of administrative control in modern nations,"[18] all these combined to formulate the idea of a single-sexed body.[19]

Within the medical discourse the aim, when confronted with "terror-inspiring monsters," was to "strip the body of its anatomical deceptions" and anchor it within a determining, single sexual identity.[20] Frank Mort also notes how, using a more contemporary example, this most severely nonnormative (hermaphroditic) body is subject to regulation, that is, talked about in medical circles but solely in medical terms.[21] It is a body desexualized, totally naked, stripped of identity through the black obliterating mask/bar over the eyes. In medical photographs it stands ramrod straight against a normalizing grid, measured for abnormalities (and therefore against the "norm"). But here's the rub: The same hermaphrodite or transsexual circulates in pornographic genres ("TV" or "transvestite" porn) and is subjectified/sexualized. "It" is a body speaking to a discourse of sexual transgression, in excess, and this is presented as erotic. It is a body spoken through clothing, sexualized body language, and other vocabularies of instituted desire. What makes these two (same) bodies different is the way their transgressions (for they both transgress the boundaries of the genetic/generic sexual "fix") are deployed and institutionalized: the first is a body constructed for medical observation and intellectual arousal, the second for sexual curiosity and sexual arousal. The first is placed in a textbook, the second in a magazine for purchase in an adult bookstore. One is for the "chosen" of the medical profession (historically and still mostly men); the second is available to the "masses" of men.

It would be a trap, however, to speak of "pornography" as just another discourse on sex. That would be to hypostatize structure (as with all structuralisms) and speak only of the regulation and institutionalization of the pornographic "voice." The pornographic voice—a regime, to be sure, of "special knowledges, analyses, and injunctions"—speaks to a reader and does so in meaningful terms.[22] Foucault's indictment, however, is largely inattentive to the "subject" and the formation of desire, other than to suggest that sexual subjectivities are formed in a power-knowledge nexus;[23] our desires are formed for us and sustained in discourse. A Foucauldian challenge for feminism, though, is its insistence on problematizing the mediated body, a body shot through with strategies of signification and power.[24]

In *Hard Core: Power, Pleasure and the "Frenzy of the Visible,"* Linda Williams historicizes the pornographic genres in the contexts of their own "episteme," i.e., their articulation in an emerging framework of visual surveillance.[25] Williams uses Foucault to argue that the "positive" (not repressive) power relations in the hard-core regime are part of the modern, secular, confessional apparatus. In this case the will to knowledge, power, pleasure, and vision is embodied in confessions of the flesh; the female body, that "dark continent," is scrutinized for its innermost secrets. One of the defining features of the hard-core genre is penetration, an apt metaphor for the epistemological interiorization of femininity. This is Luce Irigaray's "speculum," the searching probe and acquisitive will-to-vision that characterize phallocentric philosophies.[26] The trope of this relentless investigation of the "other," as Irigaray points out, is its inevitable "blind spot," the unwitting discovery (the consequences of which, to Irigaray, should be the focus of feminism's most radical and deconstructive project) that the gaze of the colonizer turns back on itself, that it can, in the end, see only itself.[27] If the norm of sexual difference is biological sameness, a version of the "one-sex/one-flesh" model that Thomas Laqueur demonstrates as pervasive in medical and philosophical discourses until the late seventeenth century[28]—that is, woman defined as "nonpossession" in relation to men, whether penis- or phallus-bearing[29]—then the gaze of subjectivity and epistemology is in the end a phallic one. The principle of identity is measured against the presumption of unity, integrity, singularity, masculinity. The consequences of this are that the patriarchal subject cannot imagine otherness.

But the problem of the negotiation of sexual difference may, in the Foucauldian perspective, disappear back into the "body"; i.e., difference is assumed in its biological visibility.[30] Desire is also assumed, although not foregrounded; Foucault is dismissive of the preoccupations of psychoanalysis. Williams argues that the staging of the female body as something to look at, and the marking of it as different through fetishes, denies it "any existence apart from the marks of difference."[31] In her study of hard-core pornographic films, Williams provides an analysis of fetish transactions in an attempt to complement Foucault's insistence on micropanoptic power and pleasure with the more precise insights, with regard to fetishism, of Marx and Freud.[32]

Questions of the fetish relations of difference, and the role of difference in the logic of seduction, are taken up in the chapters on the shoe and on jewelry and lingerie. Suffice it to say for now that the fetish in Marx and Freud[33] revolves around structures and metaphors of vision. First of all, Williams locates the *sine qua non* of the hard-core regime in the "money" shot, the site/sight of male orgasm signaling not only narrative closure but the mirror reflection of phallic specular logic. This is also a key feature in hard-core magazines. The fetish operates to inscribe difference and to achieve an illusory balance between absence and the value invested in resurrecting that absence, and a balance between knowledge and belief. For Marx, the optical metaphor is invoked to indict the beguiling nature of objects, particularly object-subject relations.[34] In *The German Ideology* Marx offers the ruse of the "camera obscura" as a central trope in capitalist ideological relations. He writes: "In all ideology men and their circumstances appear upside-down . . . this phenomenon arises just as much from their historical life-process as the inversion of objects on the retina does from their physical life-process."[35] Later, in *Capital,* the visual scenario is invoked again in an impeachment of the "magic and necromancy" of commodities, specifically their imputed power to "socialize" (make social) humans' relationships with objects.[36] What one wants to retain from Marx on commodity fetishism is the emphasis on the phantom images of ideology (and it is not hard to see the slide from a theory of the hieroglyphics of idolatry, with its mockery of ideas, artifice, and illusion, to a polemic—at the very least—of the aesthetics and politics of objects); the notion of exchange relations; and the processes of exchange whereby objects (commodities) simultaneously embody "dead labor" *and* are vitalized by the way they are invested with properties beyond their physicality, i.e., are given value in exchange relations. When Marx writes of the "magic and necromancy" of fetish objects, he is underscoring other investments that inhere in fetish objects and fetish relations: investments in loss, difference, and simulated indifference. These, and their particular significance in pornographic maneuvers, will be taken up in the chapters that follow.

But in his scathing indictment of commodity fetishism and the inauthenticity of appearances or the appearance of things, Marx does not take us far enough in understanding how trafficking in symbols is actually seductive; how, through generalized exchange value, producers are simultaneously consumers (and how there can be no radical separation of subjects and objects; an essence and its obverse; presence and absence); and finally, how the sign fascinates and entices. How does the commodity, "at first sight, a very trivial thing," wield so much power in a "mist-enveloped" system of worship?[37] Or in the words of the pleasure "theorists," what of the ambivalence around the "convergence of commodity and meaning" into *signs* of pleasure?[38]

Via Freud, the pornographic fetish would be the substitute part-object, adorning the female body to disavow knowledge of female lack, and poised to allay castration fears.[39] However, in spite of establishing sexuality at the center of subjectivity and locating the fetish within distinctly sexual origins and scenarios of difference, the logic of eroticism within the psychoanalytic narrative lacks the precision necessary to account for the problematic of sexual difference, the role of the fetish in the refusal of difference, and thus its role in seductive economies. Fetish relations both straddle and refuse closure. Why is difference and/or its effacement enthralling and seductive?

The fetish is always a play on difference(s). Jean Baudrillard's critique of the "metaphysic of alienated essence," characterized by the Marxist denunciation of the subversiveness of objects, challenges the unyielding base-superstructure model whereby use value (the question of "truth") is a reflection of an anterior reality.[40] The privileging of exchange value, in which objects signify only within a generalized and abstract system of differences, emphasizes the "labor of signification" and (with the obscuring of use value) the negotiations of differences (and indifferences) in the gaps between signifiers and signifieds. Only now, what seduces are the machinations of the signifier searching for its signified(s). This indictment of the inherently bourgeois penchant for visibility and measurement (a reductive fetishism of the "seen") allows us to consider that the fetish is as much about ambivalences around absence and the repressed as it is about the immediately apparent. It is not that the signified cannot be measured: the problem is not one of locating and measuring meaning. The problem in the age of the camera obscura is finding and (mis)measuring the signifier. If the fetish embodies (in Freud, at least) simulated absence, the drive to visibility (in Freud and Marx) is simultaneously about repressions, gaps, losses—what cannot be witnessed cannot be spoken. Any fetish, combining both presence and absence, is more than just an alibi for the "real": it is about simulated relations, and, like any simulation, it offers an indictment of the boundaries between the visible and the repressed, the subject and the object, the signifier and its referent. In short, the fetish prevents closure, and it does this through partially effacing difference, not by exacerbating it.

Baudrillard argues that the abstractions of ideological labor, the seemingly endless substitutions that are elected in relations of generalized exchange, mean that any object is randomly affiliated with fetishism, not for its absolute but for its relative value. But I think there is a problem with the assumption of the "relative autonomy" of objects (no different from the perils of asserting the relative autonomy of authors). For one thing, there are favored, not random, fetish images that circulate within a number of cultural discourses. The spike-heel shoe, for example, is a staple feature in soft- and hard-core pornographic magazines, in representations that confer "sexiness" and/or phallicism, and sometimes lethal potential, on the female image. That it is not just any shoe, but the stiletto heel, indicates at the very least that particular meanings converge (sometimes with a vengeance) in a simulated relationship of difference and indifference: not just any object can be sexualized in the name of difference. The suggestion of an equivalent exchange among signifiers (or that the object is one signifier among many) overlooks the exchange relations which coalesce in the object and the ways in which they negotiate difference. These negotiated relations are dramatic plays on difference and s(t)imulate symbolic exchange. With any simulation there is no "copyright." "Simulate" (from Latin *simulatus*): "to copy, represent, or feign"; it stems from "at the same time" and "together." An object held in simulation at once refers to difference and sameness, or difference and indifference, or difference and its denial ("to postpone," from MF *differer*, is at the root of "differ"). This is not unlike the fetish—simultaneously there/not there.

Subjects and objects cannot be held in radical separation; this is argued by D. N. Rodowick and Kaja Silverman.[41] Along with this needs to be emphasized not just the significance of fetish objects, but the problematic of fetish *relations*. If the fetish is a particularly reliable, and erotic, compromise, and if as part-object it recalls an anterior "whole," it is caught in a web of relations of difference (not just embodied objects which mark a static difference) which serve to simulate something that does not exist in the real. In the case of the shoe, the compromise is between its obvious cultural location among feminine accouterments (of the last few hundred years, at least)[42] and its import as a phallic symbol, complete with stiletto, a daggerlike heel (why is a "heel" always a man?). We might say the spike-heel shoe is poised in ambivalence, or activates an erotic theft.[43]

In her discussion of the fetish in *Hard Core*, Linda Williams offers a sensitive and unabashed treatment of the "surplus value of orgasm,"[44] and underscores the argument that theories of fetishism must work in tandem. In fact, Williams argues that the Marxist emphasis on the artifice in symbolic exchange, the investment of (dead) human labor, and consequently affect, in objects and, more precisely, the socialized power which thus inheres in those objects, necessarily *precedes* the libidinal investments which structure the Freudian phallic endowment. Williams is referring to the historical and cultural divisions which valorize specular logics and the construction of subjectivity based on possession or lack.[45] Precisely how pornography and the fetish, in particular the hypervisibility of traces of masculinity, work to seduce the heterosexual reader, is not addressed by Williams. Whither the spectator in this panoply of bodily excesses? *That is one of the questions posed throughout this book.*

While Foucault's episteme is a major challenge to the Western, metaphysical subject, for our purposes it still cannot get at questions of eros, seduction, and desire.[46] Even though foregrounding "the fetish" opens onto tropes of the visible, the Foucauldian "will-to-vision" doesn't tell us enough about seduction and desire, particularly in the illicit/perverse visual moment.[47] Any disclosure and investigation of the machinations of the "fetish as absence" point to the limits of representational logic.

Deconstructive analyses of the fetish object and fetishistic relations will be taken up in subsequent chapters. Suffice it to say for now that the mere descriptive identification of "the fetish" as central to male erotic pleasure does not adequately identify the precise nature of the seductive enterprise. Where is the reader's desire? Why should castration fears be twinned with eroticism? Unless the fetish is theorized as a transaction or significant exchange involving displacements, losses, investments, and ultimately transgressions, the reader and seduction are left out of the analysis. The strategy here is to open the analysis to include the tropes of the seductive enterprise, one of which includes the masculinization of a female model for a heterosexual reader. Seduction here is a play of simulated differences; yes, an ensnarement in the image, but an image with a referent at least to a prior system of binary differences.[48] More on these later.

In other words, there are still troubles in the text, and in the spectator-text relationship. The reading offered here begins with the assumption that representation and signification are productions, systematically structured and constituted for viewing subjects, with a specific mode of address and regime of representation.[49] The questions which guide this investigation draw from work on textual maneuvers and the consumption of cultural artifacts, particularly the "visual imaginaries," which places the struggle over meaning at the intersection of language, the unconscious, representation, and desire.[50] These are the concerns of a poststructuralist semiotics which argues that the cultural artifact, the publicly circulated photograph, is a productive machinery, not a reflection of some anterior reality/meaning. Meaning is thus produced in the representation, and in each encounter with it, the reader is re-produced as well.[51] The reading subject is positioned vis-à-vis the discourse or text; with respect to the illicit and "transgressive" visual imaginary,[52] this positioning would appear to "quote" the unspoken and, in the case of photography and the fetish, the unseen, both in a seductive enterprise. The subject formed in signification "dethrones" the unified ego, "the authorial 'I,' assumed to be both the source and the guarantor of the 'truth' of any enunciative statement."[53]

A feminist appropriation of, and contribution to, poststructuralist semiotics lies with its insistence on the instabilities and contradictions in the mediation of subjects. In this case, the focus is on the masculine subject, and the aim is to refuse phallic closure. By phallic closure is meant what is suggested by

Toril Moi, following from the projects of Luce Irigaray and Hélène Cixous, as the foundation of patriarchal, philosophical humanism and characterized by assumptions of the "seamlessly unified self. . . . This integrated self is in fact a phallic self, constructed on the model of the self-contained powerful phallus. Gloriously autonomous, it banishes from itself all conflict, contradiction and ambiguity."[54] This is the self that can't imagine "otherness"; look at it, write about it, maybe, but not *imagine* it.

The Inclusiveness of Difference

The work of Linda Williams, Laura Kipnis, Chris Straayer, and Cindy Patton and several of the essays in *Dirty Looks*[55] speak to the contradictions in the illict; in spectator-text relations; in reading positions; in identities; in the constructed body; in representing desire, the phallus, difference. This sensitivity, noting, for example, that the "point of view" in pornography is "notoriously incoherent,"[56] recuperates the feminist agenda and its concern with the structuring of sexual difference and the organization of knowledge and power relations which inhere in the social practices through which "sexual difference" is negotiated, resisted, transgressed, and subverted. Implicit in the analysis herein is a rejection of an essential core to feminine and masculine bodies, identities, subjectivities, yet a commitment remains to essential binaries[57] in matters of representing difference: in the beginning there are male and female bodies—this is all we have words for. In the beginning there is the word (the word made flesh): *alpha/beta*—*alpha*, akin to Hebrew *āleph*, "ox, bull," symbol of the father; and *beta*, akin to Hebrew *bēth*, "house," symbol of the mother. Attention to the materiality of language reveals, behind its opacity, a preference for certain signs and symboling above others, more specifically a debt to the play of difference and indifference in the seductive moment.[58]

The project of writing and rewriting involves necessarily a commitment to language, not as medium but as already mediated. The task here is to render the visual image in literal terms, and certain words—those that recur in images and in the written text that accompanies the picture—are investigated to foreground, following the deconstructive precept that there is "violence involved in settling upon a single meaning,"[59] their betrayal, their critical paradox, their critical undoing.

The poststructuralist subject, meaning, desire, and sexual identity are fully symbolic transactions. This is to say that the semiotic integrity of the photograph is challenged in (its own) relations of exchange. That is, certain possessive characteristics, under the rubric of difference, are revealed through symbolic exchange, to be fleeting or proximate properties. It is not that one *is* difference, but that one *has* difference. "Difference" is fashioned discursively, semiotically, in performative and phantasmatic sites. Difference is an investment-in-exchange whose basis lies in an originating binary opposition. The pornographic impulse fashions difference; the difference it makes, though, is difference at a cutting edge, an indifference to the phallic code of singularity (or the foreclosure of difference). It is of semiotic interest how the formal rhetorical characteristics of the sexualized image, the reliance on certain familiar, "everyday" objects, according to Beverley Brown, a "highly fixed repertoire of postures and props,"[60] are mediated to produce the "pornographic." One way in which difference is fashioned is through the deployment of fetish objects and fetish relations. "Fetish": "artificial," from Latin *facticus,* "made by art, factitious." "Factitious": from Latin *facticius,* from *facere,* "to make, do." "Fashion": from Latin *factio,* "a making," from *facere,* "to make." Form, and the movement that gives shape to the form, are preeminent in these symbolic negotiations. This movement, which allows us to talk of not objects or content but dramatic and playful relations, unsettles the fixity of binaries and straddles the boundaries it at once invokes and seeks to efface. In this case, the fetish relations in pornography are structured by traces of otherness, absence, loss, repression. The conventions of the pornographic moment[61] rely on, along with a repertoire of props, seemingly explicit genital disclosure; but, appearances to the contrary, this exposure also betrays a fidelity to the site/sight of radical binary difference. The question is inverted, in other words: Rather than "What does pornography reveal?" the question here is, "What does it conceal?"

Photofeminism

The photograph (the "presumed real")[62] is the medium of the mass-circulated pornographic magazine. When any representation enters the realm of photographic discourse, it surrenders to the possessive and nonpartisan eye of the camera.[63] One of the most common political indictments of pornographic imagery is for its objectification and misrepresentation of the "reality" of "women," through the way it deploys the identified-as-female body. But the object of scorn is the photograph, not the sexually explicit painting, sculpture, or novel. As Beverley Brown[64] and Ros Coward[65] note, it is the precise nature of the *photo*graphic regime of representation to fragment and objectify, in fact freeze and capture, the referent (or invoke the death of the object).[66] In that sense, one of the intellectual struggles for orthodox feminism vis-à-vis the pornographic *medium* is the attempt to define "erotica" as distinct from "pornography,"[67] to save the former from the signifying defiles of the latter and preserve erotica as the prediscursive, uncoded picture of sexuality. Many problems emerge in this positing of the "on sight"[68] recognition of the "clear and present difference" between erotica and pornography.[69] Gloria Steinem, in an oft-quoted phrase, writes that erotica is "a mutually pleasurable, sexual expression between people who have enough power to be there by positive choice."[70] Be where? In the photograph? This assumes that the photo supplants a "truer" reality, i.e., that the depiction is the (photographic) "negative" of women's sexual nature. It also denies the photo's ability to activate fantasy or recall the death effect (i.e., its mediated effect). And it confuses the social conditions of labor with the staged vocabulary of the profilmic event.[71] The attempt to distinguish between pornography and erotica (on moral or political grounds) is an attempt at reifying the fictive unity of the erotic, libidinal ego, seen to be distorted by the mechanisms of society's pornographic impulses. This is the fallacy of representational logic.

But at least since the work of Walter Benjamin,[72] photographic activity is conceptualized as having a productive and aesthetic specificity which allies its technique with "mass" production, indeed the "masses." Photography, characterized by the possibilities of endless deferral, is not awarded the same aesthetic value as the painting, assumed to issue from the creative vision of its author.[73] In contrast to the mass-produced and mass-circulated pornographic photograph/magazine, the "erotic," as Kathy Myers notes, is often "authorized" by its lack of anonymity.[74] There are, of course, photos which are restored to authority, for example, the work of Robert Mapplethorpe[75]—though the operative word here is "work," i.e., the valorization of production or the productive vision of the photographer (coupled with its institutionalization in galleries *and* the aesthetics of the artistic black and white photo). The mass-circulated photo is characterized by its easy, indiscriminate, and unauthorized consumption. Photography itself is indebted to an epistemology of verisimilitude, and the color photo (one *sine qua non* of the pornographic oeuvre) is invested with reality effects.[76] Erotica may be in the eye of the beholder; pornography is in the eye of the masses.[77]

Certain poststructural interventions challenge these assumptions. Brown notes that in those literatures which treat pornographic representations as the essence of patriarchy, the "everyday" is considered more galling than the exotic.[78] *Hustler* and hard-core, for example, are often singled out as the more offensive or "truly" pornographic of media.[79] And they are profoundly everyday: the models approach the reality of everywoman, complete with blemished bodies and slightly tarnished attire. They do not possess the perfected bourgeois ideal but flaunt their "common" appearance, complete with torn stockings, chipped fingernail polish, blemished skin, soiled hair, not exactly corpulence but undisciplined flesh. Angela Carter puts an end to class bias in considerations of the dominant sexual discourse:

> When fear, shame and prudery condemn the poor and the ignorant to copulate in the dark, it must be obvious that sexual sophistication is a by-product of education. The primal nakedness of lovers is a phenomenon of the middle class in cold climates; in northern winters, naked lovers must be able to afford to heat their bedrooms. The taboos regulating the sight of bare flesh are further determined by wider cultural considerations. The Japanese bathed to-

gether in the nude for centuries, yet generations of Japanese lovers fucked in kimono, even in the humidity of summer, and did not even remove the combs from their chignons while they did so. And another complication—they did not appreciate the eroticism of the nude; yet they looked at one another's exposed genitalia with a tender readiness that still perturbs the West.[80]

Carter's point, that sexual practice and the signification of desire are regulated within discourses and across history and class, is well taken. However, as we will see in discussions of the machinations of the fetish, tracing the history of something—a practice, the circulation of a fashionable object—does not explain how it works. In translating, and resignifying, the pornographic photo, the task is to render the visual in linguistic terms, and thus re-"write" it. Thus this book offers a synchronic reading of the systematic and conventional coding of the image, and an investigation into how (and why) elaborations of sexual (in)difference, simulated gratification, and machinations of the fetish conspire to seduce.

Our language betrays us. A good example of this betrayal occurs when men (or women), for example, reply that pornography "turns them on," or when women, or men, reply that hard-core is "vulgar." What do these mean? These vernacular phrases take us to the limits of language, or the ability of language to express "ourselves," our desires, fears, and embodied knowledge. Note the imprecision in trying to describe what an orgasm feels like; note the impossibility. In the visual imaginaries, one is presented with representations, i.e., symptoms, and thus what is offered here is a symptomatic reading. We know that porn turns some people on, and others find it vulgar ("vulgar": "belonging to the people, multitude; the common people"). Some find it both; some like it in spite of, or because of, its vulgarity. *Hustler* offends, and according to Laura Kipnis, its offensiveness is tied to its violation of a number of norms.[81] The bourgeois disciplining of bodily boundaries is shown to be a leaky system indeed: all manner of bodily substances, sounds, imagined odors, are "revealed" in excess. Political officials (of all ideological stripes) are pilloried through the reduction of public office to a common denominator of base bodily functions, acts, and "perverse" desires. Religious icons are subject to the same common ("of the people") and transgressive impulses.[82] Kipnis notes how this vulgarity commingles with a prurient interest in sexual behavior and sexual display, particularly as they might highlight hypocrisies inherent in the contradictory spaces between discourses of the public and private. The explicitness and transgressions are laced with an asceticism; this too is seductive.[83]

Deconstruction has taught us that language is opaque, evasive, ambiguous, playful.[84] But it is not simply constitutive of a free-for-all. Jacques Chevalier argues:

Language is a system of differences. By implication, the symbolic eludes the rule of the mob (chaos) and the despotism of the true message as well

(Logos). Language cannot exist on the basis of an absolute *laisser-faire* association. Nor can meaning be reduced to surface manifestations of a leading theme, an overarching concept, a creative subject, a simple-minded stereotype, or a domineering archetype. Beyond the sameness of the powers of speech gone democratic or totalitarian, there is the land of *la differance*: an enchanted dominion of playful images slipping and sliding their way through splits and crevices in the code.[85]

Chevalier offers that the fruit-bearing (as opposed to penetrating) analysis endeavors not to crack the code, but to reveal the cracks *in* the code. These points will be underscored and elaborated below. Suffice it for now to say that matters of symboling involve differences; and "difference" returns us to a sexual dualism. "Differ": "to bear, to scatter"; within difference, then, is the capacity to bear offspring ("bear," from the German—"to carry") and the scattered seeds (of deferral). Language contains its own perversions.[86]

The vocabularies of the photographic (and filmic) media, too, signify deferrals. That is, we know that what is missing from the text is as important as what is there.[87] The reader is one of the things missing from the text, and thus the analysis here is, *inter alia*, an encounter with him and the text before him. Victor Burgin notes that there are material and suppressed absences in a "visual medium" because the "visual medium" is "invaded by language in the very moment it is looked at: in memory, in association, snatches of words and images continually alternate and intermingle."[88] And Lesley Stern asks with regard to the privileging of the workings of desire and representations for arousal, both *modus operandi* and *raison d'être* of pornographic scenarios: "Pornography becomes a site of exploration . . . where explicitness is posed not as an embodiment of sexism but as an embodiment of desire. If desire is somewhat literally put in the picture, what of desire that is left out of the picture?"[89] That is, what does the text try to suppress, try not to say, try not to let in?

The Desiring Subject

The postmodern consumer/voyeur is perhaps perfectly suited for scenarios of loss in those simulated moments, involving as they do the abduction of virtual images to create a pastiche of new models. In this sense the market is saturated with mass-produced items waiting to be consumed *en masse*. Pornographies are one of those spectacles. Part of the specificity of those pornographies may lie in the way they stage parodic displays of sexual excess, *and* the way they simultaneously induce, or are part of, the seemingly inexhaustible search for "real" sex, thus speaking to a particular kind of consumer/voyeur. What Fredric Jameson refers to as the "consumers' appetite for a world transformed into sheer images of itself and for pseudo-events and spectacles"[90] suggests that the consumer is lost among the representations, searching for the promise of "real" sex, that master text gone missing. Jean Baudrillard addresses this point with exact reference to pornography: "It may well be that pornography is there only to reactivate this lost referent in order to prove *a contrario*, by its grotesque hyperrealism, that there is however some *real* sex somewhere."[91]

For whom? The analyses in this book address mainstream pornographic magazines, targeted for the male reader/consumer: for the most part, *Playboy, Penthouse, Hustler, Club International,* and a host of lesser-known titles emanating mostly from the United States (gay pornography is discussed in the Conclusion). There is a plethora of hard-core titles; again the sample is mostly American (store clerks say that the glossy magazines are conspicuously, though not surprisingly, without masthead, advertisements, and classifieds) with a variety of names, and most bearing the inscription "Volume 1, Number 1": *French Pussy, Cunt on Delivery, Anal Fantasy,* for example. While it is acknowledged that there are pornographies produced for the lesbian market,[92] and that heterosexual *couples* may rent and "use" videos and magazines,[93] what is presented here is a consideration of what an ideal heterosexual male reader might invest in the photo. If straight women "use" or are aroused or seduced by mainstream pornography, that is not to say that the text works the same way for both men and women.[94] To return to Baudrillard's quote, the (patriarchally) masculine subject may be reconstituted in scenarios of loss and re-membering: this recuperative move that characterizes the inaugural scene, the re-enactment of impossible authenticity, is the fundamental problem for imagining otherness.[95]

So how do pornographic photographs work? What can one say of the photo and the reader and the ways they intersect to coalesce around "the pornographic"? Behaviorism and humanist feminism preserve a binary distinction both in the photograph and in a determinate readership. These assumptions posit that pornography is a vicious elaboration of what we already know: men and women are constructed as different. The feminine discourse, within the pornographic oeuvre, is one of exhibition and sartorial display, a fashionable marking of "otherness" as a sexual spectacle. The masculine discourse, by contrast, possesses the gaze, invoking power behind the look of the reader/voyeur. The masculine and feminine presence then are premised on a relationship of what the oft-quoted John Berger has called "surveyor to surveyed."[96] But this is to accept the "woman as sign" hypothesis, i.e., that representations of "woman" are anchored around sexual difference, immediately recognizable and centered on configurations of the body. But how do we know that what we are looking at is a "woman"? Is the pornographic model female, speaking/spoken through the feminine language? How do we know? And does this discursive arrangement equal the tenacious "sexual fix"?[97]

The arguments fleshed out here focus on the spectator-text relationship, with a view to exploring the specificity of this illicit exchange, by privileging an investigation into the textual organization of desire as well as the reproduction of meaning in and through the text, and through the subject. This involves considerations of language as a coded sign system. This in turn implies that meaning is constructed not by speaking subjects—the fictive authors of enunciations assumed by behaviorism and humanist feminism—but through linguistic nominations in a discursive context. Meaning thus is not fixed and is without a stable referent. With respect to understanding the machinations of the pornographic image, "what we need is the description of a textual circuit articulating 'positions' of masculinity and femininity through processes of identification, the maintenance of these positions being the work effected by us as subjects each time we understand the meaning of a sentence, each time we 'get' the joke, each time we 'make' the film make sense."[98]

One of the instabilities of the pornographic phototext centers on the negotiation of sexual difference. The analyses in the following chapters look at how difference is both managed and transgressed, how desire and difference are impurely negotiated transactions. For example, pornographic texts may stage illicit sexual scenarios for a "masculine" reader and buying public; this may involve, on the surface, the representation of woman as "other," in the text and for the reader. But the signification of difference opens onto an especially dense problematic upon acknowledgment of the omnipresent fetish accouterments and their supposed role in allaying castration fears.[99] For if the female must have the fetish to represent desire and difference, and the fetish is a stand-in for the penis, then challenges are put to the orthodoxies of representational logic, and the concerns of psychoanalytic semiotics are extended and underscored. The fetish dresses up the woman in partially phallic terms. It fictionalizes pure difference, in the text and in the reading subject, if he must look for phallic replacements and traces on the female in a mimicry of corporal plenitude, and if this somehow suggests a desirable and seductive transaction. Hence, Elizabeth Wilson comments on the pornographic spectator-text relationship: "Far from being the celebration of male power, pornography sometimes seems designed to reassure men and allay fears of impotence."[100] Although this ties in with the "fear of castration" thesis, a thesis that contains its own (in)difference, it moves the discussion into the realm of the subject and its inherent instability. Annette Kuhn also notes that "certain kinds of pornography may combine pleasure and unease—perhaps even at moments threatening to disrupt, rather than confirm, the spectator's masculinity."[101] Andy Moye, Susan Gubar, and Lynne Segal all mentioned, as early as the mid- to late eighties, masculine "anxieties" in relation to the pornographic text, having to do with the structure of fear. Segal suggests that there may even be masculine "paranoia" in textual gratifications.[102] Claire Pajaczkowska and Susan Barrowclough both hypothesize that because strategies of identification, and signification, are unstable and often contradictory, it is possible that the male reader of the pornographic text (film or photo) is positioned *passively* in front of the artifact, and/or identifies with the female in the image.[103] These are all useful proposals.

Gilles Deleuze, in *Masochism: Coldness and Cruelty,* advances a picture of the masochistic position as male, in a sympathetic elaboration of desire in the pre-oedipal period.[104] Deleuze's focus is the relationship between (powerful oral) mother and son; the father is, not to say dethroned from significance but repudiated as symbolic phallic authority. The (male) masochist, in desiring an enduring alliance with the original nurturer, refuses phallic, paternal identification in the hopes of a return to plenitude with the mother. The specificity of the fantasies of the masochistic subject, then, emerge with his reconstruction of the "good" mother, and divestment of the father's punishing superego. This likeness of the punitive father, expiated by the (masochistic) child, is internalized symbolically, "miniaturized, beaten, ridiculed and humiliated," by the masochist.[105] This father image threatens to return, hence the "waiting and suspense" that are characteristic of the masochistic aesthetic. One crucial aspect of the masochist's phallic disinheritance is his corresponding renunciation of adult genital sexuality (for this would jeopardize the desired union with the pregenital mother). Thus, and relating to this and the abovementioned "suspense," orgasm as the penultimate pleasurable release is deliberately delayed. The male masochist is not in search of pain that is simultaneously pleasurable; he contracts punishment and suffering and waits for the pleasurable reward.[106] Gaylyn Studlar applies Deleuze's theory of the masochistic aesthetic in an analysis of "von Sternberg/Dietrich" films, with a view to challenging models of spectatorship, voyeurism, and sexual difference which posit an impulse to mastery behind the gaze, narrative progress, and fetishistic scopophilia, and which assume the castration drama and oedipal desire to be at the center of both the "objectification" of women and cinematic pleasure.[107] The questions posed by Studlar are important ones, especially as they refuse the classic formulation of the gaze and structures of identification in much orthodox feminist film theory.[108]

However, pornographic maneuvers are about difference, linguistic difference, difference(s) *both* negotiated and denied. There isn't a refusal of genital sexuality; in fact, representations of genitalia (his and hers) are explicit in soft- and hard-core. The orgasmic experience in pornographic photographs is also necessary to ensure narrative closure. Pleasure is not delayed; signs of pleasure are in excess. In soft- and hard-core, the women betray facial signifiers of simulated pleasure. The hard-core narrative culminates in visual depictions of the male's orgasm, "an essential . . . punctuation of the sexual narrative."[109] Cindy Patton is right in saying this, although the ellipses have been added in her quote to underline a point of departure from her argument. The original reads "an essential and essentialist punctuation of the sexual narrative." But instead of imputing a pornographic strategy "ground[ed] . . . in biology,"[110] what are emphasized are representations and signs. For example, in the hard-core genre, signs of his orgasm are preeminent. Not only is this a "perverse" move for the heterosexual reader; taken *as a sign,* and deconstructed, semen and the detumescent penis are, it will be shown, a representation of the "spent" male subject. Not punishment as a prelude to an erotic union, but testimony to his "petite mort," not after the fact but, as it were, during the fact.

To underscore the oedipal moment in pornographic negotiations, Freud's essay "A Child Is Being Beaten" should be briefly mentioned, which sets out a prototype of phantasy structure, masochism, and thus sexual "perversion."[111] Many others have commented on and reworked this essay and retain from it, among other things, its critical elaboration of the inherent shiftiness of identifications, the inseparability of subject and object positions, and the potential utility of understanding the role of masochism in the masculine avowal/disavowal of sexual difference.[112] The oedipal injunctions are clear if one recalls that "perversions" ("turning aside from truth or right") depend on binarism, the code, or, more to the point, an insistence on the code and simultaneously its subversion. However, it is not the law per se which is subverted, not phallic law which is renounced, but the phallus is subsumed under the "structuration" of Oedipus, or the "cut" (which is discussed below).[113] The oedipal moment of difference encompasses transgression within the binary code: transgression "always represents some kind of response to what it repudiates."[114]

The Sexed Subject

The following thesis is taken from Jacques Chevalier's *Semiotics, Romanticism and the Scriptures.*[115] Just as the ascetic discourses characterizing, indeed constituting, the biblical and romantic codes are replete with the subversive threads of eroticism,[116] the obverse is true of the pornographic moment. The explicit and the illicit maneuvers which contribute to pornographic signification appear to reveal all. The surface exposure, and the exposure of the surface, is really a poor attempt to hide pornography's asceticism, that is, its ritual sacrifices, forfeitures, renunciations, and disavowals, and these of the masculine subject. It is the responsibility of the ensuing analysis to render visual images, photographs, into linguistic terms. The attempt is not description or oppositional analysis, but a deconstructive analysis which confronts the image on its own terms, from within. Hence, Chevalier's insight for our purposes is his formulation of a theory of symboling which relies on a logical "translation" of the sentimental and historical dimensions of language, "the schemings of time and desire in the act of coding."[117] The process of symboling, he argues, consists of an "interplay between the overt and the covert—between the explicit, the implicit, and the illicit" which moves beyond the strict logic of similarities and differences.[118] The translation here is derived from the fourfold method he outlines. First, the surface narrative is probed for "the dominant signs chosen in preference to all other meanings potentially invested in the same imagery." Second, "signs forced out of the literal text form the underside of the narrative, an underground 'plot' comprising all the unspeakable fears and latent anxieties subsumed in the visible text." Third, no banning of the illicit is possible; slips of the code are everywhere. And fourth, transgression is contained within the law: "Licit expressions of language are in the habit of subsuming illicit meanings under the dominant code, which is but one way of reinforcing the powers-that-be in the realm of speech."[119] As such, Chevalier's work challenges the hermeticism of structuralism, the apolitical rule of the mob in semiotics (its privileging of the free-rein of polysemy), the transcendental subject in psychoanalysis, the limitless deferrals of deconstruction, the ignorance of the "play of passion" in feminism. As a "translation," or "reading as translation," *Semiotics, Romanticism and the Scriptures* is playful, poetic, and profound. It is, among other things, about (re)writing, and the following is offered as but one example of how its style merges with content to render a linguistic sensuousness that even Barthes could not achieve:

> Beyond the overdetermination of the symbolic and the indeterminacy of *l'imaginaire,* there is the narrative "scheme" that comprises all the frameworks and the frame-ups that readers are expected to mind (attend/censure) while being moved by them. Scheme analysis is mainly concerned with battles of words. This perspective centres on the conflicting pathways of wayward signs that belie all expectations of thematic unity. Accordingly, the reader proceeds through a maze of byplays, byroads and crooked byways that can convert the most familiar saying into a contemptible byword. . . . Words in dispute, however, should not be assimilated to a verbal brawl. The semiotic artifact is never so contradictory, diffuse, or *hommelette*-like—"a little man and also like a broken egg spreading without hindrance in all directions" (Coward and Ellis)—as to preclude the masterly intervention of an *homme-lettre,* a man of letters versed in the law. (77)

In the chapters that follow, several conventions of pornographic genres will be isolated and discussed. This is done to identify the dominant themes in pornography's regime of representation. The textual organization of the photo operates with a logic of seduction, a moment which implicates the reading subject in negotiations of desire, sexual difference, and the illicit. The questions guiding this investigation concern what constitutes this seductive moment labeled as "pornographic." Castration as a figuration of difference and conjoinment of fear and (unspoken) desire is a central metonym, and trope, for machinations within the text, and for a reader placed "at the keyhole" to these illicit representations. But I will argue that it is the (male) reader who is divested of phallic privilege—in spite of the appearance of "castrated" female genitalia.

For other things visible, and linguistic, complicate the stability of gendered categories and positions-in-representation: the vocabularies of the body speak to cultural and psychic transgression. Anal signifiers destroy the pretense to possessing difference; the gaze, penetrating and incisive, is the property of the female model. There is the presence of male models in soft- and hard-core.[120] And, as already mentioned, fetish accouterments and fetish relations stage an erotic theft. The circulation of an object recalling embodied fear and forfeiture, within a seductive economy, suggests a conspiracy between castration and eros, or thanatos and eros.

Thus the arguments contained here address the construction of sexual difference "in" seduction, and attempt to take us beyond the simple theorization of the hegemonic production of "woman" as "other."

We now turn to an elaboration of "the subject" which breaks with the humanism of both the behaviorist and orthodox feminist accounts. "The subject" is constituted by, in this case, a visual imaginary, not constitutive of it. And because the visual imaginary in question dramatizes sexual difference, the account below is necessarily sensitive to the acquisition of sexed identity, particularly the struggles and contradictions involved in this process of signification—in the text and for the reader. The discussion begins with, and is to a large extent informed by, attention to what Kaja Silverman calls the "cut," that moment (doomed to be perpetually relived) when the sexually differentiated subject undergoes those losses necessary to the processes of differentiation.[121] The losses associated with (sexual) differentiation, necessary for the emergence of the sexual subject, are sacrificial and painful. However, because they are necessary to cultural integration, they also constitute moments of pleasurable recognition. The induction into structures of sexual difference, replayed upon encountering a drama of sexed signification, is thus a struggle around shifting identifications.

The "Cut"

How can one explain why difference is seductive? The fascination with, and in looking at, configurations of sexual difference? Problematics in poststructuralism, psychoanalysis, film and discourse analysis have questioned the specificity of the formation of the subject within gender relations of difference, particularly the construction of the subject in relation to cultural technologies. This entails the study of the role of unconscious structuration in the production and reproduction of meaning, mediation through language, and the social and psychic workings of desire.

Pornography reveals a language of seduction. To penetrate the enigma of pornographic discourses is to enter the machinations of sexed subjectivity and its representations: that is, desire in language. In encountering the representation, the male reader is affirmed as separate from, and simultaneously addressed by, the model(s) before him. Pornography thrives on a system of coded differences based on the appropriation of gender differences. Pornographic photographs (particularly soft-core) are to a certain extent a play on the feminine form for the masculine reader. But it will be argued that ambivalence, i.e., tensions around difference and indifference, the subject who desires and the subject who longs for narcissistic in-difference, might be more pronounced in negotiating subjectivity in the pornographic text. Kaja Silverman (via Lacan) uses the formulation of the "cut" to embellish the notions of both agency and repression in the emergence of the subject.[122]

The "cut" is a two-edged manipulation. It is the process whereby the subject is fashioned as both distinct and separate from cultural representations (texts designed for the "ideal" reader, or "ideal I") and at the same time defined by them. In the "phantom character . . . [of] the suturing function,"[123] the subject experiences the ambivalence of absence and re-presentation in the reading of a text. The subject stands in for what is absent in the diegetic space. In the words of Jacques-Alain Miller, suture is "the relation of the subject to the chain of its discourse."[124] The process of suturing marks the incision through which the subject is cut out of the text only to be readdressed as part of its operation. In contrast to classic cinema, in pornography the reader is directly acknowledged, through the gaze of the female model, as, among other things, the complicit consumer/sexual spender.

The "cut" refers to the discursive structure which speaks to a subject formed amid "phenomenal loss and cultural recovery."[125] The "cut" can be used to demonstrate the centrality of loss in the negotiation of sexual difference and relations of desire: it is the discordant coupling of two moments. One side of the "cut" insists on the severance of the subject from an imaginary plenitude. This effects a partial guarantor of identity ("one" as different from an "other"). "Identity": "absolute sameness" or "sameness of essential or generic character in different instances." "Identity" is from the Latin *idem*, "same," which comes from *iterate*; and *iterate* is from the Sanskrit word *itara*, meaning "the other." Contained within the etymological affiliations around "identity," then, is the other side of the "cut": the workings of simultaneity. The subject is granted "oneness" only in separation from an "other," and one is always the "other" against and through which another subject's identity is constructed. Subjective cohesion is but a fiction, an imaginary wholeness. If "one" is defined only in relation to an "other," loss always looms in identity: to be "one" is always to take the position of the "other." Identities are thus relationally constructed and involve giving up something of oneself to "see" oneself from the position of the other.

The "Cut": Visual Otherness

The "cut" first of all establishes a system of binary differences. It is the fully social instance of self-recognition, the subject perceiving itself as "other than" (i.e., "one"). And the "cut" implicates both the "visual" and the "linguistic" in paradoxes of presence and absence. Anyone familiar with the pornographic discourses (as with, *inter alia,* the horror film) will know that intense fascination and pleasure in looking often accompanies disgust and horror.[126] This recalls the time when the subject is *en miroir,* dominated by an "imaginary equation" which helps define it as "other," first within a scopic regime.[127] The captivation and allure of the visual imaginaries partly recalls this scenario whereby subjective cohesion is simultaneously an alienation. The "image" granted the subject at this early stage severs him/her from its imaginary and indifferentiating omnipotence and grants it an imaginary coherence, through its distinction—separation—from the reflection or point of view of others. Paradoxically, this "self"-identity (how the subject "sees" itself) is constructed, through discongruity, as a fictive plenitude. The subject assumes an image as separate from, and defined by, others (those who "hold" or manipulate the "mirror").[128] Its reflection is only a totality in alienation, a misrecognition or meconnaissance. The subject's "imago,"[129] or ideal image, is delimited by the vision—and desires—of another. The illusion of coherence supplied by the external, mediating work of the "mirror" is the work of culture. Silverman argues that the mirror phase is not the offering of an empty space which the subject fills with his own reflection; rather, it is reminiscent of "traces of cultural intervention."[130] The "ideal I" (the idealized self-image) is part of a value system which precedes and mediates between structure and subject. This is the pleasurable perception/reflection through which the first steps toward "identification" and the anxiety of severance begin.

What is important to retain from the above is an emphasis on the losses involved in the emergence of the prelinguistic and linguistic subject. The sense of completion granted by the unifying mirror, or that which gives back a reflection, also produces a corresponding effect of alienation. The loss is generic to the individual and confronts him/her at the various stages of his/her reconstitution as subject. Lacan writes that the subject is formed amid an essential division occurring with the first rupture as the infant is separated from the maternal body at birth.[131] Another "splitting" occurs with the inauguration of the sexed subject: "In the psyche, there is nothing by which the subject may situate himself as a male or female being. . . . At sexed reproduction . . . the living being, by being subject to sex, has fallen under the blow of individual death."[132]

Certainly the pornographic spectator-text relationship is reminiscent of the mirror stage with its dialectic of vision: i.e., in "looking," one is given back a rendition of one's self—which makes him "other" to his image, and thus the subject oscillates in (and from) positions of "otherness." Jane Gallop elaborates these machinations of interiority and exteriority in referring to the mirror stage as a "totalizing ideal" which forms the subject's relation to himself as thereafter always mediated "through a totalizing image that has come from outside."[133] The mirror phase is one of both "anticipation and retroaction"; the child "jubilantly . . . appears *already* to be what she will *only later become*."[134] Gallop is careful to underscore the ambiguity of the corporal image/sensation. She notes that the mirror phase takes the "body in bits and pieces" and grants it a totality, a whole body image. But Gallop (with Laplanche and Pontalis) argues that linear time is subverted; that is to say, the mirror phase, properly conceived, does not provide coherence to the body first experienced as fragmented. Rather, "*that* violently unorganized *image only comes after* the mirror stage so as to *represent what came before*."[135] This movement of the mirror phase is characterized by loss, slippage, and its own impossibility:

> It produces the future through anticipation and the past through retroaction. And yet it is itself a moment of self-delusion, of captivation by an illusory image. Both future and past as thus rooted in an illusion . . . the belief in a projected image. . . . The self is constituted through anticipating what it will become, and then this anticipatory model is used for gauging what was before.[136]

This is one trope of the Imaginary phase: the Symbolic resides within. Its workings are particularly salient in considering the subject's engagement with "techniques of the imaginary," i.e., moving and still images.[137] The deed of Imaginary oscillations, although the guarantor of the specular subject, is necessarily a fiction, a "misrecognition." The scopic investment (scopophilic, Freud reminds us) in, and by, the reader positions him to witness a sexual scene (a keyhole to a mirror of another kind). However, the subject/viewer is necessarily outside of the diegetic space of the photograph, there to contemplate its "presence" in the photo by way of absence and signifiers of absence.

The Subject in Language

The Symbolic is where the subject fully emerges as different and sees his desires as circumscribed by the presence and desires of the other. Difference (the constitution of the subject as "one," but not at one with the other) is a discourse of the "other," and sexual difference is the final symbolic effect of linguistic signification (the "cut").

The "cut" also refers to the linguistic and metaphorical device used to designate the creation of sexed subjects of and for culture, and the relation of the subject to textual pleasures and unpleasures. Within the linguistic paradigm it reveals the "bar" or gap (the severance) between the signifier and signified. To begin with, language names, locates, and repositions the subject vis-à-vis the "object" world. However, language is a shifting anchor.[138] Within the structural relations of the patriarchal family, the father is in the "privileged mode of presence," and from his position emanates the Law or Name of the Father.[139] This is the most lawful position in the family configuration, around which all significations of heteronormative desire circulate. The nomination, of course, exists independently of the biological father; it is a linguistic designation which "provide[s] a liberation from the here-and-now of the Imaginary" (that prelinguistic period marked by the [dis]illusion of plenitude and imaginary perceptions).[140] Language initiates a number of separations—in this case, the nomination of the role from biological disposition. This is "precisely what permits the child to take the father's place in his turn."[141] Thus the structural-linguistic axiom about discourse—i.e., "language speaks us"—is profoundly social. The Name of the Father corresponds to the symbolic function which "from the dawn of history has identified his person with the figure of the law";[142] he is the chief signifier at the head of the family table.

The bar—what stands between the signifier and the signified—intervenes to impose meaning on the signified: "The signifier answers to the function of representing the signified . . . the signifier sends forth its light into the shadow of incomplete significations"; and, "the signifier . . . anticipates meaning . . . make[s] us wait for it."[143] The meaning and word/object exist in relations of tension and friction. This "semiotic fraction"[144] instigates a splitting: it separates the "real subject" from its representation. The bar, the primacy of the signifier over the signified, intervenes between the subject and the subject's needs, located as they are in the bloated signifier, and its defiles. The signified is still but another hidden signifier.

The subject is "figured in symbolism" by substitutes (for something that doesn't exist as a discrete entity), defined and obtained only in relation to other signifiers: a father is defined against a son, although a son might be a father someday. Passing through the defiles of the signifier, sons and daughters repress desire for both mother and father and thus desire "appropriately." The subject's representation—the process by which it represents itself in language, meaning, and culture—is its division or exclusion from the symbolic chain.[145] The construction of the unconscious then is composed of alienation and repressions "through the very processes by which, in receiving a name, it is transformed into a representation of itself."[146] A subject is formed in language and a linguistic chain (in syntagmatic and paradigmatic insistence), hence Lacan's statement: "A signifier is that which represents the subject for another signifier."[147] The symbolic cut, or what Lacan calls the "cut in discourse . . . the strongest being that which acts as a bar between the signifier and the signified," is the "cut" out of the self and into representation.[148]

This cut is first an incision of the body (the "real" organic, phenomenal form and experience). It refers also to the gaps, ruptures, and lacunae which structure the unconscious.[149] As a linguistic severance, the bar in the signifying chain "verifies the structure of the subject as discontinuity in the real."[150] The cut is one determining feature of the subject's "constituent relation to the signifier itself."[151] It is again the bar, that which bars the subject from full witness to signification, its signification, representation, or at least full representation of its drives. The longing to see representations of one's desire points to the impossibility of representing desire (and the impossibility of representing the phallus, as we will see). The cut is a structural relation, tied to the fashions of the signifier, from which "everything emerges" (the subject, meaning, language, desire).[152] Hence the phrase "the cut of desire," desire emerging out of the structural organization of drives.[153]

The crucial abstractions here revolve around the structuring/rupture of the subject in absences, gaps, frictions, which sustains the subject in relation to an/other. Lacan refers, after Freud, to the "scar," the mark of the unconscious, the result of the neurotic coupling of the real and the subject, i.e., the subject's longing to remain in "harmony with a real."[154] Or, the "cut" is twofold: difference instituted (self-identity) and difference transgressed (self-denial).[155]

Hence the phrase "the cut of desire," desire emerging out of the structural organization of needs.[156] And finally, two important rhetorical strategies of the cut, in relation to the negotiation of sexual difference and the sexed subject. One invokes the psychic consequences of what is signified by the cut/bar (and subsequent mapping of psychic terrain in what follows): the cut as gap, rupture. Fredric Jameson writes: "Language learning comes before us as a racking torture, a palpably physical kind of suffering upon which the feral child is only imperfectly willing to enter"; language is the "tragic symbol of [the] unavoidable alienation."[157] A second strategy of the cut refers to an embodied metaphor, that of the "topological function of the rim," its parallel bearing on the "anatomical mark":[158] this is the imaginary struggle to be signified in the symbolic (to surrender to the defiles of the signifer), and the necessary cut from biological needs/drives into linguistic expression. Lacan: "the concept of drive, in which [the subject] is designated by an organic, oral, anal, etc., mapping that satisfies the requirement of being all the farther away from speaking the more he speaks."[159] The celestial charting of the body into erogenous zones summons the residue of the cut, suggesting a "margin or border."[160] The examples Lacan offers of corporal dislocation—i.e., mutilation upon entry into the chain of subjectivity, meaning, desire; mutilation upon alienation; the dislocated subject—are: "lips, 'the enclosure of the teeth'; the rim of the anus, the tip of the penis, the vagina, the slit formed by the eyelids, even the horn-shaped aperture of the ear."[161] What Lacan calls the "grammatical artifice," the severing of the primordial drive from its expression in language, might also be termed then the "grammatical orifice."

The Cut and the Desiring Subject

The acquisition of language, the symbolic nomination of the subject from the place of language, is an ambivalent nexus of pleasurable integration into culture, and, of course, the sliding under the bar of signification, or cultural mastery.[162] Kaja Silverman re-reads Freud's allegorical tale of the mastery of unpleasure, the observations of his grandson's enactment and re-enactment of the disappearance of his mother, in the form of a game.[163] The game involved tossing a spool on a string to make it repeatedly disappear and announcing "fort" ("gone"). Whereas Freud argued that unpleasure would be merely tolerated en route to the "pleasure principle," Silverman's point is that the child is gratified, if not enthralled, in the re-enacting of the unpleasurable scenario. She locates the "fort/da" episode within a dialectic by establishing that the child's linguistic pronouncements—"fort" ("gone") when the spool is out of sight, and "da" ("there") when he reels it in—activate the unconscious. "Fort" and "da" signify only in terms of the other; in particular, "da" surrenders to "fort." The idea of the alienation or "fading" of the subject (as Lacan calls it) is strengthened when one notes, in Freud's account, that the child enacted the first part of the game ("fort") more often than the completed version. The oblique suggestion is made by Freud, explicitly by Silverman via Lacan, that the child was actually involved in making *himself* disappear along with the toy. Hence, the "first signifying coupling . . . enables us to conceive that the subject appears first in the Other, in so far as the first signifier . . . emerges in the field of the Other and represents the subject for another signifier. . . . Hence the division of the subject—where the subject appears somewhere as meaning, he is manifested elsewhere as 'fading,' as disappearance."[164]

This fading or loss is subjection to, and subject of, the signifier, language, or culture and is the "pleasure of mastery."[165] This is the agency of the "cut" and is re-enacted every time we encounter cultural texts (themselves a play on signification, an exchange of meaning within a coded chain): "in so far as they master us: . . . to the extent that they oblige us to re-enact those moments of loss and false recovery by which we are constituted as subjects."[166]

Transgressing the "Cut": Desire and Indifference

Central to the paradigms of subjectivity discussed here are the forfeitures involved in the negotiation of identity. Jacqueline Rose puts it well: "subject[ion] to a master image, and ultimately to the image of the master (the Oedipus complex)."[167] Thus, symbolic castration or the subjection to difference is the same side of the cut as the "negation" of the self vis-à-vis the mirror-other,[168] and the marking of the cut through the coded operations of language. This is the half of the equation that posits the subject formed in scenarios of "loss and false recovery," in systems of differences: self-image slides under the mirror, subject/signified slides under the signifier. The mirror is the master of self-illusion; the signifier, endlessly commutable and able to resurrect another signified (which then becomes another signifier). Both supply difference at a cost, and suggest a difference that is chimerical, unstable, and constructed within the discourse of the "other."

Both Freudian and Lacanian accounts of the subject revolve around the primacy of castration *fears* as the foundation of oedipal law. But to stand at the "cut" is to encounter those moments of cultural mastery (confronting symbolic castrations) which are nonetheless culturally pleasurable. For Freud, the ritual encounter with the castrated other (principally the mother) is an anatomical discovery. The "threat of castration" is the "deferred effect" of the Oedipus complex.[169] One possible form of erotic communion, and transgression, is for the male child to possess the father and displace the mother as the feminine object; another would be to compete with the father for the mother's affections. Both are, in the real, incestuous impossibilities. The latter, though, leads to the intense cultural identification with the father, and the ensuing threat of castration is unconsciously experienced as just punishment for guilty wishes to annihilate him (and therefore possess the feminine other). The oedipalization of the male subject—his cultural positioning and repositioning—is coupled with, and resolved by, horror at the glance at female genitals and the perception of embodied loss, and fear at imagined retribution. Within this model, castration fears are allayed through the fetishization of the female, the fashioning of her in terms of endowment.

To be sure, the Lacanian account elects the discursive phallus, not the anatomical penis, as the figure in scenarios of difference, desire, and the other. It is subject to the laws of signification in the linguistic field.[170] What does the "other" have that I don't have? Lacan would say "the phallus" or symbolic privilege. This is a crucial and insinuating trope, again working through absence (perception and disavowal): Lacan notes that the phallus as signifier "can play its role only when veiled."[171] The signifier, through displacement and absence, is in search of a signified to slide under. And what does it signify? Desire, the desire of the other: that is, the child's initial demands intervene in the (m)other's field of desire. The demand for love is the veiled demand to be the object of another's love, and that one's desire be the object of the other's desire. The phallus signifies the dialectic of difference and desire: "the demand for love" is "the test of desire." That is, "the phallus stands for that moment of rupture. It refers mother and child to the dimension of the symbolic which is figured by the father's place. The mother is taken to desire the phallus not because she contains it (Klein), but precisely because she does not. The phallus therefore belongs somewhere else; it breaks the two-term relation and initiates the order of exchange."[172]

What should be emphasized in this discussion is not phenomenal desire but, more appropriately, signs of desire. If the other "has" the phallus (and this is part of the "dominant fiction"),[173] it is only in discourses of the other's desire that the subject can also have access to it. But if the phallus is the mark of absence, it cannot be seen, nor can desire (the "non-representative representative");[174] one can simulate only the phallus, desire, and signs of desire. All are veiled: desire and the phallus work only through their signs. If the desire of the mother is congruent with being and having the phallus, then the child will wish to be the phallus "in order to satisfy that desire." Phallic desire is singular, exclusive, and competitive. It characterizes a relation whereby people (and objects) are desired for what they represent. Desire is thus a reciprocal play of substitutions, models, obstacles, and doubles in a chain: the rival is a model for another's desire.[175] Once again difference, or signs of difference, incites the desiring subject. Desire is not a privileged object, and not a simple relationship between subject and object; it is a deferral, a stayed engagement. The cut out of demand and into desire is a "castration." Jacqueline Rose: "Castration means first of all this—that the child's desire for the mother does not refer *to* her but *beyond* her, to an object, the phallus, whose status is first imaginary (the object presumed to satisfy her desire) and then symbolic recognition that desire cannot be satisfied."[176] The cut into language, the linguistic interruption, is also a castration. It recognizes and grants difference, a castrating and desirable transaction.

The subject as somewhere—floating, in the nonspace—in the nexus of the other-than: the subject positioned in alienation from the "other" who grants him a self-image, albeit skewed, is how the "other" sees him. Lacan notes the wrenching involved: "When, in love, I solicit a look, what is profoundly unsatisfying and always missing is that—*you never look at me from the place from which I see you.*"[177] And the subject-formed-in-distance also sees the "other" as precisely *that*. This is profoundly cultural as it places the subject in (social) relations which delimit the possibilities of desire, the knowable, the representable, and, within language, the sayable.

Important nuances have been put to the above scenario to prevent the suggestion of a humanist, unsexed, subject. Kaja Silverman, in *The Acoustic Mirror,* argues that while all cultural subjects must submit to castration, the masculine subject within patriarchy partakes of the construction of women as "anatomical deficiency and discursive inadequacy."[178] Characterized by his own sacrificial subjectivity, he projects that primal loss onto the figure of woman to disavow his own dispossessions.[179] With this in mind, and with the symbolic material under discussion, difference (castration) does not reside with women and female "lack." Phallic desire may look like the prerogative of men, not because they *are* or *have* the phallus but because it embodies singularity, the principle of one, and because it is modeled on the organ with which it is synonymous.[180] One conceit of the "dominant fiction," as Silverman points out, is this alignment of the penis with the phallus, the latter propped on the former.[181] It should be added that "phallic" is an adjective most frequently employed with negative connotations, even more so when applied to women: it usually denotes strength and focus (although it is variously deployed as "aggressive," etc.) but also can refer to a particular look or style of dress.[182] Used in this way, a phallic woman clearly suggests a departure from (proper) femininity. Why can't women be phallic? They are in pornography, or at least their body language and dress simulate the phallic code. Lace and the pearl (two common features of contemporary pornographic photographs) are seductive because they carry both feminine and masculine attributes. By this is meant that they are the currently designated apparel of women, yet (in the words of Stephen Heath), "stretched on the racks of equivocation and etymology," and history, they conceal associations that are in the domain of masculinity, as we will see in subsequent chapters.[183] To describe a gaze as "penetrating" ("if looks could kill"; "eyes like the barrel of a gun") places text and referent, whether we want them there or not, in the metonymic company of things used "to pierce" or for "forceful entry." The root of "fuck" is "to strike," thus the metonym expands to underscore the cultural essence of the body and biological significance. Eyes penetrate; so does a penis (always singular). Figuring the discursive body in language takes us to the limits of language. Why *are* penetrating eyes phallic? And the stiletto heel? "Stretched on the racks of etymology," and in the politics of signification, they are. This is the (inevitable) incomplete attempt at pure difference and its effacement which creates a simulated moment of loss and forfeiture. The pornographic model, in other words, carries the signs of his phallic masculinity: it is this play of differences, this erotic theft, and the indifference to difference involved, that seduces.

Castration and the cut evoke a fetishistic economy: it is around the fetish that many of the above issues coalesce. That is, the fetish is a stand-in, a substitute, not an object but a relation. It is a representation without a referent, in the sense that it refers to absence or loss; it points to the limits of representation. And it recalls castration fears in affiliation with an instance of sexual arousal. The fetish is assumed to have strong discursive power and the transcendental responsibility of disavowing knowledge and fear of castration, to make women the palatable other. The following are some examples from the more contemporary literature regarding the theorization of fetishistic representation, which posit the patriarchal code as a singularly phallic code dominated by the fear of and subsequent compensation for castration:

The female figure poses a . . . problem. She . . . connotes something that the look continually circles around but disavows: her lack of a penis, implying a threat of castration and hence unpleasure.[184]

Physical sexual difference is no longer unmentionable within public representations of women that are designated "pornographic." Physical sexual difference can be promoted within these representations because the fetish has been shifted from compensating for woman's lack of a penis to the finding of the woman's phallus in her sexual pleasure. . . . Both security and abolition of separation from the representation are provided for the spectator by this arrangement.[185]

The mechanism of fetishism . . . is that which provides a defence against symbolic castration and in so doing makes "woman" adequate as a sexual object.[186]

Within such formulations, difference is necessarily achieved as part of a cultural code which subjects individuals to signification whereby the signifier is always phallic and desire centers on an object: the phallic signifier. Transgressions of the code do occur; these are usually the concern of sociologists who study "deviance" and psychoanalysts who chronicle the various fetishisms which accompany "perverse" behavior. These "perversions" are problematized around, as it were, the cracks in the phallic code, the instabilities in sexual categories. And while the pornographic discourses are, it should become clear, a play on fetishistic scopophilia and scenarios of castration, phallic signification can be subsumed under the logic of seduction and desire, which presumes a structure of relations and exchanges, not objects. The evident perversions which exist in pornographic discourses are "normal perversions." That is, the logic of desire implicates a structure of loss, self-denial, surrender, castration. It is, essentially, an asceticism of will and of the body turned erotic. Investment in the fetish entails one's own symbolic disempowerment. Giving another the penis (or the phallus) entails one's own symbolic dismemberment: it is an act of self-denial. And within our cultural institutions these are pervasive perversions. The logic of the "cut" presumes that the possessive marks ("signs") of desire are sought out and surrendered. That is, there are encoded differences; but because the "cut" is desirable, there are also encoded transgressions which hover at "indifference," or the desire to give up the phallus.

Porn is about relations of desire within an imaginary scopic register. We must return to the discursive subject and his engagement by the pornographic/photographic regime. The "cut" is useful here as it is the negotiation of difference within a discourse of desire (i.e., the other). Desire is unspeakable in two senses: there are no words to describe, with precision, jouissance. As Barthes notes, "bliss" signals both the "pleasure of the text" and "a mode of vanishing, of annulment of the subject."[187] And our desires (only ever simulated) are unconsciously formed first in the "inter-dit." The exchanges which instigate the schemings of desire within the photographic regime are a series of displacements, losses, and absences—of the reader, but within the diegetic space as well. The photos are full of signifiers, but what are they signifying? What makes the photo desirable is the way it straddles the cut, a wholly ambivalent moment. Porn is about the (mis)management of difference within the visual realm.

In conclusion, desiring subjects are placed at the "cut," a synchronic alienation *and* guarantor of fictive wholeness. On the one side, full separation from either visual or linguistic signification would imply pure difference, or the isolated ego. Pure difference is an impossibility (and anyway would signal pure indifference). The alienations involved in the structuring of difference are the gaps, ever present, between the fictive self and its representation (either a coupling with the mirror or the substitutions and forfeitures which are part of the induction into language).

On the other side, full reunification with an imaginary plenitude requires the relinquishing of one's vital possessions to become one with another. It too is an impossibility; a total engagement with the mirror would signal the subject's narcissistic complement, the tragic mark of indifference, or death. The same is true of the linguistic nominations through which gendered subjects are signified by the law. The subject may be formed amid losses, but desire is not simply the longing for an anterior reunification. The losses are the culturally significant moments of pleasurable integration. What is ultimately desirable are the simulations which constitute representations of the "cut"—those moments which mark a refusal to respect full closure around either difference or narcissism.

A Different Phallus

> The One is always the same and unchangeable.
>
> —Agrippa of Nettesheim, ca. 1500

Desire is a strategy of difference; difference is strategic desire. In the play of passion, what gendered subjects desire are not objects, not even significant others, but visible signs of an/other's desire. The phallic urgency of the pornographic moment elects signs of desire to stand in for desire itself.

Jean-Joseph Goux uses the myth of Osiris and the reconstructed phallus to argue that the archetype of all simulacra is the phallus. That is, the contemporary, unconscious, structural phallus replaces the threatened penis. In the myth of Osiris, Isis dismembers, and re-members, the body of her dead husband, then institutes a simulated penis (a simulacrum, the phallus) in the place of the "virile member" she cannot find, and orders others to honor it. Goux argues that the phallus is "an artifact that simulates what is missing, at the same time rendering it sacred and larger than life to make it a cult object." It is both the break and the link—"the loss and the replacement of the loss by an idealizing erection."[188] Goux demonstrates the connection between the phallus and form, idea, logos, fertile and rational power—the first principle: "The offspring which *is* and which, multiplying, separates from the One (still beyond being); looking toward Him (the self, the autos), this offspring acquires a vital seed.

... The engendered being constitutes itself as intelligence by that seminal and inseminating vision; a gaze directed toward the source of life."[189] What is crucial here is what Goux refers to as the "trials of dismemberment" necessary for the "virile organ to become something other than matter" (49). To become a sign, in other words, a fundamental separation must occur. Access to the sign for the masculine subject requires a "bloody renunciation"; thus the phallus has detachable value. Goux's contribution to the feminist project is his insistence on the "deadly loss" and "phallic effigy in which the subject finally recuperates his integrity, his vital unity" (61–62). The search for his simulated phallic self involves two sacrifices: one of his embodied self, and the other involving a partial effacement of the (feminine) other. As Goux puts it, the phallus is returned to the mother, who is on the side of matter, so that the masculine subject can engage with eternal, phallic renewal and be aligned with the absolute, spirit, the represented, the invariable.

Pornography depicts a partial effacement of difference, an androgynous longing (a bloody reunion) but in unspeakable (unconscious) terms. Hence the excitement of the simulated moment—the simulated androgynous terms with which the pornographic body textual is written. The simulation is the counterfeit, and something of the original is always lost in the staging of mimetic desire. But total androgyny (a plenitude, being at one with one) would leave nothing to desire.

If symbolic castrations precede the acknowledgment of anatomical sexual difference,[190] the phallus is distinct from the penis. The castrations are the losses associated with separations from beloved objects (e.g., breasts, feces, the spool-on-a-reel in the "fort-da" game) and alienation in language (Lemaire: "The word is the murder of the thing and . . . this death is the condition of the symbol").[191] The inauguration of sexual difference is fundamental to the oedipal, castrating scenario under the law of the "paternal metaphor." The Name of the Father is the prohibitory, castrating function; and this foregrounds the move from nature to culture and, within the oedipal scenario, institutes the phallus as the signifier of value and loss. To assume an identity is to assume the other; this is the approximate loss of self (the "cut"). The paternal phallus (or the father's phallic desire) is the organizing principle, the gap, producing sexual desire. To want the father's phallus/desire (unattainable in the real) is to desire castration/sameness. One cannot possess the phallus, but one can (and does) yearn after its absence (the longing to desire no more), absence which is a dialectical play on presence. Sexual difference, determined by who is perceived to have or not have the mythical phallus, is then a play on possession, and fears and desires for dispossession.

The ambivalence of the phallic code of desire is this friction around fears, and desires, of dismemberment, both of which must be disavowed; and the longing for a surrogate to stand in for the missing desire. All these transactions involve fetishizing the female form, endowing the fetish with the projections of what the male does not have, his longing for the "cut": hence fetishizing masculine desire. The fetish, that is, takes the place of something (is an "other," Lemaire's murder and deathlike symbol, the lifeless site of desire), and it disavows that which it resurrects, *at the same time.*

Sexual Fixations

Pornography is about textual, transgressive bodies. "Sexual difference" is not the unproblematic assumption of an immediately visible binary opposition. Porn, perhaps in particular, apparently re-presents a text of difference where the actors take their place on one side of the sexual divide: the women are women and the men, if any, are men. This is because on the surface, porn is about bodies and embodied difference. But pornographic bodies are dressed up in the fabric of culture's desire. Pornographic bodies are set into discourses of seduction and difference, although the boundaries of difference are continually transgressed, and this is the pornographic affinity, precisely. Foucault is useful in demonstrating this. The "TV" body demonstrates "the textual" best as it presents a body upon which difference collapses—but to which a precarious and erotic difference is restored through adornment. And the rules governing how the body is staged—as masculine or feminine—through clothing form a discursive structure which takes over where biology leaves off and which exists beyond the conscious whim of the individual reader. Hence, again, a public dream, and without an author.

But the body in "TV" porn is, admittedly, the textual excess of sexual boundaries.

The "straight" genres (soft- and hard-core) also simulate an androgynous code which signifies in the pornographic chain of command. "Otherness," whether on the "TV" or straight body, threatens to cancel itself and collapse in indifference. It will be argued that the pleasurable moment that is pornography is the simulated movement between difference and indifference, signs of desire coded as significant in an approximation of androgyny. As Chevalier argues, the machinations of desire require those sacrificial signs which indicate a longing to possess and to be possessed, a "wishful simulation."[192] In this process, the sacrifices constitute one's dispossession; in a semiotic play, this is the dressing *up* of the body in signs of the other's desire: she, the simulated phallic model, is poised to penetrate the partially feminized/objectified reader. At its most explicitly sexual, this involves trading places in an erotic communion which resembles a simulated androgynous union. For example, in a scene from *Penthouse* (February 1986), "Toni" is described as "determined to star in major movies. Still the tough city girl, she tells us what her dream role would be. 'More than anything, I would love to be a female Charles Bronson type. There's no doubt in my mind I could play a tough-guy role as well as a man.' Is there anyone out there who wouldn't line up to watch her in 'Death Wish Part V'?" Dressed to kill, indeed.

A symptomatic reading identifies the recurring images and associations which insist on being spoken. The pornographic text "speaks" through fixations on the "body" and the "fetish." Four conventions of the pornographic photo have been isolated. They are the genital configuration and the structure of the gaze. And the recurring fetishes are the high-heel shoe, and lingerie and jewelry. What follows is an investigation of their structure within the pornographic "moment."

The Body

2 | Sexual Techniques

AT FIRST GLANCE, all pornographic genres appear to be characterized by nakedness:[1] a visual (and obscene) excess of bodies and bodily configurations, rendered objects, undignified and immodest through lack of apparel. Indeed, the essential fixation of the pornographic moment appears to be on the graphic, if not grotesque, representation of the "forbidden site of specularity and ultimate object of male desire," the female sex organs.[2] The embedded assumption in the literature is that difference is thus visible "on sight,"[3] and the genitals are an unsightly figure with which to image the female form and its otherness. This assumes that representations of biology are given. The pornographic body, however, is constructed through its discursive arrangement: the body is not naked but adorned and dressed up, is not disciplined in terms of sexual pathology but speaks to sexualities. Pornography as a discourse on sexuality constitutes the body, not vice versa.

The pornographic body and its corporal fragments are so strongly discursive that they place the body into the "meta-anatomical" and threaten to transgress the discursive limits of the biological corpus (the pornographic body knows no *textual* limitations), if not annihilate the body altogether.

In what follows, the conventions of the pornographic body are isolated and examined with a view to understanding their specific deployment in this spectator-text relationship.

Soft-Core: The Breast

The breasts are not just breasts within pornographic genres, for they too are coded beyond the materiality of their form. They are not depicted in their "natural" incarnation but are subjected to a privileging of the singular: the most common representation is of the single breast, or the breasts "separated" by jewelry or clothing, e.g., a string of pearls dangling between them. In soft-core pornography the model is usually the sole occupant of the diegetic space, and configurations of her body are given over to this display. As one of the most notable signifiers of femininity are the breasts, it is of particular interest that the single breast is the favored icon (as opposed to both pictured together).

Margaret Miles investigates the depiction of the single exposed breast in early Renaissance art.[4] She argues that the prevalence of the Virgin's/Mother Mary's single breast in religious imagery is not "susceptible to simple naturalistic interpretation." Miles writes of the Florentine emphasis on the "Virgin with one bare breast," and her thesis is that the "Virgin" is depicted as "nursing" a fourteenth-century public ravaged by "famine, plague and social chaos," and thus the single exposed breast represents the (female) body's "best show of power" (196, 205). These virginal images constitute, according to Miles, a dialectic around the ideal of the powerful Virgin Mother (with "power over life and death") and the actual material reality of women at the time. Although she is an art historian and does not speak in psychoanalytic terms, Miles implicitly privileges a pre-oedipal textual formation. I would argue, however, that the soft-core pornographic moment is reflective of the oedipal engagement with its emphasis on scripts of sexual difference and the dramatic play on desire and loss. The pornographic scenario is decidedly sexual, but the privileging of only one breast is a curious technique of the body charged with confessing all the sins of the flesh.

The breasts, of course, are profoundly feminine: fleshy protuberances on the female body, icons within sexual discourses. Flügel notes: "With the greater freedom of emotional life that distinguished the Renaissance . . . and from that time onwards . . . the bosom has always been a centre of special interest in feminine dress"[5]—and, referring to Miles's thesis, a maternal source of comfort and life. They contain a liquid, a life-sustainer, milky white (indeed, "jugs" is slang for breasts); the maternal and the sexual coalesce in the breasts to render them feminine.

Having said this, the pornographic discourse then takes the breasts and subjects them to a singular, phallic principle. The preferred configuration re-zones that aspect of the feminine corpus and re-presents the single breast (no fidelity to the anatomical rendition). One is offered the single "tit," as it were. Eric Partridge, in *The Penguin Dictionary of Historical Slang*, tells us that a "tit" is both "a girl or young woman . . . the female pudend" *and* "the penis." As well, a "tit" is "a foolish and ineffectual man." The individual "tit" then has the symbolic properties of both masculinity and femininity: it is a simulated androgynous offering. The uniform breast is a marriage of two instances of the feminine, the maternal and the sexual. It also invokes the masculine, anticipating the phallic code in a conspiracy: the feminine form contains milky secretions that resemble the seminal flow.

The single breast parallels the single erection: there is only one phallus, one erection, and it strains to be represented, to be significant. The breast in pornography is represented alone, protruding from the body. The nipple is erect, and most often when the breast is displayed in this singular fashion, it is offered to the viewer *on its own*, without competing for the viewer's attention with other visual offerings, e.g., the genitals. The single breast is a simulated phallic offering, a masculine writing on the female form. The model is penetrating the reader but not to "nurse" him.

The "breast-as-phallus" is one of the body's "best shows" of power, but also its best show of desire: erect, taut, and peeking out from behind a blouse, brassiere, or other form of lingerie. Like the fetish (itself a simulacrum, the part standing in for the whole, and a disavowal of the knowledge of what it stands for) it is the body's part-object, either always there or always threatening to peek out and greet the reader. If the breast pokes out from under a shirt, it appears not as part of the body but as an appendage, with an object status all its own. And like the fetish it is held in fascination, by both reader and model. She, for example, gazes longingly, and with intense passion, at the exposed breast: it is an object of fascination for *her*. She touches it, often licks it, thus reinforcing its visual status; indeed, the skin is often wet or oiled to heighten the part-object's specularity. This seems phallic or at least masculine in the sense that the single breast is subject to a curious organizing principle and is fascinating, to the model and to the reader, in the way the penis typically is in hard-core. The breast "fascinates" in the sense of being "irresistible," "enchanting," "charming" (Latin *fascinatus:* "to enchant, spell, witchcraft"). Both model and reader are "bewitched" and under the "spell" of this projected fantasy. In this sense, the single breast may be the body's part-object, part-of-the-body, and thus a precondition to fetishistic relations of significance.

The glimpse of the single breast as a carnal fragment is not simply a tantalizing display of the nakedness to come, for we know that the pornographer's body is *not* the body divested. The artifacts adorning the body are as important as the bodily display itself, and are not used merely to indicate what will soon be exposed, or what was previously covered. The breast, in the workings of the "photographic lexis"[6]—with its own referent, its homage to death, and anxiously playing on the edge of presence/absence, the imaginary off-screen—is "a commemorative trace of an absent object."[7] If the single breast in a binary system calls into imaginary space what is absent, the image still activates another single (absent) breast. This really is the doubled play of "there/not there," a simultaneous imaging of the seen and unseen, what Metz calls the operations of a "pocket phallus."[8] The fetish and the phallus are implicated in narratives of loss ("and protection against loss"),[9] and both are part of a visual order in which perception and disavowal share the same frame. The exposed breast may then be the "pocket phallus," the part-object always recalling the whole, yet suppressing it at the same time, "replacing an absence by a presence."[10] It is the "there/not there" structure which is held in fascination within this context. The "tit," then, is distinctively and pretentiously ambisexual.

When the two breasts are visible within the diegetic space, they are often (as noted) symbolically separate: jewelry, such as a strand of pearls, falls between them. When held apart, their doubleness *and* singularity are emphasized. The conspicuous separation of the two breasts heightens the visual investment—the reader's eyes dart back and forth to accommodate this zoning of the feminine body for pleasure. This configuration of the upper body points to a fashionable ambivalence: the breast is part of a spectacular articulation of the body which re-presents femininity in partially phallic terms. It is rendered so through the transformation of the breasts from natural flesh to fetish, and through the discursive privileging of the singular. The breasts are separated into single instances of visual pleasure and partial phallic endowment: breasts straining against lingerie and clothing, and toward the camera/eye of the viewer, complete with erect nipples.[11]

Soft-Core: The Genitals

Typically, in soft-core the model's genital offering takes one of three forms. She either (1) presents a frontal and fully exposed view of the vulva, usually in grotesque and exaggerated form as her hands enunciate the vulval area to allow for the closest possible scrutiny; (2) presents a visual arrangement of the buttocks to include both vulva and anus; or (3) offers a "rear" view that is profoundly anal. These are more than merely the "exposing to view [of] certain acts or anatomies"[12] but are a curious induction into economies of difference, differences at a cutting, castrating edge.

Within the classic psychoanalytic lexicon, a male's glimpse at the female genitals prompts the imagination of the "loss of his own penis . . . and the threat of castration takes its deferred effect."[13] Pornographic images are full of castrating scenarios which dominate the narrative. The female genital exhibition is an admixture of castration (she is without a penis), sexual difference (she is other than male), and an erotic play on both (she is seductive). (This would, of course, overlay with fetishistic inscriptions and the desirous notations on the body textual of the model. She is without the penis, yet the fetish as penis or phallic symbol endows the model in a compensatory and seductive manner.) In many instances (especially in the case of *Penthouse* and *Hustler,* for example, less so in the more conservative *Playboy*) the model flaunts her genitals ostentatiously to expose, in graphic terms, the potential for penetration. Just as it is an invitation to invade her body, it is also a flirtation with a castrating scenario that should normally frighten the male viewer. He stands, that is, in front of the classic "vagina dentata."

The intersection of the "vagina with teeth," obvious castration, and a seductive spectator-text relationship challenges the theorization of the dramatization of castration as fearful. That is, the marking of difference is a writing of the body around loss, of both model and viewer. The female body marked as castrated is missing the penis (this is her inauguration, within a phallic economy, into loss). She at the same time is poised to *castrate*: this is the reader's loss. This elaboration of difference, the spectacle of not having the penis, foregrounds castration in a most indiscreet, if not brazen, way. And like anything sensational, it provokes a look. The vivid representation of the castrated form connotes a "brilliance": it "radiates," and has a specular luster. Often the vulva is accentuated by subtle beams of light which enhance it as a fascinating image. The area is highlighted and dazzles in another way: it is wet and shiny, it glistens, no doubt also to heighten the illusion of the model's desire. She wants the reader to see that she wants him. That territory of her desire demands the gaze of the reader.

This is the colonization of the body to a technical brilliance. The zoning of the body for pleasure is its spectacular prerogative, and again desire refers only to referents of desire: desire is a representation, visual in this case—which always implicates, invests, an other (the reader). Accordingly, the *signs* of desire must be present: her sexual eagerness is apparent through her bodily writing of desire.

Surely this is part of a narrative economy of sexual difference, the body as a reminder of the great divide between men and women. But so discursive a display extends beyond biological boundaries (as will be evident in "The Gaze" and the subsequent chapters on the fetish) and actually disturbs them. The model may not possess the penis, yet she circulates within phallic representations of desire which bring her close to possessing the phallus. Recall, however, that the Lacanian phallus is not the possession of "one" but a signifier which is endlessly commutable within the structures that govern the laws of desire: the phallus is always a deferral, the nostalgic longing (in relation to an "other") for a loss, what has gone missing. She may *be* sexual difference, constructed as other, but only (and always) within the context of the reader's constitution and reconstitution as other—as he is recognized from the place of the model's desire. If the model is castrated, and this has symbolic value in an erotic spectacle, she is placed within certain phallic terms of reference. The reader, sutured in absentia, is in the position of viewing a model who, although fetishized, does not cover up her castration (she in fact flaunts it). She is a play on both presence and absence. The reader, his subjectivity mediated in his encounter with the desirous/desiring model, is also in a drama of plenitude and loss. Just as the model bears the signs of her desire, the reader, constructed as meaningful in and for the representation, invests the narrative with signs of his. His investment is in seeing the model endowed with "difference"; but her visible mark of difference is at the cutting edge of indifference. That is, the reader's investment is also his divestment: the desire of the other is closest to one's own desire. As scenarios of desire are founded on loss, the reader's loss is in seeing the model castrated and yet with the phallus, the phallus which approximates the reader's and which he has surrendered in order to see signs of the model's desire. The reader thus hovers at a desire which castrates.

The imagery discussed above is a play on *both* thanatos (castration) and eros (union). Within the classic Freudian schema, the trauma of the castration scenario invites "disavowal," that "energetic action," a "defence against the claims of external reality":

> It is not true that, after the child has made his observation of the woman, he has preserved unaltered his belief that women have a phallus. He has retained that belief, but he has also given it up. In the conflict between the weight of the unwelcome perception and the force of his counter-wish, a compromise has been reached. . . . In his mind the woman *has* got a penis, in spite of everything; but the penis is no longer the same as it was before. Something else has taken its place, has been appointed its substitute . . . and now inherits the interest which was formerly directed to its predecessor. . . . The horror of castration has set up a memorial to itself in the creation of this substitute. Furthermore, an aversion, which is never absent in any fetishist, to the real female genitals remains a *stigma indelebile*.[14]

This disavowal is said to take the form of "I know she doesn't have it, but nevertheless maybe she does have something like it"; in the words of Octave Mannoni, "je sais bien, mais quand même (I know but nonetheless)."[15] To use our own symbolic material, the model clearly does not have a penis, but she is given the phallus in the form of the fetish, and other things. In spite of her graphically castrated genitals, she carries the marks of a phallic power in the discursive bodily arrangement and the body's insertion into a semiotic code. Although she does not possess the unadorned penis denoted by the pound of flesh, she enters the phallic/masculine discourse by proxy: she has the "substitute."

Or, she *is* the "substitute." She penetrates even though she is devoid of penis. The reader is witness to the divestment of her biological power, yet at the same time he gives it back to her in metaphorically phallic terms. Castration is associated, indelibly, with the pornographic moment. However, it is not so much the Freudian arrangement which realigns "belief/disbelief" around the fetish. Instead it is a scenario of wishful seduction. In desiring disclosure of signs of the model's desire, the reader is closer to the "cut" whereby the model's power is procured at the expense of the reader's loss. He gives away signs of his desire in order to see signs of hers. Desire in its metaphorical temperament is constituted as the "nonrepresentable." But the reader is constituted in this negotiated "space" between the vivid genital revelation of castration (the model's loss) and the phallus (the "impossible referent").[16] It is within this space that the reader is constructed as different/difference vis-à-vis the genital impression before him. It is where he fleshes out his desire, and is still reminded that he has the "real thing" (the precious object, the phallus). But he knows this, and knows his desire, only through representations of the other, always an ambivalent other.

The reader encounters his illusory self in the oedipal (castrating) scenario that characterizes the pornographic moment. His otherness, seeing the "cut" other, is granted under threat of privation. If desire "is opened up . . . through a structuring absence,"[17] the castrated/castrating other is the perfect meeting place of narratives of desire. The absence of the viewer, the model's penis, and the phallus instructs the operation of desire as the search for the nonrepresentable: both bodies and texts as absence.

The model is phallic equivalence in other ways. As noted, there is another standard genital feature in soft-core: representations of the vulva together with the anus. A common pose has the model on her knees, buttocks offered to the camera (a "buttock," from Partridge and the *OED*, is "a low whore," "a shrew," "a common prostitute." A "buttock" is "also a pickpocket": see the discussion, in the "Hard-Core" section of this chapter, of the "spent" male in pornographic maneuvers). The back is in a concave arch, and the posterior of the body is elevated slightly to expose both the vulval and the anal area. This is quite an elaborate exposure, a graphic spread of the genitals and anus, bodily apertures that take in and emit, open and invade. Both are organs which symbolically (and not only symbolically) trap (here, the "bowels" of the [mother] earthy model). They contain and they castrate; but they also expel, producing decomposed matter that greets the reader and the phallus. The anus is poised to expel, like a phallic ejection. So the anal phallus is wasted matter. What does that say to the reader?

The anus is poised also to devour, a posture more aggressive than the vagina dentata. Positioned to consume, it also penetrates, as if the reader were recipient to anal excesses. This anal scenario most often accompanies bodily configurations which privilege the model's penetrating eyes and stiletto-heeled foot. Again, in these instances there is an ambisexual masquerade to the body: it appears feminine yet possesses qualities which transgress femininity. This is a body which challenges the designated locations of the "masculine" and the "feminine": it is positioned for reception *and* penetration/ejection/emission. The body flirts with a dissolve around the "sexual fix"; it teases the critical edge of the great gender divide. It points to a "snarl of gender crossings."[18]

A simulated ambisexuality threatens the anatomy of binary structures which proportion gender identity on one side or the other. The body positioned to devour *and* invade (while it positions the reader to penetrate as well) hovers around a sameness which jeopardizes the categorization of other(s). It involves not so much an equilibrium (this is not a picture of harmony) but a cutting edge: otherness is resurrected and reinstated in the fetish inscriptions which, although they signify a cultural femininity, are phallic. And desire circulates as the reader is enlisted in scenarios of loss, exchange, surrender, and death. This visual imaginary calls upon signs of the model's desire—both on the body and in the fetish—and a place for the reader to insert his. But his desire is represented only in signs of his own loss—he gives away signs of it to see hers. And within a libidinal economy and economies of desire, an exchange of signs is the investment in the circuitous route toward meaning (meaning though in flux, committed to an essential referent of sexual difference).

In the world of simulation—precisely so in the chimerical zone where desire cannot be represented—the gap between desire and the straining to represent it is where seduction is fleshed out. This is a simulated moment, the space between the image and the referent, only in this case the referent has gone missing: the simulated moment has become the real. In this semiocracy the offering of signs promises that there is some real sex somewhere—real women, real desire, real men, etc. This is the ultimately pathetic, and parodic, real moment of the pornographic image. Its viciousness lies in its attempt to re-present the real, desire and the phallus, and supplant them. Reality is subverted: the representation wins.

Where is the reader in the *mise en scène* which speaks to textual and corporal castration? In this apparent dialogue of others, the reader is engaged in a narcissistic exchange, and this is most pronounced with the privileging of the anal signifier. There is an indifference to difference invoked by anal imagery; anality is an aggressive fusion of the gender/genital divide. The anus is possessed by both males and females. Hence, in these narratives, there is the partial effacement of demarcations of otherness as the reader encounters signs of himself in the textual body of the model. And anal imagery stages a castrating drama so that sameness (indifference) becomes a picture of castration: the reader meets his double in the castrated genitals of the model. This is his symbolic dispossession, the witness to the little death of the male (viewing) subject.

To summarize, in soft-core the body is organized to feature the single breast; the genitals grotesquely arranged to expose and flaunt embodied castration; and the anus poised to accept penetration, but also poised for the possibilities of devouring and expulsion. All three representations choreograph the soft-core pornographic in a discourse of desire verging on the rule of androgyny.

The breasts are the feminine principle. They are body parts emphasized and fetishized with an enthusiasm which appears to transcend history.[19] There are two of them (as against the single penis), and they embody some apparently opposite attractions. They are a maternal source of life and nurturance; they are erotic. But the single breast subverts a binary opposition and subjects the feminine form to the masculine, phallic, principle. It contains a milky substance resembling semen and is depicted in its fully erect and protruding state, like an appendage or erection on the body. Why else represent the breast alone if not to incite (phallic) desire? The seemingly ultrafeminine breast simulates the masculine code in its singular incarnation. It borrows from the feminine (the round flesh, the milk, the duality) and the masculine (the semen, the engorged and erect state, the singular), both of which come together to effect an erotic conspiracy.

The genital exhibition provides a perspective on the body which at first glance suggests an uncompromising structure of difference. The model as other is presented to the reader, and her otherness is signified by her genitals. But even they cannot adhere totally to an unyielding "sexual fix." Although their denotation in the soft-core discourse seems to be unadulterated, natural and naked, they are not semiotically unadorned and thus present some contradictory possibilities. The genitals may zone the body for difference, but they do so in a threatening fashion. Vaginal imagery is relentlessly sought out and plays on the visible absence of the penis. This goes against the grain of the orthodox scenario of castration which posits the centrality of castration fears to the formation of the masculine subject. In these configurations, the conventional iconic figure of the castrated woman and her meaning as sexual difference are pronounced, the fetish doing nothing to minimize that visual and psychic disclosure. The reader is not simply addressed as "other than" castrated. By the time the reader encounters the exposed genital configuration, he has already encountered the penetrating gaze of the model, the single breast which assumes a masculine writing, and the fetishes, themselves a phallic writing on the feminine form. The reader encounters simulated versions of his own likeness in the discursive arrangement of the body: indices of castration precede the acknowledgment of the model represented as other (knowledge which is anyway disavowed). His losses are what constitute the model in seductive vocabularies.

Another possibility is the anal invasion. This is particularly pornographic; the anal orifice is poised to both expel and devour at the same time as it effaces sexual difference. The reader is positioned to meet a representation that combines penetration with indifference, both on a female body. As a result, the feminine discourse is transgressed as desire straddles the "cut."

In hard-core, the sexual maneuvers are complicated by the presence of the male model, the male model's penis, and a reader who is engaged with a fetishistic and voyeuristic look. All conspire to render the photo vulgar, vicious, and subject to greater psychic censorship than the soft-core treatment of pornography. Why? It is to this that we now turn.

Hard-Core: "a moment of sight which fabricates the real"[20]

Configurations of the breast in hard-core compete with other organs and displays of sexual and fabricated phallic excess. The defining criteria of hard-core are erection of the penis, penetration of any orifice, and ejaculation. The single breast is occasionally represented, but just as often both breasts are displayed. Within this genre there are many other phallic codes, centering on the penis, the phallus-as-fetish, the partial masculinization of the female model through the penetrating gaze, the writing of the body as aggressively desirous through the lingerie (her "be.longings"),[21] and scenarios involving the "anal penis."[22] There is nothing surreal about hard-core (nor in soft-core, but hard-core is perhaps the strongest attempt at verisimilitude, or replication of the real).

Black-and-white surrealist photography is a play on the physical form. It renders "shapeless" the defining boundaries of the body and hence conventional meaning attached to its materiality. The "aggressive assault on reality" utilizes the "informe," the upsetting of the body's familiar reassurances.[23] The "informe" imposes a fluidity on the body's form and "redrafts" its map through the *trompe l'oeil,* the use of animal imagery, the highly metaphorical—and lyrical—visual reconstruction of the body's surface: an assault on the body *from without.* The result is a body rethought and invented to become less human, a body cavorting with animals ("The body cannot be seen as human because it has fallen into the condition of the animal").[24] It is a body without alibi—with no fidelity to a stable referent or transcendental signifier. Rosalind Krauss completes her clever essay "Corpus Delicti" by suggesting that "woman . . . is nowhere in nature," and the use of the "informe" potentially deconstructs the categories which prefigure the authority of the gender divide.

Similarly, the pornographic moment offends as it transgresses—perhaps the same boundaries—but for other reasons. Its pretense is to the real world of sex. It strains after a referent of desire (impossible in the real!); it claims to verisimilitude but transgresses boundaries anyway. Hard-core pornographic images depart from the surreal partly because they are in color. Soft-core photos are in color as well; however, in hard-core the authenticity of color conjoins with the obdurate materiality of the genital display. And the brilliant color and sexual graphics overlay in a particularly vicious offering which is parodic and ugly, leaving us wanting the surreal, the "origin without an original"[25]—a surreal that continues to lurk behind the pornographic imagery in spite of all images to the contrary.

Fear of Castration or Transgression?

Part of the hard-core regime of representation is the fragmented body (particularly in terms of the genital exhibition); this is not as emphatic in soft-core. Fragmented concentration is on the face of pleasure—hers (documented in "The Gaze")—and on penetration. The privileged signifier is more often the penis/phallus.

The visual narrative usually begins with a clothed encounter between two strangers who quickly disrobe to varying states of undress. A few conventional genital arrangements are represented. The genitals, male or female, are seldom depicted on their own (often only two or three photos per magazine, out of a possible thirty to forty). Instead the bodies are in consort, the genitals being the conduit where they meet in a kind of corporal and specular harmony. The most common deployment involves vaginal penetration by the penis, and this is often in a framed close-up, heightening fragmentation. But the spectacle has a doubling effect: the genital union appears to be an ambisexual charade. That is, the bodies' parts form a textual closure in their manifestation as *one* physical reality. There is a loosening of boundaries around the body's immanence as the female genitals appear to be merely an extension of the penis. A body doubles as its other. The two corporal entities are feigned as one, a unity in a circuit of desire, which passes through its representations: on the male body (in its turgidity) and through the fetish (on the female).

Otherness is still drawn and anchored, however, through the lingerie on the female model. This heightened visual intensity—the investment in the fetish, a visual exchange of difference, desire, the phallus—is part of the pornographic code, always a play on otherness (and misplacement of difference). The sight of genitals copulating in this close-up would be merely *that*, a faithful site/sight of the sexual, were it not for the fetish/lingerie peeking out from the edges of the photo. Genital penetration would be full sexual disclosure, but foreclosing all signs of desire. The erect penis, for example, would be the bloated representation of desire, desire straining to be assuaged. Desire needs a tension, and the pornographic tension in these hard-core photographs goes beyond mere renditions of genitals copulating for the camera.

Rather than the reader's exclusion from the scene before him, there is a space, the moment between desire's inception and its re-presentation, the space for the dramatic mimesis of the reader and his phallus. This also involves the threats against them, threats of their demise (the death of the subject). The carnal union of genitals is more than mechanical operationalization, the "self reduced to its formal elements . . . represented by the probe and the fringed hole, the twin signs of male and female in graffiti."[26] The fetish inscription of the lingerie, however—the traces of garters on the legs, the inch or so of stocking at the top of the thigh—is a nod to the pornographic, the surplus visual exchange which unsettles with its alibi status: it speaks to what is not there as the narrative moves toward closure (the referent, the real) which can never be achieved.

Which is to say a number of things. Difference is more than its biological assignment. More important, it is activated in discourses which structure subjectivity and desire. The creation of difference in the subject is a matter of separation in the service of otherness. The male reader would be excluded from the graphic depiction in front of him (i.e., the parodic re-creation of the exemplary sexual act) if the scenario were complete. The total exclusion of the reader not only would suggest an unerotic and uninteresting scene but also would point to signs of a pure phallic economy: desire fully self-contained within the text, the reader disinherited by the sexual choreography in the photo.

But the reader is enlisted within the desiring scenario in at least a couple of ways. For one thing, the text invites the reader's gaze by offering the penis not fully penetrating. The privileged visual moment is witness to an event in completion; and there's more to see. There's more difference to see: the penis's extension from the vagina is the partial union of opposites *and* desire before its exhaustion. The reader's interest is far from exhausted at this moment. Were the penis totally enveloped by the vagina, the material evidence of copulation would not be so apparent; too much would be left to the imagination in this, the most shameless and indiscreet of sexual discourses. What offends in the pornographic is the obdurate materiality of the photo and its depictions, which on the surface (and on the surface only) leave little to the imagination, purporting as they do to a representative photographic, objectifying, realism. Both are unrelentingly real, offensively so.

In this case, the part-penis is there to see, a willing suspension of belief against disbelief that the male model has got it (but is always threatened with losing it). Also visible are the male's testicles, indices of his virility (the marking of *his* difference). The testicles, however, are also the heir to signs of femininity. Not turgid but round and more feminine, these are limp connotations on the male body. Until desire is realized, the penis/phallus is forfeited to a narrative of sexual transgressions: the male model simulates femininity while the female is masculinized. The male model gives away the signs of his desire for the female, and is divested of his controlling interests (the woman, her body, its semiotic power, is her own "capital investment").[27] According to Partridge, "to do one's balls on" is "(of a man) to fall utterly in love with." Can we then say that he's got "balls on" for her, has relinquished signs of his desire to see signs of hers? (We return to these, and other, etymological associations below.)

Paradoxically, the partly introjected penis and the visible testicles phallicize the female model as she appears to be an extension of the penis, thus also protracting the specular moment. The reader is implicated and enlisted in this visual register. He is called upon, in a discourse of desire, to locate his difference within the diegetic space. He is different from the photographic narrative in the sense that he is not of it. He is spoken in terms of a text that plays out the negotiation of sexual difference. But the text also shows up the tensions around sexual difference and creates that space for transgressions to occur and for the reader to engage in the economic exchanges which structure the pornographic moment, both libidinal and symbolic. Any exchange involves metonymic transactions which rely on relationships of contiguity, absence, and a reinvestment of desire in missing signifiers and signifieds. The subject (the reader) is placed before the cultural text and occupies that space created by metonymic associations in the text.

A second popular genital configuration involves a close-up of vaginal penetration. But rather than the high visibility of the female pubic area, the visible orifice is the anus, hers. To heighten the anality of the image, either model will separate, with the hands, the female's buttocks so that the anus is poised, not for rear entry but as an invasive orifice. It is there not to take in but to expel. It shares the same diegetic space as the penis partially penetrating the vagina. If the phallus defies representation, and if the reader is enlisted to supply it, then the "military anus"[28] accommodates the reader to an insinuating posture which treats the phallus and the reader as shit. The impertinence of the female pornographic model is her aggressive anality.

Why do we say "shit" when we are angry? Anal associations are aggressive, voyeuristic, and sadistic.[29] The "liberation of aggression"[30] in the anal-sadistic model is intrusively phallic, precisely so as another signifier—shit—signifies in its absence. And the anal moment is castrating: it can capture upon entry into the bowels. The anal delivery signifies a certain "unrestraint," a bold confrontation to the male model, the reader, and the "sexual fix," i.e., the grand orthodoxies of the sexological.[31] The model's anus (her "beastly backside")[32] is the third term which disturbs the "economy of physiological balance":[33] the anatomical display here flouts the classic heterosexual distinctions.

The anus symbolizes the repression of difference.[34] It is ambisexual, both container and content,[35] as it potentially expels as well as traps. It expels feces, with part-object status: if part-object, anal expulsions are fetishized (like emissions from the penis). Perhaps they are the perfect fetish in that they are not seen, only imagined and symbolized; thus feces-as-fetish are metastasized by their elusiveness. The reader is again reaffirmed in the search, the longing that instigates the endless interrogations of the female body to restore the missing phallus. The fetish is by definition an alibi organized around absence. In this case, the "unseen" feces-as-fetish has a doubly phallic hyperinscription: the invasive stamp of the anal matter and the peculiarly metonymic structure of the fetish places it within a "phallocratic habit."[36] In hard-core the "other" is the woman whose body textual is rendered aggressively indifferent through anal signification. This is a disavowal of femininity by endowing women with the phallus and the "trap-anus,"[37] set to devour.

The pornographic body is a configuration of part-objects. The breast, anality, the gaze, and the shoe and jewelry, and all they may connote, offend the regulation of sexual discourses by fetishizing the body, desire, difference. They also set into place the dangerous edge, the "margin of disturbance,"[38] a cutting edge which establishes difference but at a cost—symbolic castration[39] or the threatened loss of difference. To be sure, the avowal of difference is what constitutes the creation of the subject upon entry into culture. One thus desires difference, a difference twinned with desire and the impossibility of its representation. The imperative of difference is an injunction to dispossession. For the man this means to be dispossessed of his (masculine) properties. This is never achieved without a struggle, and the desire for narcissistic fusion (the primal nondifferentiating relationship) is the subtle, yet vicious, undercurrent to the sexual scene.

It is within anal imagery that one sees the erasure of sexual difference, a sadistic (and perverse) denial of all difference.[40] (The rectum *is* a grave.)[41] The male reader rather viciously harmonizes—difference with a vengeance—with the "maleness" of the model: her "anal universe" is poised to eliminate differences, and thus she is granted a host of masculine attributes.[42] At the same time as she is phallicized through the fetish, her otherness slides under the sign of the fetish, the anal signifier. This is to say that masculinity is not the standard against which otherness is measured; rather, otherness is the nexus where the phallus and the "cut" are negotiated—it is a formal structure, not the reflection of content. This libidinal exchange is self-referential in the sense that signs work through their reference to other signs (like modern power) and desire is a semiotic performance: a threatening and seductive pull of otherness.

Anality is invasive and acquisitive, thus overdetermining its phallic insistency on the predatory and the colonizing. Anal emissions/ejections are symbolically shared by the phallus: a child is the "spitting image" or "dead spit" of his father, a "speaking likeness" (Partridge). (Germaine Greer refers to the female body as a "human spittoon").[43] "Death" and bodily refuse are metonymic twins, as are penile emissions and decayed matter. The anus is the death knell to difference. Forceful bodily emissions are also in the cultural domain of masculinity; notice the "dead spit" on the sidewalk. A close-up of the anal orifice aspires to balance differences between the sexes, and between the properties of intrusion and immurement. The anus is always hers (signified by the bejeweled hands which separate the buttocks), never his: that would be the literal homosexualization of desire, a close-up too close for comfort.

The other visual perspectives are the coupling of the anus with the penis partially consumed by the vagina, and the testicles. The metonymic association of the anus with the incomplete introjection of the penis puts both organs in the orbit of an insinuating exchange. Both anus and vagina coalesce around the fetishistic structures of the seen/unseen and represent a duality of expulsion and introjection. The spectacle centers on balancing the possibilities of elimination (dispossession) and intromission. Regarding intromission, the "trap-anus" parallels the vagina: the anus has the potential of ingesting its prey (or decomposing it) while the vagina *is* actively consuming.

In *Anal Fantasy* ("the intimate confessions of a beautiful woman!"), the female model's anus is described as "winking out" at the male model (and thus placing the reader under surveillance). Her anus (and this is most common) is referred to as her "bung." A "bung" (from Partridge, Webster's, and Oxford) is a stopper or plug (traditionally used with casks of beer); the anus; and "a blow, a punch." The term is derived from the Latin *pungere*, "to prick—more at 'pungent.'" And "pungent" is akin to Latin *pugnus*, "fist," *pugnare*, "to fight," Greek *pygm*, "fist; having a stiff and sharp point . . . sharply painful." The model with the "bung" is positioned to penetrate "stiff and sharp"; as we will see, this is reminiscent of the incisive and predatory gaze. Both orifices are also phallic, castrating, and are implicated in voyeuristic discourses. The "bung" as a plug or stopper signifies a displacement or affinity between the anatomical mechanism of the anus and the associated fears of its power (as container and content: to ingest and expel), hence the rush to "plug" it ("Bung it!" means "Stow it!").

The penis, while perhaps "stiff and sharp" itself, is partially obliterated/ castrated, in visual terms, by the vaginal enclosure. The juxtaposing of this representation with the doubled performance of the anus—i.e., it is poised to project, expel (it must be "stowed"), defile, and penetrate, and at the same time is an organ set to contain, seize, and capture—is an incitement to castration. The "pungent" anus, "sharply painful," threatening to become unplugged, is the metonymic twin of the phallic projectile. And the fetishized penis, visually a part-object engulfed by the vagina, is "cut" to reveal more of the testicles than the penis itself. Both representations set up the reader to be absorbed, engulfed, unmanned, hence partially feminized.

The male model's penis is also a surrogate for what isn't there: the woman's penis. To give the penis to the other is to phallicize her: she can't really have a penis, but she can have phallic substitutes and phallic desires. It is in that suspended simulated space—where boundaries are chaotic or drawn with invisible ink—that desire is created and sustained. The there/not there structure of the fetish implicates the body's part-objects (of desire) in the form of the missing yet symbolically renewable feces, the fractional penis, i.e., what is not seen but *could* be seen, what is perhaps better left unseen so as not to disturb the reader's sexual integrity, the fiction of his phallic self. However, precisely because that integrity is a fiction, it is continually under threat, especially when confronted with visual imaginaries that straddle the invisible threshold between difference and indifference.

The emasculatory anus, paired with the both "there and not totally there" penis, redounds back upon the reader. The reader, reconstituted for, by, and in the text, must be reassured that he can be the donor of phallic satisfaction. He has got the real thing, but that status is continually threatened with loss. If the model is castrating and phallic, she embodies the reader's desire to be dispossessed of his phallus and his masculinity. His desire is double-edged: yearnings for difference and indifference are part of the same perversion, and both are central to the mechanisms of the "cut." That is, the desire for difference—to be differentiated by the text, to be positioned as "other" to its textual desires (and the textual desires of the model)—is to encounter the rupturing effects of separation, but also independence and loss (insofar as one is transformed from "one" to "other" and the alteration of body image that that implies). The desire for indifference is a surrender to castration and a narcissistic death. Desire must then originate, or is imagined, in the transgressions of difference, and in simulated otherness. And the reader is enthralled with the pornographic moment, simultaneously mundane and fascinating. The desire for transgressions and the longing for loss are what sustain the reader's interest in this most vicious flaunting of the official, symmetrical, sexual discourses.

The body in pornography is a discursive composition of part-objects. In hard-core this is especially true of the penis. Thus, the third most common image in the pornographic bodyscape is the penis and oral sex. In terms of bodily fragmentation, and in refutation of the humanist assumption that a person's humanity is effaced by his or her fractional representation, it is the male body which is sexually compartmentalized (while the female model, in fact, resides with the humanist equation of the head with the whole person). A popular sexual disassembly of the male body involves two versions of an oral sexual encounter. There is either a close-up of fellatio, i.e., the female face and the penis, or a middle-range shot of fellatio which includes a view of some of the rest of both bodies (complete with fetish). The close-up of fellatio includes two possibilities. Either the penis is partially eclipsed by the model's mouth, and the shaft is visible, although partly occluded by her hands, or oral sexual activity is about to happen, and is a suspended visual moment. The penis is disembodied, distended, and about to be "taken in" by the female model. Again, this implicates desire and the impossibility of its representation: the heightened visualness of the phallic projection is the self-importance of desire. The bombastic strutting of the cock, a part-object itself, is a prelude to the ultimate in narrative closure: visible signs of orgasm, or semen. The typical resolution to the text incurs the detumescence of desire (his) as witnessed in its corporal form.

The female model performs the vernacular "blow job" on the male model. I cannot find any historical, slang, references to the cultural roots of this phrase, but in piecemeal fashion a certain narrative emerges. One association with the word "blow" is to lose money or spend it recklessly. The *OED* notes one definition of "blow" as "to lay out or get through [money] in a lavish manner; to squander." In the vernacular, "to blow one's wad" is to forfeit all one's money, and to ejaculate. "To blow through" is (of a man) to copulate (Partridge). So also is "to blow in one's pipe"; and "pipe" is slang for "female pudend" (Partridge). Thus the affinity is deployed between "to blow" and the *male* sexual subject: a man is "blown," a woman is not. Similarly, these depictions contain the prelude to exhaustion, depletion, the draining (or death) of the "spent" male model, his "petite mort." He is getting ready to "blow" all his money on her (indeed, the pudend is also a "money box"). He will pay for her, and he will pay for it with his little death (more on the semen/money connection below).

The reader encounters a truncated version of his own body, at its most fragmented, fetishized, and sexual. This is a most perverse posturing for the heterosexual reader. If we assume that the scenario reconstitutes the oedipal drama, and the reader is ensconced at the keyhole, he is clearly positioned from the vantage point of loss. He is excluded from the visual text. Within narratives of loss, he is witness to a re-creation of the oedipal coupling, the original binary exclusion, and that which fully locates the sexual subject vis-à-vis the vicious triangle: mommy-daddy-me. The reader then is nominated as "the one who looks";[44] the alibi for his observer status is precisely his exclusion from the scenario, his access to the "cut." That material and symbolic space between the reader and the text is the necessary distance to create the reading, desiring, subject. But it's a space which can never be filled, other than with the re-enactment of loss or the preoccupation with incision. It points to an eternal recurrence which brings the subject back to his ordination as the empty phallic signifier, the one whose potential to be castrated lies in giving up signs of desire to see the desire of the other, without his loss ever being absolute.

What the reader sees in pictures of fellatio is the phallic protrusion of the male model, and ultimately oral assimilation by the mouth of the female: a "thankless mouth" is the "female pudend" (Partridge). So is "the mouth that cannot bite" or "says no words about it" (Partridge). But the mouth that does the fellating definitely has teeth and, in many senses, speaks volumes. Discursively, it is a central signifier in the production and reception of pleasure, an orifice that takes in and emits. In terms of the accompanying written narrative (a standard feature of hard-core), it is almost without exception the woman who controls the speaking voice: "Suddenly I had the urge to get down there and suck on that squirming dick of his. Maybe he thought that he had everything under control when in reality I was the one holding the reins all the time. When it comes to sucking cock then I am not going to let anyone stand in my way!" This speaks to a phallic mouth in two senses: it is a picture of the classic "vagina dentata," the organ with teeth poised to suck the life out of the paternal signifier. "Fellatio" comes from the Latin *fellare*, "to suck." (A model in the June 1988 *Hustler* is described as a "cock-muncher": thankless indeed.) It also contains its own phallic protrusion, the tongue. And the tongue signifies in phallic ways: in scenes where the model is about to orally introject the penis, her tongue is extended in phallic celebration; and penis and tongue sometimes meet in a kind of phallic communion, one approximating the other. "Tongue": *lingus, ling*—Sanskrit, "penis."[45]

But it is all a *mock* phallic display, the penis itself a mere stand-in for desire.

This is a parodic performance where everything passes as a masquerade of the phallus and of phallic desire. What the reader encounters is a representation of the male model's ceremonial (and pedantic) state of sexual excitement. Visible signs of *her* desire appear to be absent as she administers pleasure and, we are to assume, receives it from her laborious activities. Indeed, she often does bear the look of labor—eyes closed in concentrated effort as she studiously works at extracting the pearly promise of his sated desire.

But appearances to the contrary, desire, like modern power, can work only through its representations. The reader encounters at least one version or representation of desire: that of the male model whose disembodied penis symbolizes a truncated desire. It doesn't stand alone but is quickly attacked by both the hands and mouth of the female, eager to tame its imperious intrusion. The standard narrative begins with a meeting between two fully clothed actors. By page two of a typical magazine, an article of clothing is stripped away to reveal some body part. Physical maneuvers quickly accelerate to all manner of exposure and penetration, climaxing with visible traces of the man's orgasm (his spit): this is perfect narrative closure. In *French Pussy* a man and woman begin their sexual choreography with the simulated introjection of her (single) breast into his mouth. What we actually see is his extended tongue meeting her nipple; phallus to phallus, as it were. The scene heightens the phallic associations of the single breast, and thus its perpetual visibility. What follows is an exchange where his tongue meets her vagina (her genitals are spread apart, rendering a view more appropriate to a gynecological exam). She in turn "tongues" his nipple, and then the "blow job" begins. The cock is grabbed by the female's hand and is held at a proximate distance from her mouth; but this, in diegetic terms, is quickly followed by its intromission into her mouth and then the penis's disappearing act. The organ is partly consumed by the mouth, and the tactility is intensified by her hand (Freud notes that "seeing . . . [is] an activity that is ultimately derived from touching").[46] In subsequent photos there is a graphic orchestration of various sexual positions, exposures, and penetrations, the majority of which are close-up renditions of, as already mentioned, vaginal or anal penetration. (The medium long-shot affords a view of many fetishes: shoes, stockings, lingerie, garters, etc.)

Other transactions accompany phallic intromission and insinuation. Typically, couples never actually kiss, but oral contact offers a certain phallic affinity. One protruding tongue grazes another protruding tongue. Body contact is afforded maximum, yet surface, visual intensity. Maximum in the sense that everything is revealed. But what is there to see? Surface in the sense that the bodily contact points are merely a conduit of desire, and difference is a slow dissolve to a pallid remark on a surface sameness. The contiguity of the tongues is an endless duplication of the sign, in the sense that Baudrillard writes, a surface reflection where "the reality of the bodies is erased by the resemblance";[47] although within economies of desire, one has to note that they are never fully erased. The extension of the female model's tongue (always hers) connotes sexual eagerness, a further visual intensification of the extraction of (her) bodily desire.

The narrative returns (most often) to oral sex, which then leads to the completion of the picture: traces of his orgasm, semen, which become part of *her* corpus. As he "comes" on her face/neck, or on her pubes/stomach following vaginal penetration (or in the anal region following anal penetration), her body contains visible signs of his desire—now in its exhaustion—and possesses a significant and tactile mark of otherness. And then death. His "petite mort" is her possession: in pornographic films, the vernacular for male orgasm, in its visual eminence, is the "money shot."[48] It is the male's final payment, his milky secretions. From Partridge, "milk" is "sexual spendings." "To milk" is "to cause sexual ejaculation," and "to gain possession, or sight, of by trickery or artifice." "To give down one's milk" is "to pay"; and "the milking pail" is the female pudend. He has been milked dry. And we have proof of it.

This final event (the orgasm) is perhaps the quintessential *indifference* in the sense that the representation of the end of desire (the milky secretions) is the real thing. It is impossible to represent desire other than in its simulated form, as endless re-production, repetition, and a play on the signifier. This is the pornographic specular technique: desire on the surface of the body, not *in* it. Orgasms (his) take place outside of bodily orifices, the signs of which must be seen, witnessed.

What does this mean in psychoanalytic terms? The spotty, milky semen is the extraction of signs of desire from the male body. As these signs are substitutes for desire, the repertoire of images circulate within a generalized phallic equivalence and exchange. The "real" for the reader is knowable only through these representations and as he witnesses the ritual milking, the exhaustion of the male model at the mouth and hands of the female. This is the curious climax of his own desire, desire upon the death/loss of the phallus. This seductive moment is the reader's phallic inscription into an economy of indifference. Clearly at this stage in the narrative the models are indifferent to the reader; but only after he has already been enlisted, by the mechanisms of the "cut," into a transgressive scenario. That is, he has already been constituted as "other" in relation to the spectacle before him. The perversion (or one of them) in these instances is that the reader has to give away so much in this tedious and predictable seduction: he is lost in the simulated orbit of desire, just when the male model has "spent his money recklessly." What does he have left? He's broke? Not totally; narrative closure restores the phallus with the reader.

Recall that in *French Pussy* the ritual death was delayed. The format begins with fondling, teases with the "blow job," then embellishes with penetration before a return to the blow job, and then his orgasm or "money shot." There is still the final picture, however, the back cover, and it is this which engages the reader again. Just before he is in danger of certifying his homoerotic desire, he is invited back into a dialectical relationship with the text. He is constituted, as it were, as subject for the objects in the text. A number of possibilities are presented to enlist the reader. The back cover of *French Pussy* and *Hot Black Boxes* restores the reader to a position of, albeit cynical, desire. The male model is once again reduced to his most significant part, his penis, and the female is "blowing" him (she's about to make him lose his money again). But she's also gazing at the reader with a look that speaks to a detachment from the (male) model, or at least his representative (the cock). It signals her boredom as well as full knowledge of her duplicity (in fact she knows too much, another one of pornography's textual excesses). She is no prude, as she is jointly engaged with the model and yet directs her gaze out of the diegetic space to confront the reader. And she confronts the reader with *his* duplicity in the text, for the text, and with the illusions of his own desire. She's mocking the model and the reader, saying to the latter (the reader who is reconstituted for the text): "This is just a penis (and one that's already been spent, no less); you got the (my) phallus, the true sign of your (my) desire. This is just a stand-in for the (your) real thing."

This is what gives pornography its pathetic urgency: the inability of the representational apparatus to capture the workings of desire as the search for a lost object. Both the reader and the text are implicated in a discourse which represents desire in its exhaustion, drained and signified only in its deathlike form. And this is also a transgressive moment. Signs of desire can operate only through their visible representations, or substitutions, that surpass or double for reality. Desire always involves a loss, an investment, a forfeiture; in this "moneyed," libidinal, and phallic exchange, the reader is the taken-for-granted witness to the sexual scene in front of him. As witness he takes up the position of spectator seduced by the image, a testimony to his desire. As he surrenders to the image, he becomes object to its fetishized subjects; he gives up his desire to the artifice of desire, to see its contrivances in the photo. What he sees is the self-conscious and self-referential nature of phallic desire—including the model's extensions. It looks as though, for example, the cock extends out of her mouth (just like the anal penis or the tongue). And there is a certain expression of the male's desire, at least in its truncated form: the penis is partially concealed by her mouth, hands, or both. The reader, as witness or donor of phallic knowledge, then is called upon to complete the circuit, to supply what's missing from the text.

But this picture betrays its own logical contradictions. If the reader is at the keyhole (mastered by his voyeurism), fills in the absences in the narrative, and is addressed as "other" to this visual imaginary, then he might supply the missing feminine element or be feminized at his point of entry into the text.

He is seduced, "stripped," penetrated by the model with the "cock in her eye" (see "The Gaze"). Recall, too, his shared affiliation with the anal region and what is ultimately a statement (its emission) of his yearning to be unmanned. The imagery transgresses the sexual fix: the phallic exchange within the text masculinizes the female and creates a surplus of phallic associations. If the narrative is a subversive play on "men fucking men," then the reader is a man desiring not men but women with men's desire. His simulated feminization completes the picture.

The partial "feminization" of both the male model and the reader is rendered precisely when he (the model) is penetrating, about to enter the nether regions of pornographic pleasure. Just before he spends it, loses it, the male penetrates the female, both vaginally and anally, and the visual tension revolves around the there/not there axis. The top half of the penis disappears into the vagina, her anus is poised to envelop/invade (both castrating scenarios), and his testicles are brought to the fore, enlarged beyond the phallic rule.

Why the balls? We learn from Partridge that "ballock" (according to the *OED*, a version of "ball") is a testicle. "Apples" is also slang for testicles, as is "nutmegs" (hence "nuts"). The last term is derivative of *noz* ("nut") plus *muscada* ("more at muscat"); from "musky," "musk," and refers to "cultivated grapes." The etymological roots of "grape" lead to "cradle" and "basket." "Basket" is akin to the Old French for "wooden vessel," Latin for "dishpan" and "necklace." The symbology is more feminine and uterine than phallic: these are hollow objects, and the necklace is composed of hollow beads or precious jewels. "Necklace" is composed of "neck," which is akin to "nut," and "lace," one root of which is "delight" (see chapter 5 for more on these).

Further, "musk" is from the Sanskrit *muska* or "testicle . . . akin to mouse"; and "mouse" is slang for a "woman or a timid person." "To knock out an apple" is to "beget a child" (Partridge). These fruity associations place the testicles within the feminine half of the ambisexual territory: an "apple" is also a woman's breast, an "apple dumpling shop" is a woman's bosom; an "apple monger" is a "harlot's bully" or a "male bawd" (Partridge). Linda Nochlin points out the metaphors around "prime *topoi* of erotic imagery: [the] comparison of the desirable body with ripe fruit," most specifically the "likening" of women's breasts to apples.[49] Nochlin uncovered a nineteenth-century photograph, entitled "Achetez des Pommes," of a woman wearing low black leather boots and black opaque stockings to the thighs but who is naked from the thighs up. She is holding a tray of apples at the level of her bare breasts. The associations are with feminine sexuality and harlotry, hence with the "bawdy" one whose sexual wares are ripe for the picking, but at a price.[50] The genealogy of "nutmegs" also indicates that when the male model's "nuts" are on display, he's revealing his feminine, fruity, even "mousy" analogue. This is balanced against the penis and the simulated masculinity of the female model. As well, testicles are like breasts: both are metonymic apples and both contain and emit a milky substance from a pouch (the "jugs") which is a source of life. Again, the "pocket phallus" could be the breast.

The model has "got his balls on." "To do one's balls on" is "(of a man) to fall utterly in love with." In checking "balls" we are referred to "cods." A "cod's-head" is a fool. A "cod" is "the scrotum," "a pod"; a "pod" is "probably an alteration of cod bag—more at 'codpiece' "—and "a seed vessel or fruit . . . an anatomical pouch." Indeed, Partridge locates "cod" with "a purse (. . .) whence *cod of money.*" Recall the visible traces of the male orgasm, the "money shot," the model "spent"; the discursive biological form is akin to the feminine or uterine symbology of the bag, pouch, pocket. Flügel notes that men carry "what is needful" in their pockets (women of course use purses).[51] Notice how common it is for a man to "play" with, or jingle, the money/coins in his pockets; money talks. In this case he's anxious to spend it. And Thomas Laqueur writes of the ways in which the codpiece is a metonym, in Renaissance medicine and poetry, for "womb" and "swaddled child." As well, "a codpiece could also be an appendage to the female attire worn on the breast." Laqueur also quotes from a medical text of 1672 which refers to the "female testicles."[52]

Marjorie Garber notes that "to cod" is "to chaff, hoax, humbug; to play the fool." Quoting from Partridge, she adds, "It has been used colloquially for 'pretence, or mock'—e.g., cod German, cod Russian. So, 'cod' means both scrotum or testicles, and hoax, fool, pretence or mock. The anxiety of male artifactuality is summed up, as it were, in a nutshell."[53]

There is a final component to the hard-core regime which overlays with the Foucauldian arrangement of the sexual, confessional apparatus. Although not a dominant motif (sometimes five to ten photos per magazine), cunnilingus is an interesting feature among the repertoire of possible exposures. On the one hand, it presents a picture of insinuation. Typically, in an exhibitionistic pose, the vulva is displayed in terms that resemble more properly the gynecological domain. The male model spreads the vulvar lips with his hands and extends his phallic tongue toward the female's "money box." Thereby one is offered the perverse, hyperclose examination of female genitalia. The genitals are rendered obscure and given over to a physicality that visually privileges folds of flesh, reddish, purplish, wet, and ultimately indiscernible. All is revealed, and still one is given the impression that there might be more to see: the male approaches the vulva with his mouth and both hands, unrelenting in his investigations.[54] Some of these close-up shots are so detailed (imagine a close-up of the labyrinthine workings of the ear, for example) that they are devoid of fetish. At the same time they conjure up the "structure of absence" so necessary for the construction of the simulated reality, and also for invoking the status of the "fetish-as-lost-object." The male model appears to be searching for the lost object, the fetish, the penis, the phallus. The female appears to be presented in castrated form, upsetting the conventional wisdom which assigns negative anxiety to "the threat of castration and a protection against it." But Freud does go on to suggest that the fetish "saves the fetishist from becoming a homosexual, by endowing women with the characteristic which makes them tolerable as sexual objects."[55] The fetishistic relationship has already been established by the time the reader encounters the tortuous anatomical structure before him. At this moment he is once again implicated in the management of fetishistic transactions which employ that balance between belief and disbelief, the seen and unseen, imaginary presence and absence. The exposure of her genitals, to render apparent their internal mysteries, also presents another possible orifice for sexual intrusion.

Given that penetration could take place in hard-core (indeed, it is one of its defining criteria and has already occurred within the diegesis), why doesn't it? Why this graphic surplus of imagery? Could it be that the cunt is strangely phallic, capable of expulsion itself? It is castrating, of course; along with the mouth, it engulfs the cock, cuts it off, rendering visible the balls. But it also circulates with a certain phallic meaning in two ways: it is visually paired with the tongue of the male model. That is, he fully extends his tongue, a phallic protrusion, and places it very close to the vulvar area, taking care not to conceal the orifice. This economy of substitutions sets into place a phallic exchange; his tongue, in this case, is a curious stand-in for the phallus. More important, the clitoris (Greek, "homologous to the penis") is exposed. The clitoris is another female protrusion, a visible sign of yearnings of the flesh. Unlike the vagina, it does not envelop and contain but is that sexual appendage which is tumescent and noticeably turgid with desire. It is most apparent when there is vaginal penetration; so it accompanies the "penis part-object" and the visible testicles. Its erect state is a contrasting statement to the partial "feminization" of both the male model (via his testicles) and the reader. The vulva is phallic and castrated at the same time.

This seems to be an eroticization of her castration; the threat to the reader's coherence is erotic as well. Linda Williams argues in "When the Woman Looks" that in horror films there is an affinity between the female heroine (the "silent screen vamp") and the monster or Phantom.[56] She suggests that "when the woman looks" or tries to look, and actually sees, she encounters ("within patriarchal structures of seeing") the mutilated body of the monster—really her double, her representational other—and is inscribed into a masochistic drama. Williams's ideas here are intriguing and useful, but I want to invert them. That is, the pornographic reader is the one who confronts the provocative (partially castrated) spectacle of the women in the photo. Perhaps there is no "safe distance" which "ensures the voyeur's pleasure of looking" (86). In any case, the mutilated ("cut") body is that of the *female* model. Is it not possible, then, that when the reader looks, he encounters the freak, his "other" mutilated body? And flaunts his identification with it? Certainly the model flouts the normative sexual order by disturbing the feminine scenario: no repression here, no shameful pudenda (Latin *pudere:* "to be ashamed"). There is nothing bashful about the pornographic cunt (Middle High German: akin to "prostitute"); nor is her genital overture a modest entreaty. As mentioned, the vulvar area is brazenly displayed, a simulated emasculation. These close-ups do disclose the brute physicality of the mutilated folds of flesh which is the feminine form. There is no penis here, and occasionally there isn't even a fetish disguise, only the obtrusive anatomy of difference. In hard-core porn, the woman, in her bold genital exposé, is a vicious yet scrutinized reminder (the clitoris can be located) of the other's loss in conjunction with the other's desire. Williams suggests that the monster "is remarkably like the woman in the eyes of the traumatized male: a biological freak with impossible and threatening appetites that suggest a frightening potency precisely where the normal male would perceive a lack" (87).

I would substitute "woman" for "monster." In the pornographic spectator-text relationship, the (male) reader also looks at the sometimes phallic, sometimes mutilated body and genital zone of the female. This is a horror or vampire version of his desire to be dispossessed. The vampire (read: woman) sucks blood, "the life fluid of a victim." Williams draws comparisons between this and "milking the sperm of the male during intercourse" (89). She also points out that the word "nosferatu" (the Transylvanian bloodsucker) means "splashed with milk . . . the word connotes a homosexual allusion of 'sucking for milk' " (99n17).

Williams's impression of these films locates the vampire (the male in the films) as difference from "a phallic 'norm' ": i.e., the vampire/monster is feared by both the male and female spectators but represents to *men* what castration *would* look like at the hands of the all-powerful mother. Difference is thus mutilating. These are suggestive meditations and for my purposes offer at least an exploratory angle on this genital exposure which combines castration with the phallus. Part of the seductive scenario which is pornography is the relentless visual interrogation of the dismembered, wet genital flesh of the female. If he sees his mirror reflection in the grosteque display of the "monster-model," sees his castrated "other" wielding the potent fetish and the "little penis," then the moment, and the model, are quite powerful indeed, if not perverse. The reader is brought closer to the "cut."

To conclude, the discursive body in straight hard-core centers on a hyperbolic visual excess. The genitals in couplet, aligned with the fetish, are the main attraction. The vulgarity of hard-core lies in a number of things. The two sexes depicted elaborate sexual distinction: but the difference threatens to collapse around the array of possible perspectives on penetration and the way the genitals are put to use in the service of hard-core.

The reader is positioned as voyeur to the sexual scene. But his exclusion from the diegesis and the photo is incomplete: that would mark the total fore-closure of desire. Strategies of identification and pleasure vis-à-vis any cultural technology are always complex, and particularly so in the case of sexual iden-tities and the illicit. In spite of the viewer's apparent absence from the text, there is still a way in which he is enlisted into the machinations of eros.

The voyeur is not simply controller of the authoritative gaze but is actually mastered at the keyhole.[57] As will be argued in "The Gaze," one way this hap-pens is through the unsettling gaze of the model, the gaze that says (among other things): "I know you're watching." Another way this is done is through the transgression of the "sexual fix," in the name of both otherness and dif-ference. First of all, codes of fragmentation in hard-core are in no way restricted to the female of the duo or trio. The truncated body of the male challenges the reader to a fascination with his own loss. He sees the penis of the male model; and often it is a penis displayed only to be partially "cut" out of view, whether by the mouth, the vagina, or the anus. Significations of the male model's desire meet signs of the female's desire for him. This involves the partial emasculation of the model and representations of his simulated femininity: his testicles are his feminine property. What the viewer also sees is the partial phal-licization of the female through the way she is discursively positioned to pene-trate. These arrangements play on an exchange of difference; however, they are poised at an indifferentiating edge as they are combined with the nonaligned anus. That is, the anus is nonaligned with gender but its affiliations are with penetration, aggression, expulsion. It moves toward abolishing difference (and transgressing the "sexual fix").

The "TV" body appears to be nonpartisan as well. But a closer examination reveals that the perversions lie in attempting to simulate not androgyny but difference.

"TV" Pornography

"TV" pornography—both soft- and hard-core—commercializes the her-maphroditic or transsexual body. In the case of *soft-core* the narrative is the solo effort of the "ultimate she-male." S.he is alone in the diegetic space; and her body is again a discursive configuration which makes a mockery of biology and the artifice of gender.[58] The body is in excessive evidence of perversity, but it contrasts with the genre of the medical photo in which "the body" is standard-ized and calculated against the norm. The perverse body which makes it into the medical textbook institutes the desire of nondesire, the body strategically disciplined to reveal its physically depraved state. It is abnormal, maybe, but not sexual, and not displayed in a state of sexual desire. And it is objectified in two ways: it is stripped to be measured against an organizing principle of sexual difference (and against other normative systems). The eyes are typically blackened out to conceal the subject's identity, but with the effect of obliterating identity, subjectivity, and power: we can look at them but they can't acknowledge us as voyeurs. That body is pathologized, not sexualized, in spite of its sexually deviant status. The medical photograph of the sexually abnormal subject conjoins with photography to construct a realist code, and it's understood there is a manifest dialectical relationship between the representation and the real. The photos are supposed to refer back to the anatomical hegemony of sexual difference in the real.[59]

The hermaphroditic body strains after a stable referent. It and the "TV" body, at the same time, show up the flaw in the real: Where is the referent? This body insinuates itself, discursively, into a slippery signification whereby meaning won't stick, where the photo and the discursive body are saturated with meaningfulness. With what meaning(s), though? There are no fidelity claims to a transsexual status in the real; the representation is no alibi for the real: instead, it is a medium capable of reproducing itself. Also, the pornographic model (TV or otherwise) is subjectified through "her" desire, her gaze, her ability to bring the reader closer to the "cut."

Having said this, there is more than indifference operating here, as the model is identified as the "*she*-male"; difference remains a *sine qua non* of desire.

In "TV" *soft-core* the "she-male" is a biological and discursive oscillation between masculine and feminine, male and female polarities. She possesses male and female secondary sex organs, both of which are visually prominent to the extent, at least, that the reader knows she is in possession of both. In one photo layout, "Sulka" is introduced to us in centerfold fashion. In a two-page spread, Sulka is surrounded and partially draped by black gauze and heavily endowed with fetishes: a black leather corset to just under her breasts, garters, black leather gloves which extend to mid-bicep, a silver snake bracelet wrapped around her upper arm at the top of the glove, and a silver-studded black leather collar. Her ample breasts are apparent, although one is slightly and suggestively covered by the gauze. It just barely peeks out; the other is the single breast with phallic pretensions. The black netting also conceals the genital region of her body, creating the illusion of a certain femininity. But the reader knows that Sulka the "she-male" (who has built her reputation on her bi-semic body) is about to disrobe to reveal the concealed penis. Who is s.he kidding?

The photos on the next three pages attempt to contain the gross enigma that is the "TV" body, and to contain that compelling contradiction: after all this is "TV" porn, an acronym for "transvestite." The transsexual model, under the nomination of "TV," suggests that what signifies pornographically is the body dressed up or the way the body and the fetish objects operate together to viciously collapse, and at the same time resurrect, sexual boundaries.

As the narrative unfolds, the model's breasts are given exposure along with the penis. Her hands placed at her genitals, usually around the end of the penis (sometimes to totally occlude the testicles), ensure that the photo "moves" in such a way as to privilege both sexual sites, the feminine breasts and the masculine penis. The eyes of the reader travel between these two areas—is he asked to believe this is somehow real? The ambisexual model is restored to discursive femininity through the fetish accouterments which place the body more firmly within a textual sexuality. Her "she-ness," s.he the "she-male" (not the "he-female"), betrays a "textual fix" (without a "sexual fix"), a location designated by her lingerie and her exaggeratedly feminine hairstyle and make-up.

The reader is spoken through the prototypical heterosexual matrix. That is, he is a consumer of the straight soft-core genre. These photos comprise an insert in, for example, *Club International,* originating from Britain and with a slightly modified version for distribution in the U.S. and Canada. Here the reader encounters certain cultural fictions. One involves this impersonation of femininity through the cultural arrangement of clothes, a hyperbolic pose that allows the model to masquerade as female. This performance is sustained *all the while* the penis is displayed. This visual imaginary is more than a surface play of signs, more than a gender(ed) performance[60] that mocks binary distinctions, more than category confusion[61] (though it is all of the above, too). As a contemporary moment of seduction, the language of desire betrays a deeper structural transgression of coded differences—in the name of simulating indifference. No purity here (or anywhere); not even pure play, but an elaboration of the moment of incision and the chimerical zone of the simultaneity of one and other.[62] This is a curious discourse for the avowedly heterosexual reader. Thus the sexual/cultural narrative and the body textual are exposed as counterfeit. As is the reader.

This model unsettles in a semiotic performance of otherness. "Her" choreography commands the wandering eye of the reader and exposes his fictional performance. Whither belief? Whither the phallus? And what about his desire? This genre is so "state of the artifice" that (phallic) pretensions are what work. As with all hard-core genres, wherein the text includes *ipso facto* a male, a penis, phallic desire, and any number of phallic equivalents, this straight soft-core subgenre doesn't just tolerate but promotes the penis as a focus of desire. The phallicization of the "TV" model would appear to be complete: the preeminent signifier is the penis, clearly marking otherness on the body itself, and "she" modifies "male." The textual and linguistic construction designates this as a woman with a penis, not a man with breasts. But it is not so much this which is the anomaly; otherwise it would simply fit into the medical textbook, a body to be standardized against the norm. This is a body constructed "otherwise," textually in excess of the norm where the simulation/pretense is the featured attraction. The world of this "body double" is a simulated world which can never achieve any meaning in the real; it is the "impossible referent."[63]

"TV" porn shows up the impossibility of the phallus, of representing (pure) desire, subjectivity, objectivity, and difference. Although Sulka already has the penis, it is perpetually limp and is rather unremarkable anyway in assigning the model her status: s.he is a "TV," not a "TS" (transsexual). The fetish objects prevail in connoting both difference and indifference, femininity and masculinity.[64]

For example, Sulka presents her derriere, fleshy, feminine. Her demeanor connotes a demureness: she draws her shoulders together slightly (this is not a brazen, proud chest), her lips are pouty, she plays with her hair (shyly, coyly) with one arm bent at the elbow and close to her left breast. But this rear view is accompanied by the whole lower torso, stockinged legs, complete with garters and high heels. These along with her gaze ensure a certain phallic tenacity. She is a fabrication. Artifice prevails.

There appears to be a surplus of phallic endowment; why the doubled effect of simulated phallic desire with the penis? Is it that the phallus exhausts itself when it meets its supposed referent, the penis? Hence the limpness of (his) desire? This model is obviously not castrated, patently so, and her freakish nature is precisely what implicates the reader. If she embodies "otherwise," if she is not emasculated and refuses to respect categories of difference, the reader must surrender to her spectacular omnipotence, her ability to command the gaze, that is, be "cut" himself (otherwise he is without loss, and desire is foreclosed).

In "TV" *hard-core* the transsexual model engages in sexual activity with a man. In discursive, rather than biological, terms there are specific genital conventions which set up a slippery binary opposition in this sexual puzzle. The narrative, first of all, involves forms of intercourse and penetration, always of the "she-male." She, and not her male partner, engages the reader with the gaze. The male model is not penetrated himself, in spite of the presence of her penis (probably rendered perpetually limp through the injection of female hormones) and in spite of the active presence of a dildo. He is often depicted with a nonerect penis, and his body is not fetishized.

A salient configuration here is actually a form of genital suppression. The "she-male's" penis is visually subordinate to her testicles. She suppresses her penis in two instances. The first is when she is represented alone and pulls a thin strip of leather (although another phallic understudy) between her legs so that the penis is concealed, undercover, and the testicles, as it were, peek out on either side. The other occurs during anal penetration when both models face the camera as she sits on top of him, on his lap. She hoists herself in the air slightly, with one arm, and s.he pulls her penis up toward her stomach with the other hand to reveal not only his partially penetrating penis, and balls, but hers too. Thus she is rendered the more "feminine" counterpart in the photo. In contrast to the solo "TV" impersonator in soft-core, this one is not costumed in such overtly phallic terms. S.he *is* a she-male but must also conform to the sexual polarity which has "otherness" as its defining characteristic. This is still a genre for straight men. Both models must make room for the reader and downplay any enigma which would represent the literal homosexualization of desire.

A precarious difference is restored to the transsexual body, a spectacular display characterized apparently by irreconcilable differences. But in soft-core the feminization of the model is anchored around the fetish accouterments, culturally marked as feminine. Her partial phallicization is achieved through these same fetishes, along with her gaze. They accessorize the exposed, limp penis. In hard-core, the "she-male" shows up phallic otherness as necessary to the desiring subject: she has the penis, but she also wields the dildo. S.he cavorts with a man, which restores her to the status of a female. The viciousness of the "TV" genre lies in its openly straddling the cutting edge of indifference and difference.

To sum up, the genital configurations in all pornographic genres are not a simple matter of an obscene visual excess. Instead, what is "pornographic" about the deployment of the genitals extends beyond their biological designation. In the straight genres, soft and hard, the female models transgress their "sexual fix" even though their genital exposure would seem to amplify their status as "different" from the reader, different from men. But what begins as the biological demarcation of difference quickly moves into "otherness" through the textual deployment of the genitals. The approximation of an androgynous code is achieved through the masculine writing on top of the feminine form. In straight soft-core, this is contrived in the subjection of the milky, maternal breast(s), the semen-filled pouch, to the singular phallus. Even the genitals are a choreography of two partners. The sight of the castrated feminine form as "difference" becomes, under the sign of desire, an entreaty for the reader to encounter his other. *Not* in the sense that he is searching for his other feminine side, but more in the sense that in this exchange both model and reader must surrender signs of desire as part of the logic of seduction. The reader wants to see signs of her desire, her desire to see signs of his; just as he will give up signs of his for her. This is the reader's dispossession. The spectacle of castration may unsettle, but it's a complicated transaction. Because it is paired with other penetrating simulacra, and yet so clearly prominent, the anatomy of pornography enters the discourse of the other. What eroticizes the genital representation is its metonymic affiliation with the fetishes, and the "anal universe."[65] The impudent connotations of the posterior region and the intrusions of anality suggest a model poised to invade; she offers that orifice which both model and reader share. Such is the maneuver of indifferentiation.

In hard-core, ambivalence is more viciously pronounced. Hard-core partly flattens out difference through the cloning of signs of masculinity. Difference is problematized around managing the presence of the penis, the penis in intromission (orally, vaginally, and anally), and the penetrating orifices of the female. The transgressions are the borrowing from the other to incite desire. In so doing, difference is a slow dissolve toward androgyny.

"TV" pornography begins with a structure of indifferentiation. But the ambivalence which characterizes the straight genres pertains here as well. That is, difference is a play on the textual other and resurrected through the strategic genital, and fetish, deployments. "TV" demonstrates the limpness of the penis as a signifier of desire and, in general, the cracks in the phallic code which permit bodily divestment (of the male—both model and reader) in the pathetic striving to represent desire.

The next chapter investigates another bodily discourse, that which organizes the structure of the gaze. Conventions of the gaze within pornography assign the power of the "look" to the female model, inciting a spectacle that provokes, unsettles, penetrates. This marks another transgression of the "sexual fix."

3 | The Gaze

As OUTLINED EARLIER, a central feminist criticism is levied against porn for its alleged construction of "woman" as a sexual spectacle. The idea is that within the pornographic discourses (not unlike any other photograph or film which assumes a male, or sometimes female, spectator),[1] the male spectator possesses the gaze, a gaze used to appropriate if not conquer the "woman" in the representation. Within the orthodox feminist literature, this reputedly unequal relationship, based largely on the active aim of looking, is taken for granted.[2] Any notion of a mediated text is elided in favor of the radical separation of subjects and objects, and meaning that is somehow acquired outside of exchange; i.e., there is *a* gaze, this is a possession, and it is "used" in a singular way. These analyses assign a powerful scopic impulse to the male viewing subject.[3] Generally it is assumed that this drive stems from the punishing castration scenario; that is, the fantasied presence of the castrated woman marks the absence which restores the symbolic phallus to the male reader (this is taken up in chapters 4 and 5). What the feminine form lacks is supposed to structure relations of difference, based on a phallocentrism, whereby the threat that the female image generates is managed through the "determining male gaze."[4] The controlling gaze is instituted to allay castration fears (for Freud, at first a visual apprehension); it symbolically endows the woman with the missing penis and elects the fetish to stand in and, ultimately, deny difference. Thus the elaboration of the visual narrative subjects male discursive control, sexuality, and female desire to the patriarchal gaze, the eye of power.[5]

Although these assumptions (i.e., "Men look; women appear"; women are not "fully" represented in the Symbolic) are frequently still embedded in much feminist, television, film, and art criticism,[6] especially as regards representing sexuality and the body, they have received powerful correctives of late. Laura Mulvey herself treats her infamous formulation of the machinery of the classical narrative—as characterized by an implicit imperious and acquisitive male gaze which controls the erotic (female) spectacle, indeed the workings of desire itself—to a critical interrogation that turns on the question of the female spectator.[7] In "Afterthoughts on 'Visual Pleasure and Narrative Cinema' Inspired by 'Duel in the Sun,' " Mulvey suggests that the female spectator often adopts an active, masculinized viewing position but is then still a "transvestite," postponing the inevitable misfortunes of patriarchal sexual economies.[8] Kaja Silverman challenges not only the epistemological assumptions of the imposture of the possession of the gaze, but also the conflation of the "look" with the "gaze," the latter equation similar to the ideological alignment of the penis with the phallus.[9] The gaze in this critical reworking is what "confirms and sustains" identity but is not equivalent to the possible circulation of "looks," even though the gaze, as a central conduit for the "dominant fictions" or dominant "images or screens," is internalized. One sees oneself seeing oneself. Although the look may maintain the gaze, the eye (through the agency of the look) only "aspires" to the gaze, and thus the possibility of slippage is present. Silverman urges the "dislocation" of the look from the gaze, to demonstrate that the conflation of the two confirms phallic sufficiency, a project at odds with the aims of feminism. And the alliance of the look with the gaze also reproduces, in feminist film theory, the impasse regarding the imputing of the radical separation of subjects and objects. The spectator is never totally outside the spectacle "in a position of detached mastery" (74). Instead, "light . . . projected onto the subject" emanates from the gaze, and grants the subject its own screen image. In terms of the pornographic gaze, it is the possession of neither the reader nor the model(s), though it is the conceit of all genres that it, like the phallus, belongs to one (or the other). Both female model and reader look, but only one is invested with attempts to approximate the gaze, and that is the female model. In the same way she is "given" the phallus through its many substitute fetishes and fetish relations, her look is crucial to the operations of the pornographic machine. As she is aligned with the spectacle and thus has proprietary rights to the gaze, she is a "picture," in this case, of sexual availability. He, the viewer, is implicated in the micropanoptic of her look: is a sexual status conferred upon him through her look?

Sexual status as what? Silverman argues, in this essay on Fassbinder's refusal to commute the exterior gaze into interiority (a refusal of the phallic function), and more elaborately in *The Acoustic Mirror,* that the "dominant fiction" addresses the masculine subject as "plenitude and coherence" (but another hidden fiction).[10] Within patriarchy, the (male) subject, formed at the threshold of corporal and linguistic dispossessions, won't bear the burden of his own objectivity and displaces "knowledge" of his own castration onto the female form. He is "cut": this is his sexual status, reinscribed in the writing on/through the body.

Specular investments are central to the workings of visual imaginaries. The pornographic photograph is saturated with sexual significance, and it moves through its formal strategies of elaborating difference. The eye of the viewer is directed to "read" the photo in meaningful ways. But as with any cultural trope, the pornographic gaze, and its ideological and libidinal supports, is contradictory and oscillating. The look is in the discursive domain of both the reader and the subject of the representation. Designations of masculine/feminine do not represent a picture of unity but are themselves unstable, shifting, and rife with cross-currents. As noted by D. N. Rodowick, the "look" engages both "subject" and "object" and circulates within an economy of imaginary absences. There is "the *act* of the look, but also . . . the *return* of the look from the imaginary other in which that vision is verified."[11]

Visible Maneuvers

The notion of suture as providing an optical point of view is easily applicable to the photographic enterprise. Photographic spreads "move" (or direct our eyes to do so; Lacan notes how anything visual "is a trap . . . as subjects, we are literally called into the picture").[12] Similarly, any individual photograph contains a "punctum," that punctuation which marks the photograph according to the logic of its details.[13] Within classical suture theory, the logic of the narrative is revealed through the functioning of its images.[14] The profilmic event depends on absence to signify presence and, particularly, sutures the reader as he (in this case) fills in the gap created by absence on the screen—or in the photograph. This presence/absence is negotiated through the structuring of looks appropriating the look or gaze—the illusory subject position—of the reader. Oudart's phrase "Imaginary of the filmic space" refers to the interdependency of presence/absence in the creation of meaning in the spectator-text relationship.[15] The look and its containment within the gaze (this distinction is elaborated below) are central to the Imaginary, during whose reign identity is established as misrecognition, alienation, difference, and loss. The "mirror phase" is the dual-sided metaphorical mirror reflection: the subject is inscribed in difference and separation upon the granting of visual recognition and through the look returned from an "other" which signals a repetitive scenario of dismemberment from a fantasy of an initial merger with that "other."

Within the scopic economy, and vis-à-vis regimes of representation, the spectator may be activated in one of two looks (which, it will be argued, can loosen and complement each other): the narcissistic look and the voyeuristic look. Narcissism refers to a look which enhances identification with signs of one's own self or body; the voyeuristic look is allied with the look of the camera.[16] The classic narrative text involves the possibility of three other "looks" through which spectatorial subjectivity is negotiated.[17] One is the look of the characters within the visual text. Their looks at each other organize the "to-be-looked-at-ness" of a (usually female) character; the source behind a look emanates from a male character and is directed toward women, who in turn receive and are determined by it.[18] A second look is the look of the spectator, engaged with the dominant gaze in the film, i.e., that of the male character. And a third strategy is the appropriation of the look of the camera which also directs the eye of the viewer and selects "what is worth looking at."[19] These three looks structure the pleasurable narrative and suture the viewer through these visual machinations into its operations. The look which is missing is the one which would disturb the complacency and coherence of the viewer's imaginary relationship with the text: that is the look of any of the characters on the screen toward the audience. That would be, in effect, to be "caught looking." One of the determining features of the pornographic maneuver, however, is *precisely* this "fourth look": the model possesses the gaze, directly addresses the reader, and in so doing "destabilizes that position and puts it at risk."[20] This is a curious return of the look, a possession of the model which challenges her object status and endows her with a penetrating gaze, and all it may connote: "If the woman looks, the spectacle provokes, castration is in the air."[21] The association of blindness (in women) with loss or frustration of sexual desire is a familiar discursive strategy in films.[22]

The twin themes of subjectivity and desire are centered, in part, on visual moments, perceptions of "looking/being looked at" whereby "perspective" is the metaphor for signification. Different visual strategies operate in pornographic genres. Models, male and female, address each other; that is, they assume positions of desire through modalities of the structure of the gaze. The models address the camera/spectator to anchor the narrative by inviting voyeurism, narcissism, or combinations thereof. The reader is both included in the construction of the sexual narrative and threatened with occlusion through the denial of his "space" within the movement of photography.

The Gaze in Straight Pornography: Soft-Core

The key distinguishing feature of soft-core pornography is the female model represented alone. Desire and pleasure circulate around her body, its codified display and highly fetishistic adornment, and her signifying look which directly addresses either the reader or parts of her own body.

Typical of the soft-core genre is a visual narrative with its own closure. The female model is the only individual occupying the diegetic space, and photographs are arranged strategically so that the "story" reaches its climax with the centerfold. This is preceded by a spread of photographs which are smaller in size than the centerfold (sometimes three and four to a page) and contain images of models engaged in activities, some sexual (e.g., only partially clad, fondling themselves), some not (e.g., talking on the telephone, portrait shots), and in various stages of undress. This is all simulated foreplay and raises questions about the positioning of the reader through the gaze, his engagement with the construction of the narrative, and the central discursive space given to displays of the female body, symbolically adorned as gender-specific and sexual. The desiring spectator is addressed in ways which allow him to participate in and complete the play of desire of the model.

A "story" often accompanies and anchors the photographic spread, depicting the "lifestyle" of the model. It presents a general portrait of her life and her many interests, hobbies, and fantasies (not just sexual), always with emphasis on her availability (she is single) and unceasing energy for sexual encounters (often with the proviso that sex combined with love is the ultimate expression of passion and desire, even for the *Playboy* centerfold).[23] The idea seems to be that the "girls" are sexy and daring but not too sluttish, really the girl next door. They cannot be available for *every* man, otherwise the reader would be in a position of having to compete for what, in fantasy, is the continuous presence of embodied desire. And there *is* the look which acknowledges the illicit nature of the consumption of pornographic material: the sidelong, sly glance which barely whispers, "This look is for you, which only *you* can see." It connotes, in its slyness, the clandestine and furtive nature of the exchange. What is really the generalized address (any adult in the public domain can buy and read these magazines) appears destined for the individual consumer, and only him (i.e., sexual consumption is still rendered private and essentially monogamous), through the suturing gaze of the model.

Alternately, there is the "look" of pleasure: the closed eyes, the open mouth, often with tongue protruding. This is the spectacular look: it accompanies autoerotic activity, fondling of the genitals or breasts. These instances invite the voyeuristic gaze, the reader occupying the position of the camera. The model and her self-possessed look (her eyes are closed) threaten to exclude the reader through the self-satisfaction of her own desire. However, the self-contained look forms part of a larger visual narrative in which the reader has already been addressed via the gaze of the model and thus is already inscribed in sexual scenarios which demand his presence. (The model also knows she is being looked at, that she is on display, even if she is not actively catching the eye of the reader.)

The photographs offer little diegetic variation; they are constructed and move in such a way that distractions and extraneous details are kept to a minimum. The model's body or parts of it, in fact, are usually given over to the full visual space of the photograph—leaving what kind of space for the reader? He occupies the space of the voyeur, and his presence is signified specularly: as long as he can "see" her watching him watching her. Circuits of desire are in place.

The model's look of pleasure is also the look of love's labor, but it is more than a labor of love: in this libidinal economy, investments are not gratuitous. What is exacted from the model's face is the industrious look of bureaucratic administration: the functionary's ministerial efforts. In this visual moment the look is embellished and weighted with the responsibility of the display of the objects of one's labor. The laborious, indefatigable, never idle machinations are all in the service of the production of value/meaning. These are the official discourses of sex; which is to invoke Foucault's intensification and "analytical multiplication of pleasure," "power . . . brought to bear on the body and on sex."[24] Pornographic bodies are discursive bodies, and the signs of their intensification are registered on the models' faces in conjunction with the body saturated with desire (other discourses surround the fetish, to be taken up in other chapters). The face conveys the look, which in this case exceeds the image of receptive femininity.

The Epicene Eye

The visual moment in any medium (and one would argue that this is especially so with pornography) is a courtship between image and looking, the vehicle of which is the eyes, those that manage the look. In the case of pornographic photographs, there are models who look, and who solicit a series of looks from the reader. This solicitation involves an exchange circulating within a libidinal economy. The investment is in a sexual discourse privileging a commerce which is by definition ocular, not carnal. To speak of the gaze is to invoke a metaphysics of staring: the gaze is not the glance but the stare; the "gaze gone hard . . . tends toward a certain violence, a will to penetrate, to pierce, to fix in order to discover the permanent under the changing appearances, which implies a certain anxiety in the relation between spectator and object seen."[25] Her eyes, her gaze, never leave the reader.

The eye is an orifice, the window to the bodily soul,[26] an opening which takes in the perceptible world. It is the body's peephole; an eye-opener is, after all, that which shocks and surprises, a revelation, an act of revealing to view, an enlightening disclosure, "to have seen the light." A hollow organ, the eyeball is penetrable, like the eye of the needle, that through which thread passes. Its bisexual qualities are nonetheless apparent: the eye is also an agent of illumination, providing light, an orifice of projection. "To cast an eye on, lay an eye on," "to have eyes for," "to look into something": the eyes are active agents of capture, possession, penetration. They do not just receive but they project, and they do this through the light they shed. In short, the eye is figuratively feminine and masculine. Like the eye of the camera, it is an aperture which admits light; as a metaphor for looking, however, it is aligned with a masculine trajectory and the ability to extend vision to the spectacular. Ocular penetration offers up documentation of the perceptible world, hence in-sight, a visible inventory which is partisan from the start (like the "reality" captured before the camera lens).

Beauty may be in the eye of the beholder; this signifies an aesthetic or intellectual perception or appreciation. But "to have an eye for" is to submit a point of view or judgment. In this predatory way there is power in the workings of the gaze. Lacan speaks of the voracious eye, the "appetite of the eye on the part of the person looking," how "envy" (*invidia*) stems from *videre*, "to see."[27]

There is an epicene quality to the eye and its inscription in the gaze. Power may also reside in the eye of the beholder, and in this case is shared by the model who is the subject doing the looking. This is clearly visible in the pornographic photograph which organizes the eyes around the workings of desire as they permit a reciprocity between both masculine and feminine possessions; i.e., one captures at the same time as one is being caught.

Modes of Ocular Insight

The most notable opposition in all genres is that between opened and closed eyes. The opened eyes project a certain kind of look: they are beady eyes, with lids in slight descent. These are not wide open, youthful, innocent, and naive. These beady eyes are like the beads they connote: small, round, and "shiny with interest or greed." A bead is also a "small knob in the front sight of a gun"; "to draw a bead on" is to take aim at something. These eyes, like beads (also a perforated object for threading), are taking careful aim at their object. They are eyes in focus. The beady-eyed look is guilty of knowing what's going on, complicit in the illicit, a feminine surrender to the "masculinity" of the desiring subject. That is, the model bears the marks of masculinity in her eyes/look. The eyes of her desire are signs of masculine projection, an erection in front of the male viewer.

Beady eyes are "small and bright." Beady eyes do not provide the most candid view (they are not wide open to all possibilities). They are hiding something, are not without guile, and are subtly cunning: the one with beady eyes is not to be trusted. The less than candid model is the one who acknowledges the illicit exchange of sexual glances with a photograph, with a stranger. The illicit exchange threatens the stability of both subjects: the subject of the representation, she who desires to be looked at and in so doing carries the mark of *his*—the other's—desire; and the subject who is reading the representation, who is enlisted in his "feminine" surrender to penetration. The model's piercing acknowledgment exposes the nonspontaneity of the profilmic event, its staginess and reproduction (simulation) for the camera.

This desiring female subject is looking, casting an eye at the "apple of her eye," that highly cherished object. The "apple" of her eye can also, according to the *OED* and Partridge's *Historical Slang*, refer to the pupil, the eyeball, the object of one's desire (and the slang for "testicles," hence returning us to the sexual connotations of the reader). There is a symbolic rapport between the eyes and testicles which invites their sexual affinity even further. Both are associated with light. The eyes take in and throw light on, eyes "see the light." The testicles are the apple of the eye and provide the seed or the light of life; they emit fluids of seminal light. And both are claims to "truthfulness": the "eye-witness" is the one who bears testimony based on his own observation. "Testicle" is derivative of the Latin *testis,* "witness," and is thus related to "testimony" and "testify," both referring to the provision of evidence, demonstrable proof, a declaration, confession, or affirmation based on the "truth." To give evidence, to testify, to bear witness: she is witness to his virility, calls upon him to provide evidence of it, and offers up her body as testimony to his virility/ masculine desire. All of this she does through visual insight.

The slightly shut eyes, beads focused intently on the unsuspecting viewer, are not eyes wide open.[28] Again, from Partridge: "to have one's eyes opened" is to be robbed. Hence the "eye-opener" is the lesson learned, instruction for the uninitiated. The model in question, however, is already "in the know," not wide-eyed and bushy-tailed, but savvy enough to give away her desire only once she sees evidence of his.[29] This she demands; nothing can be taken from her. Thus, the look has its passive and active sides. The model in this case looks as a projection of her desires; she also desires to be looked at and solicits this visual rapport from her desiring reader.

The viewer is engaged in the fantasy of the satisfaction of his desire. This involves the visible expression of the model's desire, projections which put her within a simulated masculine discourse, the partial masculinization of her body, its positions, and its symbolic adornment. The opened eyes are the window by which this desire is read, entered. But the eyes opened (and ready for business) emit more than they take in, hence they are beady. Beads are often sacred relics, icons of religious ritual (the largest rosary bead is the "paternoster," the Name of the Father). Beads are also jewels. The beady eyes in this case are fixated and focused on the "apple" of the model's eye, that is, the "apple" of the reader: his "family jewels." The look is "eyeball to eyeball": an intense gaze, a "close confrontation." The beady eyes engage the passions of the "other." *And* the beady eyes are ambisexual: possessed by a woman who longs to be possessed by a man and exposes her yearning through a wishful simulation of the possession. In so doing she seduces. In so doing she possesses the family jewels with her insightful/inciteful gaze.

The eyes can be a projection of desire. The effect of the sexually explicit and illicit unsettles the reader (he with the open eyes) as the sole power behind the "gaze." Silverman writes: "Exhibitionism unsettles because it threatens to expose the duplicity inherent in every subject, and every object—to reveal the subject's dependence for definition upon the image/screen, and his/her capacity for being at the same time in the picture, and the point of light for another subject."[30] The model thus carries the weight of the look, even though she may be the spectacle. And, as the saying goes, "to have someone by the balls" is to have someone utterly in one's power, especially of women over men (Partridge). She catches the viewer by the eye-ball.

In contrast, the closed eyes which accompany a display of autoeroticism do not simply denote the creation of a passive spectacle. Eyes closed in simulated pleasure or ecstasy follow, in the photographic spread, the look which has already penetrated: there isn't a singular or unproblematic eye. The closed eyes prevent ocular penetration of that orifice. "To connive" is, from Latin, "to shut the eyes," "to wink" (which brings us back to the "winking bung" in chapter 2). However, although the eyes may be closed, covered by lids, sunglasses, or the brim of a hat, they are viewed in conjunction with parts of the body that *are* offered for penetration. As will be shown later, closed eyes consort with parts of the body and its symbolic adornment, masculinized to the point of being capable of penetrating themselves.

Consider two literal renditions of photographs in which penetrating techniques circulate around ocular maneuvers, even though the model's eyes in this particular shot are closed:

1. "Kathy" is lying on a small coffee table, head at one end, rear end resting at the other, her legs bent to balance her pointed toes on the floor. The view we have of her is from the side, a long-shot. This is what we see: her back is arched, her head is tilted back on the table (eyes closed), her chin is in the air, and her breasts are protruding with fully erect nipples. "Kathy" is sporting white lace fingerless gloves; her hands are resting just above her breasts on her collarbone. Her stockings are studded with small shiny beads, and ballet slippers encase the feet, similarly arched to point the toes, elongate the feet and legs, and support the upward arching of the back. Two areas of her body are "highlighted" through the use of beams of light which appear to enter from an unseen window. Each beam points to, and highlights, both the breasts and the pubic area, such that both are shiny and glowing. The former—her "high-beams"—are erect and looking to penetrate; the latter is a pleasure zone highlighted for penetration. The model in this picture does not possess the incisive gaze, but her body is no passive spectacle/receptacle either.

2. "Susan" "loves to flirt with strange, unsuspecting men by turning them on only with her beautiful brown eyes." She shades her eyes with sunglasses while she spreads her legs, bent at the knees, to reveal wider possibilities; at the same time *her* breasts are in the path of a light beam (the "eye-beam" of the reader). "Susan's" hair may also partially occlude her vision; she then sports a man's tie whose tip ends at her most feminine point of entry. Her long, blood-red fingernails, in the closed-eye shots, are placed on the pubic or anal area, signaling again points of entry, as well as the body's protrusions. The heel of her shoe serves the same visual and phallic function as she contorts her body to aim it (the high heel) directly at the vaginal orifice.

This is the masculinization of the model's desire to satisfy the viewer's desire. The closure of the model's eyes does not mean simply that she is looked at. She is in fact doing something: desire is written on her body, and her self-containment (the apparent exclusion of the viewer) is still an active solicitation of the interests or desire of the reader. The model knows she is being looked at—she has already engaged the reader through the previous exchange of looks and glances. However, she is not merely reduced to an orifice (she has put the lid on that orifice that invites ocular penetration) as her body bears the simulated marks of masculinization, male insight. Her physique carries its own projections, erections, protuberances: the breasts—or in slang, "headlights"—are prominent and thrusting outward or the nipples are fully erect. And excrescences are abundant (as previously noted, the anus is a favorite offering/invasion). This is the simulated world of sex, the "delirious surround" of the spectacular, the consumption of meaning which defies representation.[31] The display is not one-half of the real/representation juxtaposition but is itself a simulated world of signs which anticipate and shape the real. How do you represent desire, that which is only ever the desire of an Other, which exists only in a nonreferential exchange and is not the property of One? In this case it is written on the body in a series of simulated codes; the body shows up simulation only as the real reproduction.[32] The masculinized body of the woman has no referent but is a composite of signs which refers only to signs of masculinity anyway: it is hard, taut, turgid with desire, and bearing protuberances loaded with indices of wishful penetration, the desirous be.longings[33] of an androgynous commerce. A masculine code is an integral part of the female body.

In soft-core, the model's gaze penetrates when her eyes are open yet beady. The look is direct in its ability to pierce and hold the reader. It is alluring, inviting, and unsettling. The model eyes the viewer flirtatiously, slyly, knowingly. Her glances are coquettish; her come-hither looks acknowledge the dalliance of a reader engaged in the illicit. Part of the allure of pornography is this fantasization of desire involving the illusory dyad and not the woman shared by other men. The look is a "peek-a-boo" look which also acknowledges the naughtiness of the public consumption of the quintessentially private act. The open eyes are a prelude to what will follow: the eyes will close, the model will engage in autoerotic activity, and the body will be offered up for visual entry. This may explain why the reader relinquishes the privilege of the power of looking and allows himself to be penetrated, if not virtually castrated, by her gaze. Although the reader may long to be caught by her eyes, his power in gazing is partially restored when the model surrenders hers. The closed eyes are the picture of simulated desire, the foreplay which precedes the "real" thing yet to come. And what is to come, penetration of her, is signified by her body simulated with the possessive marks of her desire for this. This is pronounced and visible when she relinquishes the power behind her looking, when she, at the same time, puts closure on her "eye-hole" ("hole to look through") and the option of being penetrated *there*.

The look of the coquette solicits the reader in another important way. It is dangerous and insinuating and works diachronically toward its own antidote, i.e., the look which displays pleasure at the model's own hands, thus to the apparent diegetic exclusion of the reader. However, although masturbatory/ autoerotic sequences are very common in soft-core pornographic material, the reader may project his desire onto/into other parts of the model's body as he can see her desire written there, in his language (protuberances, projections, and be.longings). And this will occur *after* the reader has been enlisted in a penetrating exchange.

A photo spread entitled "An Evening Off" is typical of the solipsism of the desiring subject. A variety of shots and poses depict a model caressing her legs and breasts in obvious masturbatory pleasure. Of seven photographs, two contain muted glances at the camera (chin tilted downward; head horizontal and off to the side); in another scene of self-contained desire, the model describes posing "as if the camera were my lover and I was sharing my entire body with it": a body invaded by the eye of the camera. In the other photos the look is of concentrated pleasure, eyes closed, mouth open, the look of ecstasy. Her solipsism, however, is complemented by the simulated marks of the spectator's inclusion into the textual body. These are the masculine marks of her desire for the reader's desire: the long fingernails, the spike heel, the erect nipples, and orifices offered for possession, the penetrating possibilities. The look of self-containment, the exclusion of the male reader from the diegetic space of the photograph, is accompanied by full genital display or the offering of buttocks and anus to the camera—but with facial signifiers of pleasure visibly flaunted by the head turned and tilted upward, face contorted. A small narrative text accompanies the autoerotic scenes, and the model's desire is further enunciated through her own confessional statements: "Sometimes, I just have to take an evening off and really get into myself. That way I make sure I make myself happy—and boy, do I!" This occurs after she has already "gotten into" him; she now solicits *his* look.

The observations made above raise questions about identification in the libidinal/narrative economy and the exploitation of sexual difference within the pornographic moment. How and through what mechanisms is the male reader represented to himself? What, in these cases, is "the spectatorial experience of sexed individuals"?[34] The separation of subject and object in this exchange is not so unproblematic; nor is the look (of the reader) a picture of unity. It is an imbrication of both narcissistic and voyeuristic components.

Is there pleasure in this for the male viewer? Although a popular "look" is the sly one, coy and cunning, this knowing look is accompanied by a sharpness which is penetrating and which attempts to fix the viewer, and to fix him as source of the gaze. The model has a security about her, a sureness of motive, a subtle command. She is the designing woman, not without guile, whose cunning device is her eyes: the gaze attracts and locks the look of the reader, no innocent bystander he. This is how "Cindy" is described: "Her gaze demands that you be patient, that you allow her to call the shots. She holds the torch for no-one, and yet her eyes suggest a flame, fathoms deep, that is both mysterious and inextinguishable." Her eyes enter his bodily soul (which the eyes, after all, mirror): he is caught. But pornography is not about sex; and representations of the model who insinuates, and the viewer who is interpolated (and interpellated) in a perverse cultural role reversal, suggest the construction of subjectivities and differences rife with contradictions as well as the uneasy separation of subjects and objects.

How can this be accounted for in psychoanalytic terms? In terms of libidinal and symbolic economies? The discursive position of the model invokes the operations of the "cut" and challenges the "simple equation of exhibitionism with passivity, and voyeurism with aggression."[35] This is the theorizing of the will to subject-ion. In Jacques Chevalier's words, this is part of the logic of seduction that betrays a "play of passion," in which signs of desire are expressed to indicate a "wishful simulation of the (desired) union itself." In this case the pornographic spectator is male, and as noted in chapter 1, it is also suggested by Silverman, via Lacan, that there is pleasure in submission to painful experiences, in their "mastery of us."[36] Lacan's rhetorical subject is formed in alienation, visual and linguistic, from the signifying other, and sees itself from the vantage point of its otherness, an otherness effected partially by the "image/screen" of its exteriority.[37] The ego's ideal image is a phenomenological impossibility, established in separation from its picture of unity, the original plenitude which lends the subject a specular image of coherence, albeit fictive.[38] The process by which the subject assumes an image is "predicated on the painful sense of loss"[39] associated with the "otherness" which is "mirrored" back to it. The "other," bi-semic at least in its ability to signify, introduces a " 'gap' into the operations of the subject . . . keeping the goals of desire in perpetual flight."[40]

Visual imaginaries can thus reposition the subject at the point of his cultural integration. Silverman's point is that this is a nexus of both pleasure and renunciation—the pain of alienation from the other is constitutive of subjects. The receptivity of the male reader, then, at the moment of suture engages with a narrative of loss and plenitude. The photographic text implies a relationship between the shot (plenitude, the picture, the mirror) and the subject (absence, the missing element), that which perceives the shot.[41] That "missing element" (gap, loss) calls upon the discursive subject to stand in, assume the "position of a taking-the-place-of" to provide closure or imaginary coherence to "reading" or cultural integration.[42] What's missing if not the necessary (illusion of) phallic support, the masculine subject sufficient enough to fulfill the phallic function, to "be" pure difference (the phallus). In the case of these visible maneuvers, the viewer sees himself through the "representative" gaze of the model.

Pornographic photographs play on a watchful eye and a potent gaze, in the discursive domain of both the model and the spectator. The model carefully "eyes" her subject with a vigilance verging on the microscopic panopticon. The eyes of the model and her "look" may exclude the reader but activate his desire: in this dyadic relationship, model and reader have eyes only for each other. Instabilities in the masculine viewing subject position are held in view in this critical encounter. Suture, which structures the availability of the subject founded on absence,[43] entices a cultural (and psychoanalytic) re-reading of simple equations of sadism/active looking and masochism/passive display. As well, these two categories are not binary exclusives. Castration of the male (submission to the Law, language, and desire) is part of access to the Symbolic and crucial to machinations of desire. How better is this signified than by the male who, in his representational equivalent, is positioned so ambiguously?[44]

Is the gaze male?[45] What I have attempted to demonstrate in the preceding is that the manipulation of the "gaze" is central to the formal features of the pornographic genres. In so doing, I have emphasized a number of points which situate the "look" within a problematic of identity and dislocation. The pornographic consumer, to be sure, is enlisted scopically; what he looks at is problematized around the metaphorical eye. The eye, however, is never neutral. For example, if the model's eyes are shaded, they prevent entry by that orifice; at the same time, the look of the viewer may be directed toward another orifice, or fetish, or simply the outline and surface of the body. But what s(t)imulates the pornographic movement is the privileging of the model with the beady, penetrating eyes. She is the model who solicits the attentions of the reader: she makes a visual pass at him, projects her look, takes aim, incisive and penetrating, meets the reader. What makes the moment pornographic is this partial masculinization of the ocular orifice, an orifice which begins as ambisexual; i.e., it can receive as well as emit. As part of the pornographic maneuver, the eye is aggressive, acquisitive, possessive: it invades the space of the reader, implicating him not only in the activity of looking but also as the one who is looked at.

In hard-core, the "look" must compete with other graphic configurations of genital display, sexual activity, and the fetish object. However, the "look" still signifies in important ways: as a signifier of pleasure; as part of the narrative economy which directs the gaze of the reader toward the erogenous zones; and as an acknowledgment of the reader.

The Gaze in Straight Pornography: Hard-Core

The hard-core genre is the "eye-popper." In it the reader is privy to the graphic "exposing to view [of] certain acts or anatomies"[46] and is voyeuristically ensconced at the peephole. If the reader's eyes "pop out of his head" in shock, fascination, identification, and desire, he is at the same time emasculated through his visual projection and temporary loss (of his eyes, of sight). To have eyes "pop out of the head" is, in the vernacular, nearly to lose one's eyesight (and to take a lot of sight in). In Partridge, "to lose one's eyesight" implies an unexpected and very intimate view of a member of the opposite sex. Paradoxically, thus, it is the viewer who is robbed, whose eyes are wide open in taking in the gaze/spectacle, who encounters the penetrating gaze of the model, who is rendered sightless by the female "eye-popper."

Scenarios of blindness in the oedipal drama are associated with guilt and castration. As noted above, in the classic narrative film, woman's loss of vision is aligned with some other medical or sexual-pathological disturbance, or as punishment for seeing too much, for appropriating the masculine gaze, masculine critical insight, masculine desire. Metaphors of lost vision in those examples are the somatic inscription of (the wish for) a limp or repressed desire. Here, however, the reader is a peeping Tom. (The *OED* records the first use of this phrase in 1837: "The story [of Godiva] is embellished with the incident of Peeping Tom, a prying inquisitive tailor, who was struck blind for popping out his head as the lady passed.") "Tom" is slang for "girl or woman," also "prostitute," and, in Partridge, "either tom or Tom" is " 'a masculine woman of the town' (a harlot)." The instabilities in voyeurism are evident in the ways in which that position refuses to adhere exclusively to either masculine or feminine subjects. The voyeur, publicly stripped of his penetrating properties, is implicated in a nexus whereby transgressive possession is the norm. Here, the look that the pornographic model appropriates is the one stolen from the viewer: "With a cock in *her* eye: hence sexually desirous" (Partridge, emphasis mine).

The pornographer's voyeur sees a sexual encounter between two or more individuals: chance, spontaneous, and among strangers. There are three possible corresponding looks of the female model in this genre: (1) the look of pleasure; (2) the look which is directed at the genitals; and (3) the model's engagement with the camera/reader.

The look of pleasure. In straight hard-core pornography, the look of pleasure accompanies not autoeroticism but the graphic depiction of penetration of the female by the male. Men never touch or penetrate each other, except in a signifying chain: i.e., "A" (male) touches "B" (female), who touches "C" (male). (Is A then touching C?)[47] And male models do not engage the camera/reader. The reader is thus doubly excluded from the representation. He does offer his look but then relinquishes desire to the already present and erect penis, that which does the erotic work for him. Through the suturing process the viewer is tenaciously and precariously there, at once a redundant player in this ménage. The question of his involvement with the drama before him then suggests an oscillation between the voyeur's peeping Tomism and the narcissist who encounters women, men, and signs of himself. The joys of the narcissistic bond, however, are not threatened by the male model's direct visual address: that would disrupt the fiction of the heterosexual stability of the viewer. It would also upset the dominant discursive sexual arrangement which assigns otherness to women.[48] The reader thus displaces his look onto the gaze of the woman in the representation.

The look of pleasure is a look which simulates sexual ecstasy and is signified by closed eyes, open mouth, and head tilted back. It is also the look of labor, a studied, concentrated look which treats its sexual object solemnly. It is the look which signifies female pleasure, itself a predominant pornographic fetish, as John Ellis notes.[49] The face of the male model is not given diegetic dominance; when it is figured at all (and more often it is not), it bears either the look of amused or bored detachment or combinations of pain and ecstasy. As with soft-core, there is the bureaucratic exacting of compliance and a kind of autoproduction of pleasure. The emphasis here is on the feminine look of pleasure produced, and passion consumed. Again, the rhetorical (viewing) subject is enlisted as the cultural voyeur, yet his psychodrama is an oscillation between positions of plenitude and loss.

Whereas the soft-core photograph is usually restricted to only one body and its codified display is less graphic, the hard-core narrative, given its surfeit of signifiers (bodies, body fragments, looks, fetishes), is more ornate. The movement in the photograph more actively enlists the "absent one" in the suturing process. But this is done in a curious way, as the viewer is doubly excluded—by the self-contained look of pleasure of the female model, and through the inclusion in the diegesis of the already present male model.

The genital "look." The models in pornographic sequences look at each other only under certain circumstances: i.e., if they are women. If two men are featured with one female model, they are merely signified by their genitals, and their connection to each other is by vicarious association: they inhabit the same diegetic space and are there to give pleasure to the woman or extract it from her. Both men and women will look at their genitals and each other's (in union), and a circuit of desire is sustained in this signifying chain of genitals and bodies. The frontal display of genitals gives an illusion of uninterrupted narcissistic pleasure. The locking of genitals through intercourse creates a singular body: the female body appears to be an extension of the penis. There is continuous and pervasive tactility. However, strictures against male homoerotic affection are in place, and men will never touch each other.

There is a commingling of narcissist and voyeur. First, the drama of the "primal scene" is played out for the latter. The cropped photographs and fragmented bodies do nothing to truncate desire but instead channel it through the "keyhole." The "illicit" combines with a lust for verisimilitude, coalescing neatly with the eye of power, the camera. Within the hard-core pornographic moment, voyeurism and narcissism overlap, the scopic drive being essentially autoerotic: its object is the subject's own body, a guarantor of imaginary self-coherence. Identifications are shifting and mobile, involving narcissistic fantasies and, initially in the development of the subject, a search for autoerotic satisfaction.[50]

The construction of the spectacle, then, does not so easily fall into an equation of opposites, i.e., activity/voyeurism, passivity/exhibitionism. The voyeur enters the moment of sexual suturing and engages (*not* in a move of pure identification, if that were even possible) with the male, "marked as the object of an erotic gaze."[51] As well, the masochistic component is activated; that is to say the subject has taken up "multiple identificatory positions, whether successively or simultaneously."[52]

The classic formulation of voyeurism depends on a gap, a separation between the seer and the object seen. But voyeurism as mastery suffers in the hard-core genre, as elsewhere,[53] as the gaze flips on its own narcissistic vanishing point. Kaja Silverman, in her essay on Fassbinder's aesthetic, notes how any spectator is incorporated into the image and in the act of looking; thus he "fades away."[54] That is, viewing is wedded to an image: the "point of light" (that which grants the subject his own image; the gaze) both precedes and postdates the subject—the subject is incorporated into the image. Thus, what might appear to be a gap between spectator and spectacle is partially filled by the male model in the pictures. The "look" of the viewer is marked by the narcissistic gaze, and absence gives way to presence: lacunae and losses of the narrative, and the psyche, are fictively filled. Yet the look between spectator and his imago is not direct enough to threaten the dominant gaze of fixed, binary sexual identity. If that happened for the heterosexual viewer, the male model would penetrate the viewer's (very) open eyes; this is too radical a maneuver for the heterosexual matrix. The extradiegetic looks then are mediated by the exchange of looks among the models in the photograph. As well, the male body is not adorned as an object of "erotic display," and thus sexual difference is doubly sustained in the semiotic language of desire.[55]

As noted in the previous chapter, a key feature of the pornographic visual vocabulary is the "rear" view and graphic anality. A case can be made for the contiguity between anality and ocular penetration. Drawing from Freud's case study of the Rat Man, an anal obsessive whose compulsions involved the twinning of overwhelming desires and obsessive fears, Bela Grunberger argues that there is aggressivity in anal impulses, to be sure, but the perceived imperious impulse behind voyeurism can in fact be the pairing of anal castration and narcissistic seduction by a powerful other.[56] In chapter 2 it was noted that in hard-core the female model's anus is said to be "winking out" at the reader/model, another micropanoptic. Grunberger suggests, in a reversal of the pornographic equation where the bung/anus is the winking eye, that "the eye acts as a sphincter."[57] "To bung one's eye," from Partridge, is "to drink a dram till one's eyes close." Once again, associations are with seduction and the reader's dispossession: the loss of his ocular insight.[58] This too forms part of the semiotic language of desire.

Direct address. There is a look which directly engages the reader, and that is the one which addresses the camera. This third look, only of the female model, is returned to the reader toward the end of the visual narrative. It accompanies fellatio and sexual intercourse, for example when the woman, poised on top of the man and with her back to the camera, glances over her shoulder. As with soft-core, this look is naughty: it acknowledges and challenges the illicit pleasures of spectatorial sex. It has a particular place in this genre. Although men are given diegetic space in the hard-core narrative, the relay of their looks is intercepted by female models only. Direct address of the male model to the viewer might solicit unspoken signs of homoerotic identifications, thereby closing the gap between subject and representation and unsettling the viewer's/voyeur's position at the keyhole.

When women directly address the reader as if to say, "Look at what I'm doing," they strike an exhibitionistic pose. Yet this insightful look is contained in a close-up photo which is a display not of her genitals, commonly associated with the idea of exhibitionism, but of her *face* and *his* organ, for example during oral sex. Freud points out that the exhibitionist is "at the same time" a voyeur.[59] Again, as with the soft-core counterpart, this look is direct, penetrating, and this time cynical and mocking. The model, imbricated in the archeology of the panopticon, "makes visible" the reader. In that sense, the model is also doing the watching; she is in control of her own gaze at the same time as he watches her (and encounters a sign of his fragmented corpus).

To conclude, the manipulation of the gaze is a formal feature of the operations of hard-core. All three looks both elaborate sexual difference and dramatize indifference at the same time. The first two possibilities, the look of pleasure and the genital "look," direct the look of the reader at signs of the female model's desire, and signs of the desire of the male model. But it is a desire which frames the exclusion of the reader (who stands outside the representation), seduction not achieved by his own will. Difference here is marked primarily through the genital arrangement. The genital look does not simply denote the female genital display but also includes detailed signifiers of masculinity. This excludes the reader again as he encounters his stand-in in the diegetic space. The surrogate is a fragmented vision/version of his own body, usually seen in conjunction with the female's facial signifiers of pleasure. So while the reader may project his look onto that of the female model, it is a voyeuristic look which overlaps with narcissistic preservation: he searches out a look (of pleasure) affiliated with his fragmented body.

The third possible look within the hard-core genre is the female model's possession of what Paul Willemen has called the "fourth look." This is the dynamic look which confronts the reader with an eye aimed to penetrate, setting up a "relay of looks" which upsets any linear notion of "subject-object" relations within a spectator-text exchange.[60] This mode of address engages the spectator directly and brings him closest to the "cut." The "fourth look" endows the female model with the discursive possibilities of ocular penetration, ocular phallicization; her textual body borrows the masculine code. In this sense, conventions of the gaze in the hard-core genre contribute to its viciousness. Again, the vulgarity behind the excessive elaboration of sexual difference lies with the way it straddles, at a cutting edge, difference and indifference.

In the "TV" genre, sexual difference appears to collapse into indifference. Here the transsexual body itself is apparently indifferent to difference, carrying the marks of otherness within its own closed economy. Difference and otherness, again, seem to be sacrified in the name of sameness. But the structure of the gaze within the machinations of desire does invoke sexual difference—as we will see.

The Gaze in "TV" Porn

The construction of the look in TV porn primarily engages the reader (as opposed to the solipsistic/narcissistic look of the model at her genitals). The *soft-core* pictorials are contained within the straight soft genre as a special attraction or insert ("A 6 page photo set! Sulka! The ultimate she-male!"). The still photographs are one to a page (i.e., eight inches by ten inches), giving the reader a full view of the body, and the look of the model is direct. Sharp and penetrating, it is a look which cannot elude the reader and accompanies every body position: i.e., even when the model offers her "rear view" to the camera, s.he glances back over her shoulder, her look firmly implanted. The gaze is not the central signifier here, as the body is a discursive play of transgressive sexual positions and competes with the look of the model for the reader's attention. However, there *is* a direct look which is carried by the transsexual (in transvestite's clothes).

The gaze of the model in *soft-core* TV porn is not so sly, not so "come hither," but it is more penetrating. It is direct, straightforward, a look candid and outspoken. It is the gaze which tries to contain all difference, to balance contradiction. She (through her eyes) captures the eyes of the reader and controls the movement of his look. Her critical perception accompanies a body whose biological disposition subverts sexual difference. The instabilities of the model fascinate. The reader's look remains within *her* gaze, doubly relaxing his already loose sexual fix. If the body textual is written as "feminine" through the fetish signifiers of lingerie, jewelry, and high-heel shoes, wouldn't that writing render the (fully obvious) penis obsolete or at least dispensable? Phallic meaning is restored, however, through the symbolic deployment of fetish objects which are necessary to the functioning of this seductive narrative. There is so much to see, and the visual dissonance is orchestrated, in part, by the gaze of the fe.male model.

In TV *hard-core,* the simulated production of men who, in a reciprocal play of desire, desire masculinized women echoes throughout this visual text. This challenges the social construction of gender identity through the representation of subjects who, in desiring what the other desires, enter into sexual arrangements which continually tease the great sexual divide.

The narrative begins with the exchange of looks between the models as they initiate sexual contact. A few introductory photographs provide the setting for the story, which is typically about a chance encounter between a transsexual/hermaphrodite whose "true" identity is concealed (by clothing), and an unsuspecting yet persistently willing male. The story unfolds as the transsexual model gradually reveals her hermaphroditic body through the shedding of feminine attire. There are, again, three possible looks here: the "genital look" (the fascination with genitals and/or genital contact), the look of pleasure, and "direct address." With the *genital look,* one or both of the models visually engage the penis. This occurs most often with intercourse or with autoerotic fascination. Hands are a feature which partially structure this look. In the case of the ambisexual and a male model, the fascination with looking (on the part of the viewer as well) appears to take on the voyeur's aim of looking outside himself: he is again implicated in the highly illicit consumption of public sex. Sexual pathologization doubly heightens curiosity: the body/subject so discursively arranged is not just displayed in acts which should be consumed in private, but is the morally unhygienic body. It subverts a system of normative difference based on binary opposites. Penises, anal entry, *and* the literal phallus (the transsexual playing with a dildo in mock sexual ecstasy) are key signifiers: the common shot is of the "female" model spreading her buttocks to display "rear entry" (she in the "dominant" position, sitting on top of him). Or in a view of the front she covers her genitals, either in mock masturbatory performance or to hide her hermaphrodism. But can that knowledge be suspended? In a curious way we have men looking at men; and men in circuits of desire vis-à-vis men. I have argued that the female models in straight porn carry masculine attributes (and this is further borne out in the chapters on the fetish), but this resonates, is a visual cacophony, in TV porn.

The *look of pleasure* accompanies intercourse and is signified by closed eyes, head tilted back, open mouth, often with a protruding tongue or tongue licking the lips in oral and sexual readiness. It is a look of pleasure directed at anal penetration. Freud says of anal eroticism: "An invitation to a caress of the anal zone is . . . used . . . to express defiance or defiant scorn, and thus in reality signifies an act of tenderness that has been overtaken by repression. An exposure of the buttocks represents a softening down of this spoken invitation into a gesture. . . . Both words and gestures are introduced at the most appropriate point as an expression of defiance."[61]

So the viewer takes pleasure in looking at bodily configurations which visually privilege the anal-erotic. The "female" model, however, is the one with the "defiant" offering (the male model is never penetrated anally), and her boldness (not to mention her "filthy" offering)[62] would challenge any crude reading of phallic reference ("male domination") in this case. The aesthetic vulgarity of TV pornography may lie in the overt challenges which are put to the binary sexual system and fictive male subjective coherence. Also there is the overlapping of narcissistic identification with voyeurism as phallic signification abounds.

Direct address is the look of the transsexual (the male models never look at the camera) which meets the reader's but is not often "straight on." That is, "she" looks over her shoulder, while offering a rear view of penetration, or shifts her head, in a reclining position, to partially face the camera. Her eyes directly meet those of the reader. It is a look which says either "Are you watching me?" or "Caught you!" or both: the reader is caught in the act of watching. Both model and reader are complicit in the act; in that way the gap between image and spectator, the "absent field, the place of a character who is put there by the viewer's imaginary,"[63] is sutured by the look.

To sum up, "TV" pornography downplays sexual difference. The "TV" body cancels out otherness by signifying both sexes at once. And the gay male body either interacts with another male body or is on display for the gay male viewer. But in both genres there is a sliding into difference through obvious fetish accouterments (especially in the case of "TV" porn). As well, otherness is resurrected through the "relay of looks" generated by the model designated as other. Indifference is transgressed toward signifying moments of difference.

The gaze of both the "TV" and gay model addresses the reader as other and foregrounds the reader's desire: to be a desiring subject is to see signs of the desire of the other. In both "TV" and gay porn, this desire and otherness is, among other things, an ocular projection.

The structure of the gaze in the workings of the visual imaginaries is one feature which activates fantasy and the subject. The looks, propped on the gaze, form part of the diegetic space and partly orchestrate the narrative movement of the photograph. They also suture the reader into the text in a way which depends not just on his absence or place outside the textual operations. The look of "direct address" depends as well on acknowledgment of the viewer's position as voyeur, caught in the act of watching. He is being watched. The occupation of positions of both subject and object is one way the viewer confronts the "cut" in the pornographic moment. Moreover, he is enlisted into narcissistic scenarios; the pornographic discourses problematize strategies of identification between spectator and text.

That there is pleasure, and pain culturally constituted, in the gaze for the male viewer is perhaps an understatement. But part of that pleasurable apparatus involves the reader standing before the penetrating gaze of the model, no passive object she. Her appropriation of the threatening and active gaze works to place the model within a discourse which transgresses the normative "feminine." The reader is thus positioned in a transgressive relationship regarding the normatively "masculine." Difference is not so firmly fixed. And otherness is a discursive construction based on visible signs of the other's desire: the model displaying hers, the reader giving up some of his.

The pornographic body confounds the boundaries of sexual difference. Similarly, configurations of the fetish suggest that the objects which adorn the body are a transgressive site, fabricated under the sign of erotic theft. The high-heel shoe enjoys a stubborn presence in all straight genres. It is to the exploration of this that we now turn.

The Fetish

4 | The Shoe

A Note on the Fetish

As ALREADY NOTED, the pornographic body is a textual body replete with fetish inscriptions. The favorite fetishes of the contemporary pornographic discourses are the high-heel shoe, and lingerie and stockings. An analysis of these objects will show how they might function in the logic of seduction. Situating the cultural emergence of particular fetishes proves to be a difficult task. Their historical appearance is frequently no more than itemized, along with other fluctuations in fashion, in the literature on the history of clothing. Elizabeth Wilson, for example, makes only passing reference to the shoe in the fourteenth century: "Shoes became exaggeratedly long and pointed."[1] She later quotes Daniel Defoe (writing in 1725), who describes the transformation of a "country girl" upon her occupation of a "fashionable town house," made visible in her appropriation of the sartorial style of her employer. Defoe notes that her "neat's leather shoes are . . . transformed into laced shoes with high heels; her yarn stockings are turned into fine worsted ones with silk clocks . . . her poor, scanty, linsey-woolsey petticoat is changed into a good silk one four or five yards wide."[2] The initial association between rank, wealth, and certain styles and fabrics is made: silk and the high heel are for the leisured classes, the bourgeois classes. This phenomenon might suggest that there are some anachronistic, transgressive affiliations between an object and its symbolic status in the photograph. For the pornographic model is a slut, speaking street language but in what were once the clothes of the drawing room.

Valerie Steele notes, however, that by the mid-nineteenth century, lacy undergarments (no mention of the shoe here) were the prerogative of "women of easy virtue."[3] By the 1880s, the idea that the "respectable married woman" might also enjoy "decorative and seductive" underwear was in vogue.[4] This meant there was a certain cultural, and sartorial, tension between outerwear and underclothing: the Victorian cult of virtue ("a ballet-dancer's fragility of looks . . . they wore their hair parted in the centre and demurely sleeked down and looped to frame a madonna oval face")[5] fashionably covered over the hidden eroticism of lingerie. This, 1890–1914, was the "great epoch of underwear."[6] One can speculate that these tensions center on contradictions around the public and the private, and emergent redefinitions of both, during the Victorian period. The growth of an erotic emphasis in women's underclothing, designed to be seen in private, flouted the public ideology of prudery. It cut a flirtatious edge: the naughty sexual expression at a time of hypocritical social tyranny. What might elect lingerie as an enduring fetish is its appearance in late Victorian England, when it straddled that line between the visible and the hidden (designed to be seen but not always; in other words, simultaneously "there" and "not there"), the illicit and the acknowledged. This is the period Steven Marcus writes of in *The Other Victorians.*[7] It is that contradictory undercurrent of sexual subculture, he suggests, which gives the Victorian pornographic novel its purchase. In fact, in one of his most interesting chapters, Marcus discusses the recurrent theme of flagellation, "a veritable flood," in these novels. He outlines the structure of the beating fantasy; it very typically involves a boy or man being beaten by a woman, the latter experiencing pleasure from the transaction, the former a mixture of pleasure and pain.[8] But Marcus makes the crucial point, and this relates to any discussion of the fetish as a symbolic artifact, that because conscious role-playing is a common feature of these narratives, and because the point of view and first-person voice shift through each beating scenario, "differences between the sexes are blurred and confused."[9] The ambiguity is what Marcus emphasizes and is what I would retain to help explain the power of the fetish. The fetish objects which I discuss in the thesis are, I argue, objects which suggest an erotic theft in the way they simulate qualities of both femininity and masculinity. That some of these objects appeared during the age of so-called sexual repression might make them all the more ripe for fetishization, for even as they enjoy mass circulation, they embody the illicit. In short, they mark the struggle between emergent tensions around redefinitions of the public and the private, the social and the sexual, production and consumption.

There is still a marked shortage of explanatory material regarding the ideological function of certain fashion statements. Historians typically supply endless details and documentation about the vicissitudes of lingerie or stilettos. But they will also slip into a contemporary mindset when they impute "natural" meaning to the appeal of specific articles. For example, Flügel writes that high-heel shoes "make a great difference to the whole position of the body when standing. They render impossible the protruding abdomen . . . but by the upright carriage that they necessitate they tend to give a corresponding prominence to the bosom."[10] Similarly, William Rossi, in *The Sex Life of the Foot and Shoe,* argues that the spike heel positively emphasizes the contour of the legs, ankles, and feet while at the same time thrusting the bosom forward.[11] While these might be functionally the case, we must remember that the objects in pornographic photographs endow the image with exchange value, not use value. As such, their symbolic language complicates and loosens the original referent.

Scopic Investments

A clichéd formulation within both psychoanalytic paradigms and contemporary film theory suggests powerful associations between the fetish and castration. The metonymic affiliation or semiotic contiguity based on "part-objects" and substitutions[12] assigns fetish objects a compensatory, and erotic, quality that serves to disavow knowledge of feminine "lack" ("castration") and allay the perceived threat this knowledge brings. The castration complex, and its attendant representational apparatus, is the attempt at reconciling knowledge upon observation that girls don't have the penis with the "conviction . . . energetically maintained" that this cannot be the case, or in the famous words of Octave Mannoni, quoted in chapter 2, "je sais bien, mais quand même (I know, but nonetheless)."[13] Surrogates for the missing penis take on a fetish character and endow the female body with textual features, assume a "writing" on the body, and a writing *of* the body, or the body coded. The negotiation of sexual difference based on possession/nonpossession of the penis relies on a visual investment, and thus theory which informs work on the visual imaginaries is concerned to uncover the fetishistic endowment of the female body as an erotic spectacle. The tension between the pleasure in looking and the threatening glance at the "castrated" female body is managed through the performance of the fetish.

As previously noted, however, the scopic moment may combine aspects of the castration scenario which are both threatening *and* seductive. Certainly the surfeit of fetish signifiers *alone* would testify to the empowering of the female body and the consequent psychic disinvestment experienced by the male. The (male) reader stands in relation to the signifying power of the female textual body and in encountering the fetish, allows it (or belief in it) to work for him.

Freud cites instances of the fetish masquerading with phallic proportions and locates a favorite organ and object in the foot and the shoe. Again, an "uncanny and traumatic" moment is invoked in the fetish—and allayed by the same. The fetish represents more than fears of castration; it is associated with a partial phallic endowment of women. Precisely how the "uncanny and traumatic" operate informs the thrust of this book. One must ask, for example, if there is possible pleasure in this painful recall of recognition of castration. Or is there seduction in the recognition of moments of "loss," and the relinquishing of signs of desire?

The Fetish Cuts Both Ways

The popular assumption in the psychoanalytic literature on the fetish is that in searching for the lost phallic object, the masculine subject is trying to close in on lack. But the phenomenal fact in pornographic genres is that the fetish and the fetishized body of the "female" model—which carries signifiers of masculinity—are associated with both castration fears *and* seductive and prohibited pleasures. If rhetorical subjectivity is refashioned in narratives of plenitude and loss, the circulation of the fetish suggests that its meaning lies in the way it speaks to both coherence and dispossession. Fetishistic transactions thus provide the dialectical movement around contiguity and distance between reader and text, subject and object, desire and the representation, the viewer and the object.

Visual pleasure, the fetish (and photographic syntax), depend on a "missing element" (a loss, or that which has "gone missing"). The fetish fills in the gap between belief and disbelief; it is a stand-in for the missing element (the reader, the phallus, desire). This missing element, or the inauguration of the "cut," comprises oscillations between absence, separation, and imaginary plenitude: the "cut" is at the center of both separation and merging, or the suturing/ "sewing in" of the subject. The "cut," just as it fragments an imaginary, corporal coherence provided by the fetish site of specularity, also arranges the subject discursively as he is integrated culturally. Dialectics of pleasure and pain coalesce around meaningful objects, those that viciously suggest both presence and absence.

Death and the Fetish

It is common enough to draw associations between photography and death.[14] In "Photography and the Fetish," Christian Metz persuasively argues that the photograph also overlays the fetish.[15] The photographic picture is not just the "capture" of the person but the continual displacement of the object/ person photographed: "that moment when she or he *was* has forever vanished . . . 'dead for having been seen.' "[16] The eye of the camera appropriates its object(s), is a "take," "immediate and definitive," "the instantaneous abduction of the object out of the world into another world, into another kind of time."[17] The photographic objects are testimony and *timelessness,* incapable of ontological change, their meaning will circulate only contextually. They are timeless (and unchanging) because of their associations with stillness and memory (harking to that abduction). Metz argues that photography is "a cut inside the referent, it cuts off a piece of it, a fragment, a part object, for a long immobile travel of no return."[18] The objects then take on fixed and fateful qualities, *preserved* as fragments of the past, and a simultaneous *activation* of it. With the photographic medium this is insurance against loss, a symbolic investment in the photo, the object, and "the past," and their ability to recall part of the whole. In that way, photographic objects are still in memory, refer to the death of the object, the freezing of time, and they simultaneously resurrect (from the dead) the displaced object.

The fetish, too, cuts into a referent and survives its death only through its refusal to forget. Like the photograph, it is twinned with repression, absence, and loss. As within all systems of exchange, the fetish object is a stand-in for an original or prior motivation. It embodies "loss," absence, an immutable association with "death"; and it preserves the re-presentation of that death. Fetishistic recall thus points to a profound investment in "dead objects." Objects which are precisely dead are also a delivery to the past through a presence. This presence suggests a narcissistic attachment to the object based on its death-like claims, so that the object's significance continues to live on in its death. Freud notes the strong affiliation between "the work of mourning" at the death of a loved one and, in terms of the will to survive, a love for "this object *as dead*."[19] Photography, the fetish, and death are implicated in a reliable compromise such that the "livingness" of a thing is preserved in its stillness, is a stand-in for "the living." This is a symbolic redundancy: it represents a cut to the referent (what the fetish represents) and a cut out of the living, a return to the living via death, a desire for the cut.

But why an *erotic* compromise? Although the fetish may be a masculine prerogative, and phallic in its properties, the pairing of the fetish with castration fears is questionable. That is, the marking of "woman" as different is a dual maneuver: on the one hand, the fetish preserves the fiction of "otherness." In that sense the fetish is like a mirror: the reader sees himself in the phallic death wish. But on the other hand, that otherness—the writing that signifies the feminine—is a partially phallic discourse which allows for a "delicate" difference, like the high-heel shoe the model sports: a precarious balance. So pleasure is in difference, but difference at a cutting edge: the collapse of difference into androgyny would be the death of desire (and anyway is the "impossible referent"). Simulated androgyny, however, plays on the edge of death, and this seduction is the discursive construction at the heart of the pornographic moment. The shoe condenses androgynous properties to coalesce around a moment which is erotic and s(t)imulating, and a fetish object which contains signs of the other's desire.

The Shoe as Weapon

Oedipus: Gr. "swollen-footed"

A fashion editor at *Vogue* magazine describes the appearance of the stiletto heel in the mid-fifties as "fashion with a vengeance."[20] This most telling accommodation of feminine adornment with revenge conspires, I would argue, to make the pornographic spike heel the "fetish with a vengeance." The arrival of the stiletto heel on the fashion scene is announced in a newspaper article "with daring new words like pinpoint, needle and stiletto."[21] Lee Wright notes that other names, such as "spike" and "spindle," were often substituted as nominations for this new heel.[22] But "stiletto" was, and is, the most common epithet. Wright, in her study of the intersections of materiality and ideology in design, and Elizabeth Toomey, in a 1953 article, "Paris Shoes Have Pointed Heel and Toe," place the cultural circulation of the stiletto heel within a decidedly postwar, utilitarian context by locating its origin in the "kind of steel built into airplane casings."[23] Wright notes that the heel does indeed have a metal core; but the name "stiletto" ("the thin-bladed knife") preceded the invention of its metal core, suggesting the name's undoubtable connection to sign value rather than use value.[24]

Wright goes on to describe the shoe's "stylistic" features in terms which put it within the discursive realm of masculinity: its "antisocial reputation increased as it became more pointed"; it was "more aggressive and seemed to be *breaking* with those early ideas of femininity"; it had a "defiant gesture . . . [of] rebellion," representing someone who was a "go-getter."[25] At the same time, Probert writes that the shoe is the "zenith of the very feminine look," and Toomey wrote that the heel is "slivered to the slimmest shapes to make us all look as dainty and delicate underfoot as a Cinderella."[26] These linguistic and ideological nominations, connoting, as Wright notes, both fragility and strength, suggest a noteworthy sexual ambivalence. Wright points to the associations of the stiletto with symbols of "liberation rather than subordination," symbols that are "progressive rather than retrogressive," conveying "rebellion and dominance."[27] The shoes are feminine in terms of vestmental codes, but within the agencies of sexual representation they are coded as ambisexual. The pornographic shoe is for a Cinderella with power. It is a *fetish* with a vengeance in the sense that the spike-heel shoe is fashionably ambisexual. It is unmistakably feminine (in cultural terms: delicate in shape) yet carries the weapon. It is transcendent in its ability to recall the fetish; in popular film, television, and other cultural artifacts, women in spike heels signify danger. Danger is an enduring feature of the fetish and its associations with threats of absence, loss, and castration. The shoe embodies difference, is a strategy of its containment; in the pornographic instance, what makes it signify is its masculine heel, but a heel within a feminine frame of reference. The foot is shod, furnished, or equipped; the footgear, however, is a balancing act between the foot clad and partially exposed. There is the hardness of the leather and heel and the shaky footing provided by the spike heel. Most often the shoe's delicate quality is revealed by its lack of support: the shoe is a feminine sandal, open-toed with thin straps of leather covering the instep; the toe protrudes phallically from the front. And the heel causes one to totter—no sure-footed model here.

The Shoe: Soft-Core

Steele notes that the shoe is symbolic of a bi-sexuality: it carries the phallic heel and toe, and it "could also symbolize the vagina into which the phallic foot [is] slipped."[28] The tension between the "active" and "passive" components of the shoe and what it can symbolize fetishistically contributes to an androgynous writing on the body. It is an economic balance of two parts: a womblike enclosure and the phallic extremity.

The shoe in soft-core is the high-heel, also called the "spike" or "stiletto" (the exceptions are minor: in a subgenre, models simulating young girls wear sneakers and/or knee socks; or a model may wear cowboy boots, for example, as part of a "Western" motif). The stiletto-heeled shoe is accompanied by nylon or silk stockings and some form of lingerie or undergarments. And it is prevalent: regardless of the scenario, whether the model be in bed, on a couch, in a bathtub, or photographed in a "nature" setting, the shoe is visible within the diegetic space.[29] The spike heel elongates the leg, but it rezones the body for pleasure in another way as well. The pornographic model is not typically depicted with lower limbs extended; more often than not, her legs are bent at the knees to point the foot/heel at the genital region and thus create a triangle. The framing of the legs and heels in this way invites the movement of glances from genitals to heels and back again. Alternately, the heel is poised in the direction of the camera/reader.

TAKING AIM

This configuration—heels aimed at the reader—most often accompanies the rear end offered to the camera. However, it is not just fleshy buttocks which are on display; rather, the anal region is given full exposure, and one may say that the psychological terrain is anal as well. One need look no further than the vernacular for evidence of associations between anality, anger, and aggression (and of course money). What are the shared characteristics of the tight-fisted and the tight-assed?

The metonymic association between anal signification and the spike heel should be underscored. Anal affiliations are aggressive, as well as voyeuristic and sadistic. Both Grunberger and Chasseguet-Smirgel locate anal representations within a seemingly "perverse" order.[30] Like all Freudian derivations, perversions are part of "an original and universal disposition of the human sexual instinct."[31] Anal associations are phallic as they incite, in absentia, content and form: specifically, anal matter in the form of projections. In the "Rat Man" case history, rats are symbolic of many things, among them money, feces, and the penis: all of these are implicated in scenarios of loss and thus circulate within scenarios of castration as well.

Grunberger's "anus-as-trap" refers to a perverse "role reversal" whereby the (male) child engages in passive homosexual fantasies about the father and invests in a masochistic identification with the mother. This fantasization entails anal introjection of the father's penis, a defense against the "positive" Oedipus complex. The result is a sadistic impulse: the "anal penis" and anal castration are themes in which the father (his penis) is "devoured" by the anus, a dual fantasy/fear. In a further perverse twist, the phallic mother must be castrated. This anticipates a voyeuristic and fetishistic incitement to "search for the phallic mother"; in this pursuit penises are attributed to the woman and are ritualistically removed or denied.[32] Grunberger suggests, however, that this obsessive provocation (the confluence of anal sadism, voyeurism, and the "phallus") is a structured fantasy, a play on transgressions. That is, the voyeuristic search for the phallic mother may be a "search for the father's penis detained by the mother and introjected through devouring."[33] What these fantasies reveal is the complex interplay between the simultaneity of visibility and absence, endowment and loss, the fiction of corporal plenitude and an investment in the body's part-objects which transcends fixed positions of masculinity and femininity.

The anus is both form and substance, "the content and the container,"[34] able to take in (introject) and expel. As discussed in "Sexual Techniques," anal significance calls upon an avowal of absence as well as a blurring of subject/object distinctions. More precisely, it merges subject and object. It represents thus a "narcissistic fusion" and a narcissistic confirmation: the castrated father (or castration of the "phallic mother") represents the perverse attraction. Freud does appear to align his arguments with an ideological disposition to the laws of heterosexuality. "Perversion" here implies a move away from the oedipal erotic narrative. "Perversions," writes Freud, "are sexual activities which either (a) extend in an anatomical sense, beyond the regions of the body that are designed for sexual union, or (b) linger over the intermediate relations to the sexual object which should normally be traversed rapidly on the path towards the final sexual aim."[35] Although this definition seems to suggest conformity to the hegemonic code regarding sexual union, there is the subversive reading of which Freud was, of course, not unaware. Kaja Silverman, drawing from Freud, notes the "diversionary and decentering character" of perversion.[36] It is this "radical challenge to sexual difference," the unsettling of sexual (genital, symbolic) hierarchies (organized around symbolic genital investment, and difference as the code), which places anality in the realm of the "disruptive" perversions.[37]

Such transactions take on a renewed peculiarity when paired with anal significance and fetishistic relations. Anal significance in this case reveals castration fears and desires, again, as the effacement of difference is symbolized by the introjection of the father's penis via the "trap-anus closing in on its prey."[38] Anality, the possession of both sexes, is the "universe where all differences are abolished." This symbolic loss of sexual difference is a universe where men resemble women (and vice versa); it is an impossible healing of the narcissistic wound.[39]

Anality, and all it may connote, is in the diegetic, narrative, and symbolic company of the spike heel. In these photographs the heel of the shoe circulates among an exchange of equivalences. First of all, it is long, hard, and phallic. It is offered on the same visual plane as the anus and (this is one of the perversions) is equated with anal invasions, anal protuberances. What is a shoe? In functional terms it walks on dirt, mother earth. Linguistic associations are loaded. A "shit-shoe" or "shit-heel" is "derisive to one who has bedaubed his boot" (Partridge). "Shit" is a term of contempt, applied "rarely to a woman" (Partridge). In these photos, the model's body is positioned so that either she "moons" the camera (i.e., leans over and exposes the buttocks to a rear view) or she sits with knees bent and pulled toward her chest. In this frontal view the anal region is revealed. The model's hands, with long fingernails, often are placed to spread open the buttocks and further display not so much a point of entry but another penetrating possibility. The eyes are also their most beady and incisive, surveying the reader with a vigilance that lets him know he's being watched. The watchful eyes, the stiletto aimed at the reader, and anal invasion all belong not to a supine body but to a body's text which is exhibitionistic, voyeuristic, defiant, and phallic[40]—but all the while "female."

Why the phallic and anal endowments? Pornographic discourses *are* perverse, but the perversions are located within a structure in which the laws of sexual difference are continually transgressed; i.e., women are positioned as men, men search for the phallic mother and want to castrate the father. This is a structured play on difference: the desire for difference, the desire to abolish it at the same time, and the tension between a narcissistic fix and desires dependent on a referential "other." Which is to say there is a reader in/for all this. As he sees signs of another, and, more important, signs of another's desire, he encounters his own phallic projections, longings, and desires. What he sees, and what is pleasurable, is a simulated rendition of his own masculine possessions. This is another trope, and one most pointed in symbolic transactions privileging anal configurations. That is, the emphasis should be on "possession," not in the pre-Foucauldian sense of a stable object (forever in opposition to a coherent subject). For example, it is not the case that "she" *is* the "asshole," but in a circuit of exchange she *has* the "asshole." But so does *he* (the man, the reader). That these "possessions" become part of her bodily text is what makes them desirable. The heel in this scenario is another possession, the simulated phallus, and speaks to the male reader's forfeiture, dispossession, and loss, all within a scenario of desire.

A PHALLIC SLIP

The other possible configuration of the shoe fetish involves the arrangement of limbs (the legs) to position the spike heel toward the genitals in mock phallic effect. In such instances the body is contorted to aim for penetration—but only aim, for the heel/phallus is merely a stand-in and capable of limited phallic proportions. In such instances the heel is poised at the vaginal and anal orifice, which share the same visual plane (sometimes this may be the heel of the foot itself, unshod but covered by stockings).

THE HEEL

The stiletto heel is a fundamental part of the contemporary pornographic code. What is a heel? Flügel writes of the "unconscious phallic symbolism attaching to the heel."[41] Krafft-Ebing regards shoe fetishism as a "latent form of masochism," representing the "desire to be trodden on."[42] In the vernacular, a "heel" is an "untrustworthy or despicable person," "contemptible," the morally impure *man*. Associations are with domination and power: "to be at the heels of" is to be close behind, under control or subjection. "To be heeled," as is the model, is to be armed with a revolver. The heel is also affiliated with money, wealth, and status. The "well-heeled" are those supplied with money (the filthy rich, no doubt). Those "down at the heel" are slovenly, shabby, without status or wealth.

Finally, a "stiletto" is a short, thick-bladed dagger. A spike is a sharp point, a large nail; in slang, "spike" means "hypodermic needle" and "action potential." As a verb, "to spike" is "to pierce or impale" or "to render a drink potent" ("spike it") by adding something highly reactive (alcohol).

The pornographic model who sports the heels and confronts the reader with her stilettos is well-shod to the point of being filthy and rich, in two metonymic affiliations. First, the proximity of the spike heel to anal imagery conjoins the body's projections with the aggressive impulse. Second, Freud's "connections between the complexes of interest in money and of defaecation" aside,[43] the model subjects the reader to the text of her well-heeled body, and, of course, the text (the magazine) for which the reader has paid money. The model is but a fee-male.

These are heels with the potential of piercing and penetrating, and thus have powerfully invasive qualities. This is a model with the power of intrusion and a model worth paying for. Why is this erotic for the male reader? Why the seductive surrender to the phallic extensions of the model?

THE HEEL AND PHALLIC DESIRE

In soft-core, phallic equivalence is written on the female body. That is, if there are men in the photographs in this genre, they do not signify their desire through erections or penetration. They are instead erotic accouterments themselves; their presence is scarce (yet flirtatious), and depictions of desire are given over to the "feminine" form, the female body, the fetish and the peculiar way it masculinizes the female body. The fetish is a stand-in, a simulation of the reader's phallic properties, and a dressing up of the model's desire to be possessed by the masculine body—the reader's. The gap between reader and photograph is wide in this genre. The reader is able to see himself only in the hysterical inscription on the model's body. What is desirable for the reader—the visual display of the model's desire—is a semiotic reference, referring only to signs of desire. Desire is a simulated offering of signs of masculinity: an approximation of the seductive yet potentially annihilating effects of an androgynous union.[44]

The simulation of desire (only representations of desire being possible) is a dramatic re-enactment of that which cannot be achieved. The sexed positions of spectator and spectacle within pornographic imaginaries are unsettled (and unsettling); as already noted, "female" models also possess the gaze and in so doing operationalize the codes of power. The spectator is implicated in a discourse which treats its subject(s) to a dialectic of eros and thanatos: i.e., this erotic communion involves moments of separation and loss, mastery (by the "object"), and the re-enactment of the sexual subject amid contradictory positions.

DESIRE AND THE FETISH

The female body is a textual excess, in excess of its own femininity. There must be an Achilles heel in all this, though, a vulnerability suitable for a woman and fitting a (male) reader seduced by the pornographic moment, which in the last instance cannot be totally threatening (a total divestment of the reader), but merely "la petite mort." The femininity of the model is a cultural demarcation in the economy of sexual difference. This representation of the female desiring subject is an engagement within a "mimetic paraphrase of desire";[45] her enunciations speak to the enigma of his (the reader's, the "other's") desire. In this case the enigma is a phallicism that can't be represented. What we see may look like "enunciation under the force of a woman's desire,"[46] but from her discursive position as "desiring," she carries the wishful marks of *his* desire for *her*. The model's desire is thus married with *his* enonce (the origin of this discourse).[47]

Mary Ann Doane has noted that in "women's films" from the forties (although one can argue that this may still be the case), femininity is aligned with pathology, and the enigma which resolves the narrative is the woman's "cure," usually a somatic shift for the viewer from an "erotic gaze" to a "medical gaze."[48] Her body is the site of the clinical, masculine gaze and the "manuscript to be read" for indications of feminine hysteria or the problematic question of women's desire. One enigma of the feminine subject revolves around her discursive inability to desire. Lea Jacobs has written about feminine discourses of desire in the 1942 Hollywood film *Now, Voyageur,* noting how codes of the body shape its fetishization and inscription into a larger sexual order. Jacobs's analysis of *Now, Voyageur* reveals that the "cure" for the "spinster," thus her initiation into sexual desire, "is to transform the ugly oxfords and thick stockings of [the] initial shot into high heels and stockings which show off Charlotte's legs."[49]

It is acknowledged (by Doane, Jacobs, and others writing under the rubric of "feminist film criticism") that woman's desires and narratives are part of a dominant fiction which constructs the "other" and which is a slow dissolve into what is ultimately a master—masculine—discourse. However, just how phallic this desire, or this shoe, is, is not emphasized strongly enough. Both carry with them, in the context of the pornographic shot, a "violation of the categories of sexual difference."[50]

What exactly is the discursive space the shoe is penetrating? If the "sexual fix" is transgressed, then two possibilities present themselves, both having to do with desire and the lost referent/origin. First, in the suturing, viewer positions oscillate around a number of distinctions: seeing/seen, desiring/desired, voyeurism/narcissism, subjectivity/objectivity. Within this circuitous economy the reader may still be implicated in a decidedly phallic discourse whereby "woman's" desire is still knowable only in phallic terms, from the point of view of *his* writing of the "other." His desire is for her phallic expression (of his desire for her phallic expression . . .). *Her* desire may remain an enigma, yet it is hardly written in passive terms. Thus, the fascination is with this perceived feminine silence, or getting it to speak. The fetish fascinates and penetrates that space/silence between reader and text, Imaginary and Symbolic, and is necessary for the representation of desire. Her enonce, "statements" and fetish objects of desire, puncture him/his desire, so in represented as desirable, she is also desiring.[51]

Second, desire has no natural referent, nor is there any way of representing it except in its repressions and displacements. So when Linda Nochlin suggests that the "reality" of woman in a masculine discourse is the "ultimate-meaning-to-be-penetrated," she is talking about the limits to representation and desire.[52] To represent an "ultimate meaning" within a mimetic scenario of desire, the model must carry marks of both his and her desire, and thus simulate an androgynous union of opposites. She wears the stiletto heel, often poised at the genital orifice to penetrate her, and just as often aimed to penetrate *him*. She desires and in doing so is desirable. This is a sexual *dis*location.

The shoe fetish in soft-core plays on absence; that is, the model is a spectacular sensorium whose textual body is a visual projection *of* the reader and, with her masculine vocabulary, a projection back *to* him. In all this there is a space for the reader. He stands in fascination at the spectacle, this simulated moment which has relinquished any faith in its realism.[53] The fetish is a hysterical display to foreground, against the figure of the model's body, a symptomatic desire. The marks of sexual longing—the fetish objects of her clothing—are implicated in a circuit of desire: the reader's desire to see the likeness of her longing to be possessed, signified in a bodily vestmental code. This is a phallic investment in which the reader's desire—to see hers—is exchanged for the commodity object (heel, money, shoe, etc.). The meaning, as in any semiotic chain, is exchanged for the object. And the repressed meaning in this instance is (his) phallic desire.

Absence signifies desire in a number of ways: the reader must surrender some properties of his desire to witness/conquer the desire of the model. Loss and the fetishized relation are the terms of castration, the fetish as surrogate or part-object for anxieties (comprising fears and perverse pleasures) around the "missing penis." So the real penis is absent, but the fetish recalls that absence in perverse and seductive ways. The distinguishing absence in this genre is a representation of the reader (the model typically stands alone) as well as (as Metz notes of the reader vis-à-vis any photograph) his look or gaze: yet the fetish recalls them. And they are solicited by the model. The reader lends his gaze to the image, is robbed of his manly penetrating properties. He is simultaneously stripped of his phallic properties as he dresses up the model in the image of his desire. That is, the fetish shoe is modeled after his penetrating and incisive image, and is a weapon-extension on the female body.

Absence is signified, most subversively and again in castrating terms, in the loss of a phallic referent. There is no natural referent for desire, no natural way of representing the terms of its form except within a "dialogue of lovers," a parenthetical space in which desire is imagined.[54] The viewer is realized only through his liquidation; his partial recovery is achieved through the fiction of the fetish as substitute, and the recall of the traumatic moments of loss. Paradigms of loss signal a repression (a loss hearkening a nostalgia and hope for recovery), and hence the fetishization of what is missing, a desire for repression.

The ritual adornment of the foot with the stiletto-heeled shoe is one way of lending the body its pornographic status. This, along with the gaze, genital choreographies, lingerie, and jewelry, confers a hypersignificance on the terrain of the physical. The shoe is in excess, often given to greater visibility than the breasts or genitals. As a fetish, the spike heel structures the narrative around difference and its partial effacement. It locates the female model on both sides of the sexual divide; i.e., it is a shoe only women wear, thus evoking cultural femininity. It also structures and sustains the reader's look. What is there for him to see is a difference with a vengeance: the phallic extension. In contrast to hard-core, where the reader meets his stand-in in the form of a male model, the fetish in soft-core bears the responsibility for creating otherness. If the fetish domesticates the threat of otherness, it reinstates it at the same time, and in phallic terms.[55] The shoe is a sign of the female model's desire. The shoe recalls the phallic properties in the inscription of the model's desire: it steps into the discourse of the reader's desire. Emily Apter speaks to the phrase "I would not want to be in your shoes" and argues that it once again "ironically projects the deeper nuances of castration anxiety." Apter plays with the etymology of "boot" (elaborating on a discussion of the contiguous nature of fetish substitutions—in images, in language—in French literature, in this instance "the way in which servitude, erotic submission, and foot fetishism are curiously enmeshed within a complex system of representation centering on the maid,"[56] particularly the latter's body-text):

> *Bottine,* the diminutive form of *botte,* has as its root a condition of podalic deformity, or clubfoot (bot), also active in the peasant's sabot, which, since the Middle Ages, has connoted a vulgar, ungainly worker's shoe. The conjunction between lameness and the social underclass, with the associations ranging from one-leggedness (boiteux), signalling beggars or pilgrims on crutches, to the wooden leg (jambe de bois), described by Krafft-Ebing as a standard prop of the bordello, is only reinforced by the innuendos surrounding a secondary meaning. As tube, barrel, or drainpipe . . . the *bot* projects images of fecal evacuation and the maid's habitual corvee of emptying the chamber pot.[57]

Castration anxiety, yes, but I think the porn reader *does* want to step into her boots. Again, the shoe is in the domain of corporal and semiotic dislocations; it is a sign of his corporal desire, but it is her possession. Simulated difference is intact.[58]

The Shoe: Hard-Core

The spike-heel shoe in soft-core plays on absence, both of the viewer and of the phallic referent. This pornographic moment is the simulated world of seduction, wherein the fetish is a stand-in for what is missing. In hard-core, the scenario is more complex and the female model less of a solitary spectacle. For the fetish in hard-core is not the only sign of masculinity. The distinguishing feature of the hard-core genre is the diegetic presence of men and the "penis as a phallic symbol." Thus, there are two impulses to this scopic moment: first, the spectator is a voyeur at the peephole, privy to a re-enactment of the primal scene, or at least a public viewing of the quintessentially private act. And second, the voyeur's fascination overlaps with his narcissistic investment.

The spectacle in hard-core is staged fascination in a phallic exchange (not fascination with the sole female model), which circulates, seductively, around a surplus of masculine signification. The "woman" already possesess a penetrating gaze and carries the stiletto heel. As well, there are male models who already occupy narrative positions within the photograph, usurping the place of the reader. He within the photo re-presents the reader to himself. This is a narcissistic image for the reader and a double exclusion: phenomenologically he is of course outside the frame. And, the reader's "presence" is replaced by a part-object, Metz's "pocket phallus."[59] This "present absence" points to a phallic redundancy and a phallic displacement which is the partial exclusion of the reader—only partial, though, because he can still see himself (or signs of his desire) in the fetish-heel: it is her phallic properties that embody his desire.

The high heel in hard-core signifies in important ways. It is one of what Beverley Brown calls pornography's "non-transparent features . . . a repertoire of milieux and costume," an everyday object given specific form within the pornographic regime.[60] The shoe *is* a curious feature of the pornographic imagination, a surplus investment in the body and a superfluous aid to the sexual act. It is an investment in the body which disinvests it of any essential power; it exposes noncorporal desire. But how *does* one represent desire, itself always a referential exchange? The shoe/fetish adorns the body not to equate the body with objects (to "objectify" it), but in a way that vitalizes the objects, makes them work in a "process of ideological labor."[61] The lifeless object, the commodity/shoe, is a fetish of the "code," in Baudrillard's sense. In *For a Critique of the Political Economy of the Sign* he writes of the structural properties of fascination, valued and sustained in exchange. Fetishistic forms are dominated by the code, not the object, and are charged with the marking of difference ("epitomizing a whole system of differences") within a system of value propagated by a generalized exchange. The shoe is a marker of sexual difference (it is feminine), but its materiality slides into signification as it takes on the ideological properties of otherness and difference. The female body as castrated, and the continual seductive reminder of this, is held through the hysterical inscription of difference on this textual body. But the object-shoe is "difference" in a more perverse way. That is, the hard, slender extension and protuberance is sharp, a projection on the female body. This stiletto is the heel (that masculine object) of the female body, its instrument capable of penetrating, cutting. It is a phallic writing on the "feminine" surface, or a colonization of difference.

But it is difference within an exchange which threatens to cancel out otherness, collapsing difference into simulated indifference. The shoe in hard-core is metonymically and spatially twinned with the penis. It accompanies the fragmented body (usually his), visual signifiers of her pleasure, erections, penetration, and ejaculation. The shoe is a surplus signifier, a companion to both scenes of genital display (a readiness for penetration) and the graphic penetrating act. The spike heel is visually associated with the female genitals. The legs of the female model are bent at the knee, her genitals are exposed, and the shoe and heel are partially or fully included in the diegetic frame of the photograph. The open genital spread is exchanged for the foot and the heel of the shoe in a simulated economy. In this semiotic interference, sexual opposition is a partial collapse on the body's surface: the very body to be penetrated carries its own phallic extension. During scenes of explicit genital intercourse, the heel is a simulated phallus, a redundant sign whose referent is still only a *representation* of desire. The body is contorted so that the heel is aimed at the reader; thus the "feminine" stiletto is intrusive while the body is already locked in genital exchange.

ABSENCE AND THE FETISH

Fetishistic negotiations mock the reader at every turn. In a parodic display of otherness, both reader and male model are framed within a surplus of signification, a rhetorical space where something is real only insofar as it can be (mis)represented. Both reader and models are superfluous, subordinate to phallic signification *in excess*. Both bodies (male and female) in this genre are surrogates for phallic (dis)investment. Hers is named under the sign of the fetish through its masculine vocabulary; this is a writing of desire in its simulated code. In that sense, her "androgynous" encoding is an ephemeral possession which betrays a tenuous "sexual fix" and is poised at the seam of the "cut." To be positioned as a desiring subject, the female model "speaks" in the terms of the "other."

But a total effacement of sexual difference (androgyny) would be the death of desire: "otherness" is central to all the repressions which constitute the subject in language/desire. Its semiotic demise would signal the "impossible referent." The incorporation of the fetish in the hard-core genre is a "cut" into indifference, a simulated androgynous space: penis exchanged for heel exchanged for phallus. All this in the service of representing desire. These misrepresentations do, however, allow for the reader to insert himself into that void (more on this below).

The anatomically masculine body seems less potent than the body culturally designated as female. Its biological discourse includes the penis, of course; but the penis, too, is only as good as what it can represent: an inflated desire which is merely the prelude to its "petite mort." Narrative closure is thus achieved through the waning and eventual death of desire: seminal traces on the woman's body are the male's denouement, the draining of desire in its corporeal form. There is a natural terminus to his desire; not so for the female model, whose semiotic performance represents the "infinite repetitiveness of desire."[62]

Where does the reader fit into this phallic exchange which privileges a simulated order in which the "real" is surpassed by its representations? As voyeur outside the diegetic space, the reader is witness to a narrative which excludes him as the donor of phallic pleasure. He does, however, have the "real" thing which is activated in the service of desire. He fits into that indifferent void, that side of the "cut" which transgresses the sexual fix and works by divesting the subject (the reader in this case) of signs of his desire.

As narcissist, the reader has a visual investment in the doubling effect of the fetish/phallus. Hard-core is not a visual discourse which celebrates masculinity in its "original" and obdurate form (via the penis). It is instead a quest for the missing referent, the lost phallus. These representations try to cover up the flaw of the real: (mis)representations of desire are more desirable than desire itself—which anyway cannot be represented. Masculinity here is the lost referent; thus the reader of the hard-core genre is in a profoundly ambivalent relation to the fetish relations of significance in the photograph.

Fetishistic transactions cut both ways; that is, hard-core heterodoxy is a radical play on otherness. The fetish object instills the threat of difference and manages it at the same time, thus effecting a partial collapse around sameness. Hard-core is more subversive than soft-core, not because of its vicious elaboration of sexual difference, and the reinforcement of the phenomenal masculine subject. Instead, it problematizes sexual difference around his rhetorical alienation through the structure of fetishism and phallic redundancy, as "both there and not there, nothing to see and nothing to hide."[63] The reader's complicity in the exchange is *his* "little death" in the midst of all this nothingness. Nothing exchanged for nothing: his desire is invested in the deflated representations and lost referentials of desire. Thus, the reader and desire cancel each other.

"TV"

If the straight hard-core genre is a radical play on otherness—in the sense that the exteriorization of the viewer's masculinity is written all over the place—"TV" pornography would seem to be the most obdurate collapse of sexual difference sustained on the body. In "TV" porn the "she-male" body is a textual surplus of signification. And while the high-heel shoe is worn by the fe.male model, it is, along with the other fetish objects, a hysterical inscription on a body which is *already* a play on difference. "TV" porn is all about appearances and the suspension of belief (but seemingly without absence): it *appears* to be a significant in-difference to the binary biological opposition yet still a semiotic concession to gendered signs.

In "TV" *soft-core* a single transsexual model occupies the full diegetic space. S.he is adorned as culturally feminine in exaggerated style. The reader is witness to a symbolic construction of the feminine subject on a body doubled as its other. The fetish adornment of the body anchors the model's gender identity: through this enunciation of comportment codes she is a female poseur. She is on display, as is the penis: she holds it as if to emphasize the masculine component of the body. Her demeanor is coy. Her sexual allure is displaced onto her erotic accouterments: the stockings, the garters, the corset, the stiletto heel. Thus the model is phallicized beyond "her" natural biological overendowment as the high heel circulates through a generalized phallic equivalence. The penis, although on display, is subordinate to the body dressed up and adorned as "feminine." It appears to be an attachment to the feminine body, a masculine facsimile of what is really the discursive figure of femininity. The penis is soft, a physical understatement of desire.

What makes this body different is its wishful disregard for sexual opposition and the way it flaunts transgression of a fixed sexual location. What makes this discourse seductive is the way the body is adorned to deploy gender, but again in lawfully transgressive ways. The model is partially phallicized, i.e., in a position to desire the reader and to solicit his desire for her. In granting the model certain phallic terms of desire, the reader is suspended in loss, having given up signs of his phallic properties. The model is "other," and in the symbolic legislation of sexual difference, the reader is reaffirmed as "other than" the model, but it is an otherness that "cuts." Fetishistic maneuvers sustain phallic equivalence on the body, inciting an exchange that straddles the impulse to deny *and* endow. This otherness, expressed in phallic terms, is a seductive scenario for the reader.

The model is missing something, in spite of her prodigious biological frills. Her indifferentiation violates the sexual fix, and it would seem there is no "otherness" to desire. Difference, however, is resurrected to counteract her lack of corporal difference. The she-male's transgressive body is restored to one side of the binary cut through her feminine, fetish, apparel. This apparel, of which the shoe is an important part, is the "true" simulation of androgyny, of desire, and of what she's missing: representations of the reader's (phallic) desire.

"TV" *hard-core* also operates within an economy of excessive visibility where there are no surface absences. The heel in this genre takes its place among the surplus and simulated phallic investment: the presence of *two* penises. That is, there is also the dildo grasped by the she-male in mock phallic display. On top of all this, the transsexual is culturally feminized through erotic accouterments. The dual nature of the spike heel harmonizes with the body that doubles as its other. It appears to be a suitably feminine article of clothing, but it carries both masculine and feminine properties, and the heel's metonymic associations suit a masculine code; i.e., a "heel" is a man. In this genre masculine signification abounds, all the while within a feminine frame of reference; indeed, the transsexual model is referred to as a "she-male," teetering precariously on the fine line between male and female, masculine and feminine, the discursive and the real.

Where is the reader in an economy of desire which appears to be foreclosed? How is he redeemed in his position as desiring/desirable subject? First of all, the transsexual is coded as feminine not just through the lingerie and make-up, but also by virtue of "her" interaction with another *male* model. In that sense, the two models perform in a heterosexual dyad, a coupling which, although perverse, is within a sanctioned discourse. Although *his* signifier of masculinity, the penis, and facial or genital signifiers of his pleasure are subordinate to the diegetic and semiotic space of the she-male, "her" penis is still perpetually limp, unable to achieve phallic heights. She simulates desire through the fetish accouterments; in this case the heel of the shoe is the perfect stand-in for that which cannot be achieved but can be only represented. This limpness is a pathetic concession to a phallic economy in which the feeble misrepresentation has surpassed the real. This insistence on loss allows the reader to take up that space created by the phallic slip-ups: the limp signifier.

As noted in chapter 2, testicles are an advertisement for the feminine counterpart to the penis, and there is yet another connection with the name of the shoe/boot. Emily Apter points out the derivation behind "boot/booty," that being, as already mentioned, lameness and deformity/castration, along with "purse or money" (the "money shot"), and "in vulgar parlance, [booty] refers to the scrotum."[64] The "booty" makes way for the fetish as part-object (partial to her loss and his desire) and creates a space for it and for the reader. The penis, as the ultimate masculine protuberance, is not so readily available, apparent, or *active* in the service of sexual difference or the signification of desire. The heel may be, then, a "penis symbol," taking up the place on the she-male's body of a lifeless rendition of the cock.

The heel is a penis extension on the body: harder, sturdier, even, than the frail penis (visually subordinate anyway to the testicles). The reader is then enlisted in a choreography in which he might still become the final donor of phallic pleasure, the life-giver in a fetishized exchange. At the "margin of disturbance"[65] that characterizes a fetishized economy, the fetish carries its own conditions of fascination. It is structured in terms of "there/not there," hence implicating the anatomy of absence. In those oscillations between belief and disbelief there is a place for the reader, wishfully granted the real thing: the real phallus, more than just a penis symbol, and symbolic of a desire to satisfy the desire of the radical other in the form of the (fe.male) model.

The reader's inscription into the photographic memoir and the fetishistic narratives of difference and loss are part of the "immobility and silence" which accrues to the photo and its death effect.[66] The space, the silence, and the vacancy (the fetishistic overlay) are filled in by the reader. Filled in are phallic misrepresentations, part-objects of desire, proportionately greater than (and unrepresented by) the limp biological possession of the model.

FASHIONING THE FETISH

The recuperation of difference is a reinvestment in loss. Difference is established in the transsexual's biological and sartorial narrative. But it is a difference whose name is femininity, dramatized through vestmental codes (lingerie and shoes). The femininity of the model is also written on the body's surface through a limp penis, a bogus phallus: merely a masquerade for desire. Desire is then signified by the erotic accouterments donned by the transsexual, and at that seductive edge: the "margin of disturbance" in which impersonations of masculinity/femininity play on a partial annihilation of difference. Difference is, however, recovered (covered up) in the outfitting of the model as feminine. This is a fidelity to categories of *gender* opposition (not biological oppositions and signification; those designations are already inscribed on the body). And an inscription into narratives of gender is the reader's surrender to desire and the loss of some of his phallic properties.

In "TV" hard-core, the "she-male" eludes phallic perfection. She is hence dressed up, her body fetishized beyond its biological construction (already a fetish deployment in the way it activates formations of "there/not there"). Masculinity and desire are simulated; the ultimate masculine protuberance is not so apparent, although never out of sight. Fascination is perhaps at its most spectacular in this genre, fascination with the "irreality"[67] of this contemporary spectacular site. The imagistic "body double" subverts the traditional authority of the sex and gender divide: structures of difference are exhausted in a choreography which strenuously defends belief against disbelief (and all the embodied "losses" therein). The "ultravivid mode of fascination" is the consumers' orgasm in a culture of seduction/simulation.[68] What defies representation— desire, the phallus, an origin—is given shape in a spectacular style, a "parodic rehabilitation of all lost referentials."[69]

Nostalgia and the fetish associations with death combine to fascinate and thrill. In a seductive economy of "sheer text[s] . . . without truth content," the spectacle fascinates, Foster argues, as it participates in the loss of the real (i.e., the phallus) while simultaneously assuaging this loss through the circulation of the fetish.[70] And the spectacle fascinates in its power to submit the reader to the illusion of the perfection of the image. *In so consuming,* the spectator is partially excluded/consumed, like the "passive position of the dreamer," and as with the commodity, "all traces of productive labor and material support are erased."[71] The reader, however, is never fully excluded, nor is he ever in full possession of the image. His loss is also his desire. Perfect narrative closure, the double exposure of the hermaphroditic body, would eliminate otherness and its referent: this would be the death of desire.

The reader is presumed—mere flattery—to have the shoe on the other foot: i.e., to have the real thing. This pornographic genre, although circulating within a partially phallic economy, can only hover, teeter, around its articulation. The "TV" body is symptomatic of the tension between the erasure of difference and a longing for it at the same time.

The fetish in this genre is the impossibility of representing pure difference, hence the invoking of the phallus; the shoe is the perfect exemplar of this. There is the nostalgic reconstruction of masculinity as the lost referent: representations of masculinity are thus fetishized; i.e., bodily configurations are a surplus of phallic writing. The male body in this genre wears the penis as part of its biological dress code. It interacts with a body, that of the fe.male, that flirts with difference on the body's text. Is she or isn't she? Is s.he a she? *That* body's fleshy configuration carries a signifier that won't go away. But it is a signifier which is a mockery of the masculine, as much a put-on as the lingerie. This penis-signifier is not masculinity at its most turgid. Rather, it is a potential exhaustion of desire: sustaining, still, a space for the insertion of "the phallus" (as a reference to the reader). The penis, the testicles, and the phallic attributes of the she-male model compete with each other. The phallus wins all the time precisely because it can be represented only symptomatically, like the hysteric's corporeal enunciation. The fetish-as-masquerade heightens the phallic exchange so that the body is outfitted in (simulated) androgynous terms: the spike heel and lingerie are cultural statements of femininity, yet at the same time are the artifice of desire (and therefore a reference to the symbolic construction of masculinity).

Freud wrote that the "normal prototype of fetishes is a man's penis."[72] However, in the coupling of the penis with its phallic reconstruction on the body of the transsexual, the fetish character of desire aligns the excessive marking of the body as different with the phallus, not the penis. The fe.male is both feminized and phallic at the same time: the ultimate other.

In conclusion, the discourse of the transsexual model (and the penis-signifier) enters the simulated world of fascination through the fetish(es) which serve not to suspend belief (that the fe.male has been castrated) but to domesticate, and eroticize, the threat that phallic desires pose to the male reader: the fetish eroticizes her castration. But the fetish objects disavow the annihilating effects of the model's (and the reader's) castration (which would, after all, be the death of the subject). At the same time, castration in its simulated/desirable form is offered in the acknowledgment of sexual difference.

It would seem there are no absences in this genre, no losses, no "fright of castration at the sight of a female genital."[73] The simulated world attempts to put a hermetic seal on perfect phallic equivalence: the fetish and the phallus appear to be aligned as one, men fuck men (difference with no loss) who simulate women, or men desire women with men's desire. But the fetish again sustains difference, and in this case is the signature of its allure as well. The fetish accouterments disrupt the perfect symmetry of the "androgyne" and place the body within a discursive context: it is culturally assigned as feminine and semantically as "transvestite." They create the threatening image as well as overlay it with desire, a "seduction before undressing."[74] The reader, not even needed to satisfy the model's desire (and how *would* one satisfy the doubled desire of the ambisexual?), can still locate himself at every turn within an economy of difference elided in favor of a balancing act: phallic projections compete with feminine fashionable statements, as the body doubles as its "other."

5 | Jewelry and Lingerie

The following comments apply to the soft-core genre. Pornographic bodies, as noted, are dressed up in the language of desire and are "spoken" through transgressive possibilities: the corpus of the model threatens biological and discursive boundaries, showing up biology as yet another discourse, a malleable one at that.

Normative pornographic display is one of adornment, not nudity, and plays upon the ambisexual nature of otherness and the ambivalence around the cutting edge of seduction. Representations of the female disrupt conventions of the spectacle; the female model wears the "modest" immodestly. She exposes her undergarments, her lingerie (the seductive signs of her desire), and borrows the language of the street, i.e., the iconography of the hooker—the spike-heel shoe, the fishnet stockings, the cigarette—to turn the private into a public discourse.[1] By contrast, the male model in gay soft-core is more often completely nude and quietly contemplative.

In *The Psychology of Clothes,* Flügel writes that "clothes resemble a perpetual blush upon the surface of humanity," bodily adornment being a balance or ambivalence between "displaying our attractions" and "a means of hiding our shame." As such, clothing is discursively positioned to negotiate culturally neurotic symptoms.[2] This combination of ambivalence around modesty and display, and neuroses, allows us to imagine forms of bodily adornment as transgressive and marked by a dialectical interplay between the wearer and the wearer's public, viewed and viewer, subject and object. The neurotic symptom is

> something of a compromise, due to the interplay of conflicting and largely unconscious impulses. Some symptoms of this kind seem indeed to serve as a compromise between almost exactly the same tendencies as those which find expression in clothes. Thus the attacks of psychological blushing, from which some patients suffer, are, on the one hand, exaggerations of the normal symptoms of shame, but, on the other hand, as psycho-analytic examination has demonstrated, at the same time involuntarily draw attention to the sufferer and thus gratify his unconscious exhibitionism. In terms of this very close analogy, it may indeed be said that clothes resemble a perpetual blush upon the surface of humanity. (21)

We have already seen the erotic compromise effected through the discursive body, the shoe and the reader enlisted into representations of difference and indifference. Another concession to the ascetic, in the sexual, exists in women's lingerie and jewelry. Flügel also notes that a central modern difference between the sartorial make-up of men and women is women's "double weapon of exposure and of decoration" (106). This statement aptly characterizes the deployment of fashion statements on the pornographic body textual. The "double weapon" is a curious endowment of the female body in this sexual scene, especially when implicated in discourses of desire (for men). For jewelry and lingerie are objects as well, which effect a simulated androgyny in a seductive fashion. The interaction between the selective exposure of nudity and the appointment of sexualized beauty through jewelry constitutes another fetishized transaction in the pornographic oeuvre.

Jewelry

It is the protocol of all straight and "TV" genres to elaborate sexual difference through the use of jewelry. This kind of costume is related, as Flügel notes, to the display of wealth: "Wealth in a more readily exchangeable form may be carried in the shape of ornament. In civilised societies the most common approach to this is the wearing of precious stones as jewelry" (33). Jewelry connotes wealth, possession, currency, ostentation, and vainglorious display. Customarily, in the late twentieth century, women still wear more jewelry than men, and of a different sort.[3] It is not uncommon in cultural practice for women to wear actual coins or imitations of coins, on charm bracelets, necklaces, belts, etc. Flügel writes: "Coinage, or its equivalent, may be carried, not only to show that the wearer is rich, but actually to enable him to buy what he requires" (33). Although the relationship is complex, it does suggest that purchasing power resides with both reader and model and that the models are fee-bearing.

There are slight variations in what each (female) model wears: a ring, a bracelet, sometimes earrings, seldom nothing at all. As with the shoe fetish, some form of jewelry is present as a microfetish, or at least part of the symbolic organization of femininity-in-seduction. There is a recurring motif in neckware. A necklace often draws the gaze upward toward the face/eyes—and separates the upper torso, i.e., the breasts, from facial signifiers of pleasure and desire. This is if the necklace is small, short enough to rest on the collarbone. The more popular version of ornamentation is the longer necklace which extends between the breasts, serving the purpose of individuating the breasts, separating them visually to singularity, thus the simulated phallic principle.

The Pearl

The article with the most currency is the string of beads, notably pearls. The immediate fashionable associations are with the feminine: pearls are worn by women, never men. Doris Langley Moore writes that pearls worn by women enjoyed great vogue in the seventeenth and late ninteenth centuries. This has been "eclipsed," she notes, by even more widespread fashionable use of the pearl in the twentieth century.[4]

This wasn't always the case. Byzantine royalty, notably Emperor Basil II, wore red military boots sewn with pearls; as well, their crowns consisted of a double row of pearls.[5] Red leather shoes set with pearls are also recorded of Japanese emperors.[6] Male Venetian royalty in the sixteenth century wore pearls knotted into their beards.[7] Male Indian royalty wore a sash of pearls.[8] King Charles I wore a pearl earring in his left ear all his life.[9] In Elizabethan England it was more common for *men* to wear pearls, and one pearl earring was popular among young men.[10] Whereas "men have, in their time, worn great pearl-studded ruby collars, or shoulder knots dripping emerald and sapphire and pearls; pearls have been sewn into their tunics, hung from their hat ornaments, embroidered on a coat, or set in an order worn as studs or pinned in an ascot," the pearl has over time crossed the gender barrier.[11] Women now wear pearls, but it is the traces of the masculine other that assign the pearl not only to the sphere of feminine adornment, but to its contemporary use in discourses of seduction and (transgressive) desire.

Why the pearl? A pearl is "a dense . . . and lustrous concretion," "a gem . . . choice or precious"; "smooth, hard, roundish, formed around a worm or foreign body within the shell of an oyster"; "akin to [OE] '*heel*' " (my emphasis). "To pearl" is "to sprinkle or bead with pearly drops," "to give a pearly color or luster to."

A number of considerations emerge from these associations. The female model is adorned with a precious or semiprecious "gem" (her jewels), an "object of great beauty or worth; its choicest part or prized thing." And the gems have "luster": "gloss, refulgence; shining surface, brilliance, bright light . . . distinction"; "radiant in character or reputation." The pearly gems are a specular prize, their luster commanding attention. As a prized thing or choice object, they connote an object of desire and a mark of femininity: they are like a glimmering trophy, feminine in their to-be-looked-at-ness. But they are also distinctively radiant, a shiny beacon to the one who looks. In their specularity they project to, and reflect, the reader.

The *OED* notes that the designation "pearl" is "used in reference to shape." The genealogy of "pearl," however, indicates (absent) traces of the masculine in the overtly feminine object. The etymology of "pearl" is, immediately, "haunch, sea mussel, akin to heel." Descending into "heel," one is referred to "hock," and from "hock" to "skeleton." A constellation of "hard," "shallow," and "dry" (from "skeleton") produces (from "hard"; there are no related terms for "shallow" and "dry") "strength," which yields "strong" and "strain." "Strain" leads to "halter," which leads to "helve," which produces "half." "Half" branches in two directions. One denotes "to *cut*" (my emphasis), from *cutten,* "to penetrate." The other yields "shell," which produces "to hoe, hew." The etymological associations—remember that these all stem from "pearl," the hyperfeminine jewel worn in this sexually explicit context—confer an androgynous configuration on the object. Taking this further, "to beat" is the root of "hew," the first definition of which is "to cut with blows of a heavy cutting instrument," followed by "to fell by blows of an ax," "to give form or shape to, with or as if with, heavy cutting blows," "to make cutting blows." Finally, one finds that the root of "blow" is "penis." From "pearl" to "heel," to "cut," to "penis." From "pearl" to "penis": this feminine gem as partially phallic object is another instance of the masculine masquerade.

A "transferred sense," from the *OED,* is the "pupil of the eye." The pearly, light-filled beads are akin to the beady eyes. Their polished hardness is a masculine complement to their round feminine connotations. This is how one historian of jewels, Mab Wilson, describes pearls: "Solitary and unpierced, a pearl seems oddly complete: a small, self-contained, self-absorbed, light-enveloped universe. Pierced and strung, the most beautiful pearl loses its separateness at once and becomes a smiling part of an indivisible whole."[12] This eloquent praise for the pearl captures, in part, its dual status ("the Eros and Agape of jewels; the most earthly and the most unearthly") as self-referential ("oddly complete") and destined for union with others (by being "pierced and strung"). The same author emphasizes that men have worn pearl earrings, but never pearl necklaces. The pierced *ear* (surely the singularity here is significant), to a degree, by now, mainstream, has been the prerogative of the gay male and the prostitute (as with the cigarette, the sex-for-sale connection being clear with the latter).[13]

Furthermore, pearls insinuate themselves within the oyster, itself slang for *both* female pudend and semen (Partridge).[14] The root of "oyster" is "shell" and "bone," overdetermining again the ambisexual significance of its emission. Partridge also notes that "oyster" is a low colloquial expression for "a gob of phlegm." This too suggests that the feminine pearl resonates with symbolic properties that are shared with the masculine argot. Recall that in the discussion of the genitals and the sign value of semen, it was noted that the "issue" from fathers is referred to as his "dead spit." And Germaine Greer referred to women as "human spittoon[s]."[15] As discussed below in the section "Leather," there are shared linguistic properties between oyster/phlegm and "black," the preferred color of the leather garments worn by the female pornographic model. Each contains the etymological association "to burn," a caustic affiliation.

If "the world is your oyster," as the saying goes, you've "got the world by the tail"—your potential, fantastic desires shall be realized. A "tail" is also both penis and female pudend (Partridge). There are a number of other colloquial phrases associated with "tail." For example, "tail-feathers" is pubic hair. "Tail-flowers" refers to the menses. "Tail-fruit" are children, "tail-juice" is urine or semen, and "tail-wagging" is intercourse (Partridge). It appears the oyster/tail has its erotic and ambisexual component as well—as does the oyster/pearl, in other ways. For example, the oyster is both hard and soft: hard shell, soft lining, hard pearl. Pearls as jewelry (the family jewels) are round and threaded; the round, uterine-like pearl is simultaneously pierced to create a string of pearls. It again carries a doubled disposition or capacity for uniting a binary opposition; i.e., a string of pearls is a combination of hollowness and hardness, a unity-in-difference.

Why the pearl? It is the oyster's emission, and this gives rise to at least two possible renditions of its significance in the pornographic oeuvre. (1) The pearl resembles semen. It is white or whitish; in its luster it adopts a sheen, a surface brilliance. It looks wet. The pearls which drape the model's neck and extend between her breasts resemble the pearly drops of semen which, significantly, will adorn her body in hard-core (and often his): this is his excretion, his precious thick "liquid seed" (*Anal Fantasy*); these are his gemstones. In fact, a "pearl necklace" is the slang phrase used in pornography to refer to instances of ejaculation on the female's upper torso. In that sense, the pearls are a motif of sated, spent desire, the product of his being "milked" ("I intended to tease her for as long as possible, but there was no question as to who was teasing whom. . . . She continued to squeeze and milk me" [*Penthouse*]). (2) The pearl is contiguously related to shit, which is, as we have seen, another mainstay in pornographic magazines. The product of the oyster—the pearl—is the oyster's excretion, its garbage, its shit, posing as milk, or its milk posing as excrement. This elimination from the body of the oyster produces its own metonymic twin: it is a sign of both life, with its seminal luster, and death—a discharge, shit, the elimination from (of) the body—a gob of phlegm.

Corporal desire cannot sustain itself and signifies only through the representation of its death, its loss. That is, pearls appear to be ultrafeminine. But if the pearl is "akin to a heel," can one then say the pearl is akin to the oyster's phallic projection (semen/shit) and, as worn by the female, signs of her (phallic) desire? Isn't it that these jewels at their most feminine are part of the masculine charade? The pornographic moment uses the pearl as a fusion of eros and thanatos, of desire and death. In its visibility, and materiality, it signifies the exhaustion of desire, the body, and difference (for if oedipal desire is the discourse of "others," this fashionable ambivalence implicates difference as a liminal territory: at once with one and the other, difference and indifference).

If the model does not wear pearls, she is very often adorned with a string of some other beads. Articles of jewelry include earrings, rings, and bracelets, often bejeweled. The gems heighten the specularity of the jewelry (and that of the wearer), but at the same time, the diamonds and other gems are positioned to catch and reflect light, dazzle and enthrall, capture the gaze and, temporarily, in iridescence, the reader's blind spot. The effect is bewitching; it is a brilliant display, a phantasmatic body as a shimmering screen, all surface glitter (ultimately incapable, though, of being penetrated). In temporarily blinding the reader, the classic castration scenario is invoked: she is poised to penetrate.

A reading: Lisa, in a *Penthouse* spread (June 1988), is fetishistically endowed in a variety of different styles and poses, at times more scantily clad than others. In a typical scene she is sitting on the floor, wearing a blood-red dress that falls off her spread legs, which are bent at the knees. One leg is at a right angle to her body, to reveal her crotch. She is also wearing red spike-heel shoes, the heel of one placed close to the vulvar area. One breast is exposed, the other is covered by her long tresses of hair.

It is a photo evoking trickery, deception, and longing. These impostures are conveyed through the body's fashionable text. Lisa's jewelry consists of diamond-studded drop earrings, a diamond-studded triple-strand necklace, a triple-strand diamond bracelet, and a very large solitaire diamond ring. Her belt buckle is a beaded design about four inches wide. All glisten, dazzle, and reflect: she is a light show. The lighting in the photo is shaded (typical of this genre, especially *Penthouse* and *Playboy*), creating a hazy impression. Shadows contrast with beams of light which highlight her one exposed breast and her genital area. There are also beams of light on the wall behind her. She is a dangerous tease, in the style of film noir. She sports a wide-brimmed black hat which partially shades one eye, and there is a black veil (complete with fake beauty marks), both of which "mystify" her face but allow for the clear, beady-eyed gaze. Indeed, one eye is accentuated with a spot of light—a seductive twinkle, as it were. The gleam in her eye, the beams of light inspiring her penetrable but ultimately penetrating body parts, and her flashy jewelry project out toward the viewer.

The reader is caught in the glare of her optimal projections. These items of jewelry, particularly the earring (a unity-in-difference, the hard object piercing the soft fleshy lobe), are the ritual signs of femininity. Yet they are also signs of desire: they are *her* "be.longings" for him, and serve as signs of *his* longing for her, or his longing to be possessed by her desire. They embellish the textual body of desire. Within the discourse of the "striptease," fetish accouterments veil the spectacle "under a glaze of superfluous yet essential gestures."[16] These jewels are like magical icons of power with the ability to bewitch and reclaim for the spectacle its "erotic power."[17]

According to Flügel, the " 'evil eye' was supposed to harm its victims . . . by damaging their reproductive powers or reproductive organs."[18] Thus the amulet and "evil eye" are brought together via the castration drama: defensive objects (ornamental stones, precious jewels) are symbolic of the male or female reproductive organs, designed to assure that "potency and reproductive power" have not waned (74). Within the pornographic genres, one can argue, the ornamental symbols are of the simulated androgynous order. They are hyper-coded statements of sexual desire and are related to reproductive power *at least* in the sense that they obliquely refer to the biological discourses (of penetration, protrusion, etc.).[19] But the jewels are related to reproduction as well in terms of signification, the labor of producing meaning: they have reproductive power in their exhaustive attempt at signifying (for they don't deflate like the penis in hard-core), at presenting and (attempts at) *re*presenting desire. This is their reproductive power: they empower the body's text as they both engage and ward off the "evil eye" of the reader. In this sense, too, they have potency. The female model cannot be castrated; her "potency and power" intact, she is fetishized to charm. Even her "charms" (breasts) are partially phallicized, i.e., separated to form and conform to the principle of singularity. And the pearl would be the supreme example of a fetish of reproduction: it is a unity of the masculine as it mimics drops of semen and other emissions, and the feminine as they adorn the female body.

This pornographic tease is more akin to the sexual fetish, not (as Barthes would have it) the commodity fetish. The argument for commodity fetishism posits the equation of human beings with objects such that the former are reduced to the status of the latter. The part then stands in for the whole, the person identified with her jewelry—mineral objects—and their object status. But an alternative scenario seems to be at work here, as the sexual fetish may in fact serve to sexualize the person. It is not that the body is objectified through its strategic and intertextual recoding of objects, but that objects are subjectified and expected to perform the functions, and have the qualities, of emotional and psychological states. They are deployed with an urgency and invested with lifelike properties. Not unlike Marx's fetishism of objects, the objects do assume and consume a significance beyond their object status. The objects stand in for emotion—desire, longing, and the body's flesh (cf. the spike heel). They conceal the labor of signification.

Jewelry, pearls, and diamonds, notably, are desire's masquerade and identify the body's difference. The pornographic model in soft-core is culturally coded as feminine (the contemporary phenomenon of men sporting jewelry, though still not pearls, indicates a rebirth of a certain "fragment of a fashionable discourse,"[20] a public display of the masculine body), but in ways, given the signification within the photo, which speak to phallic sexual desire. Fetish objects, and fetishized relations, in the pornographic oeuvre constitute an erotic theft, an ambisexual charade. There are other staple features characterized by traces of masculinity, although coded on the surface as hyperfeminine. It is to these we now turn.

The Fingernails

The heel has already been discussed. It is a precarious balance between a feminine enclosure and a spike-projection. The pearl is the gemstone "akin to a heel." Other signifiers (of simulated phallic proportions) are the fingernails and lingerie. The hands, specifically the fingers,[21] in both soft- and hard-core, function to direct the gaze of the reader at the bodily orifices of the vagina and the anus. As such they are put to work in the service of love's labors: they spread apart the ass cheeks or vulva lips to foreground the penetrable and refigure the body for scrutiny. The "appropriately gendered hand,"[22] distinguished through nail polish and jewelry, manipulates the handling of sex in the representation and reading of its discourses. The fingers have an overdetermined significance through the invariably long and painted—usually red—fingernails. These protrusions mimic the performance of the phallus and take over from the missing penis (hers) and that of the reader. They are blood-red and slick (they look wet), and they are clearly within the danger zone. The long, extended claws are those of the wild animal. They are the fingers' weapons, daggers on the hands, extensions of the powerful body. They do not intrude on the reader (i.e., are not aimed at the camera) but indicate the body's pleasurable, and forbidden, realms. And if, for example, they are touching the breasts, they set into contrast the difference between the soft, fleshy breasts and the sharp, hard nails. Again there is a textual inscription of difference.

Lingerie

Lingerie is another pronounced and indispensable feature of pornographic strategies. The deployment of sexual technique circulates as well in the public exposure of the language of the bedroom: the female model takes and displays what are culturally designated for private consumption. These items also refer to the language of the street and the prostitute's discourse. It is one perversion of pornography that underwear is exposed to outer view. Stockings and garters may peek out from under a skirt, for example, or may constitute the complete apparel of the model. The women never remove these articles of clothing, not even their shoes, during their autoerotic sequences and/or their simulated lovemaking with either another male or female, and this perhaps more than anything else underlines their profound significance for the pornographic moment. The reader occupies that spot at the keyhole and is witness to the goings-on in the bedroom. The setting will typically be Victoriana or at least contain rather elaborate and busy details, again of the feminine genre, e.g., pink bedsheets, pillows covered in ruffled cases, lacy curtains, intricately carved furniture. The pornographic model is a self-conscious self-delighter: she unabashedly pursues sexual ecstasy at her own hands, and also unabashedly excludes the reader from her ability to please herself. But she catches and enlists him by looking at him and disturbing his solitary fantasy placement at the keyhole.

Even if the scene is not of the bedroom per se, lingerie (or occasionally some other article of clothing) is a recurring motif, and the reader is still positioned as voyeur, excluded from the scene (primal or otherwise) yet necessary to its production and reproduction. He is affirmed as a sexual, desiring subject before it, and reconstituted in its reading. He lends it his various properties: his eyes, embodied and disembodied desire. If there is a reader for every text and a reader in every text, the ideal consumer of pornography must then negotiate his textual desires and those of the model. It is here that lingerie signifies within the organization of simulated phallic desire.

By lingerie is meant pornography's stock-in-trade: stockings (pantyhose are common only in "TV" porn) secured by garters and some form of lacy camisole, brassiere, or sometimes a corset. And clearly lingerie is a statement of excess, once again, like jewelry, a strong cultural marker of femininity and testimony of difference. The model's "otherness" is a mapping of the body's terrain. Lingerie is unnecessary—if not an impediment—to the sexual act, yet clearly necessary to the workings of desire: it is the mark of difference.

Stockings

How does lingerie work? The stockings, sheer but with an opacity as well, are expressive in their specularity. As indicated, they are stockings which extend to mid-thigh, the kind that need to be suspended by garters. This highlights the vulva, of course, but the typical "gynecological" spread which provides easy visual access could just as easily be achieved through total nudity. So, why the stockings? For one thing, they offer a contrast: the flesh of the leg stands out more clearly against the color tones of the stockings (usually black or white). There is a difference held in the way the two—flesh and fabric, skin tone and color tone—are set against each other. As well, the stocking maps the body and creates a heightened visual space at the top of the thigh. The most important part of the leg, the mid-thigh to the tip of the toe, is almost disembodied and in a visual zone all its own. That is, when encountering the stockinged legs, the eyes are drawn upward toward the genital zone, but they are also pulled downward to focus on the foot/shoe/heel. As such, the stockings create visual movement on the body. They elongate the leg and they deliver the leg in its own package, the stocking, and give it its own autonomous status.

The legs then appear to exist independently of the body; they are covered. Perhaps one signifies the other: clothing "means" against nakedness and vice versa. But, more pointedly, and to emphasize their semiotic power, the stockings give the leg a protrusive, if truncated, effect. They phallicize the leg up to the point where it is contained within the shoe (which also has its own phallic heel). The stocking colors the leg in phallic terms, fetishizes the body's extremeties, endows them with meaning and seductive power.

The stocking, no fetish in itself, and without the transcendental signifying power of the high heel, fetishizes the leg. It endows it with a shimmery specularity, elects the leg, that is, as a stand-in for the phallus. The sheathed leg is typically bent at the knee (another crack in the phallic code) so that a wide view of the vulva is provided and the heel of the foot and shoe is aimed at the genitals. To give the leg its phallic, penetrating power, to signify it as more than a limb, it is fetishized to make it specular, and longer, at least as it directs the gaze both up, toward the genitals, and down, toward the toe. It is as though the leg is the penis slipped into its vagina-like accouterments.[23]

An equivalent scenario involves the long black glove, used by strippers, which extends to the upper arm. Typically these are removed at some point during the performance. Barthes, in "The Striptease," writes of "the whole spectrum of adornment" which characterizes the erotic spectacle (85). He locates one powerful aspect of the dramatization, "the shedding of clothes which makes voyeurs of the public," in its movement, or the way it calls upon memory and projection. He writes: "There will therefore be in striptease a whole series of coverings placed upon the body of the woman in proportion as she pretends to strip it bare" (84). The body's insertion into clothing/discourse presents and sustains a certain narrative. The articles of clothing invite a cover-up. The privileged gaze at intimate apparel creates a fantasy space in which to imagine the activity of dressing, slipping items on, adjusting the garters, smoothing the fabric against the skin, and so on. One can project forward to the promise of undressing. Fantasies of the past and the future give the image a diachronic status.

Lace

Lacy lingerie and leather implicate a fabric fetishism. Lace is a double play: it partially covers areas of the body while permitting partial access to the same areas. The access is tactile as well as visual. So is the fabric. Lace, like leather, is multisensory (leather and rubber, two well-known sexual fetishes, also have their own aroma). Lace provides a visual motif and is something which invites the touch. It is audible—it rustles. The fabric, too, creates movement between the seen/unseen, effecting a there/not there or there/partially there condition.

"Lace" is part of an interesting signifying chain, with a few metonymic associations. The familiar definitions apply—noun: "fine open fabric"; "cord or leather strip for fastening or tightening"; also, "braid for trimming men's coats etc. (usually *gold or silver lace*)." From the Latin *laqueus*, "to snare—more at DELIGHT"; from *laqueum*, "a noose." "Lace" is also "a cord used to support something hanging: a sword, baldrick, belt." Thus, the fragility of lacy fabrics and design also accommodates a more aggressive posture. "Delight": from *delicere*, "to allure." The body adorned with lace is poised to elicit (indeed snare), in this case, the illicit look. Verb: "to fasten or tighten"; also, "to lash, beat, defeat"; "to add a dash of an alcoholic liquor to." This is also the definition of the verb "to spike" (again, also a heel), to make something potent. From *The Dictionary of Historical Slang*, "to lace" (to add either strong liquor or sugar) is derived from "lace as an adornment," which is an interesting direction for the meaning to take. Also, a "lacing" is a flogging; a "laced mutton" is a wanton woman. All indications are that lace is an admixture of sexual enticement, danger, and loss of control (his).

The female model is the one who dons the lacy apparatus. She sports the lacy undergarments, though they are fully exposed to view. Although she could be "laced up," the more typical lingerie item is "lacy" and without ties and stays, characteristic of the "merry widow." Is it not appropriate to suggest that she is a precarious balance of being laced, fastened, but also therefore "laced" or spiked with something potent? That is, this woman is capable of "lacing." David Kunzle, in *Fashion and Fetishism: A Social History of the Corset, Tight-Lacing and Other Forms of Body-Sculpture in the West,* argues that the tight-laced corset, far from an example of the repressive horrors of Victorian society and the masochism of its female fashion victims, was an expression of sexual desire and erotic pleasure.[24] It seems that contradiction or ambiguity is one of the things which sustain the fetish, in this case visual as well as moral. Kunzle notes, for example, that the tight-laced corset looked uncomfortable, and for some women it may have been. The waist was made abnormally small, and the bosom and posterior were both thrust outward. But Kunzle, Anne Hollander, and Elizabeth Wilson note that the use of the corset suggested an eroticism of enormously long staying power—"a sexual readiness deliberately prolonged, an erotic tension stretched to the breaking point"—and thus pain and pleasure conjoin to speak the erotic.[25]

The pornographic model is a fee-bearing model who "delights": herself, in her flagrant autoeroticism, and the reader who indulges in the forbidden look. She "allures" the reader—"to allure": "tempt, entice, win over . . . fascinate, charm." A charm is a word, an act, or an object "supposedly having occult power . . . ; thing worn to avert evil etc., amulet; trinket on bracelet etc.; . . . indefinable power of delighting." To charm is to "bewitch, influence (as) by magic." And from allure: "more at LURE"; and the origin of lure is "bait . . . an inducement to pleasure or gain: ENTICEMENT," synonyms for which are: "inveigle, decoy, tempt, seduce." "Charms" are also slang for "(Always plural) A woman's breasts" (*Historical Slang*).

The above suggests that the model who wears her lacy charms enters the region of the intersexual. The "charming" model is also poised to lure, ensnare, bait, tempt. This is pretty powerful stuff, written, in condensed form, in the fabric of the fetish lingerie. The lacy fetish is associated with the threatening eroticization of feminine attire; these costumes of the demimonde are poised to allure and have the power of the fetish, the missing magical phallus. Lace, *inter alia,* fascinates, charms, bewitches as if by magic, and, like the fetish, recalls, in its absence, properties which are themselves powerfully alluring and delightful.

They (and by extension she) are powerful enough to serve as protection.

Flügel notes that the imperative behind clothing is protection, not simply decoration, protection against "discarnate psychical forces."[26] Many items and articles in popular culture have superstitious value, a holdover, Flügel writes, from
a time when decorative trinkets were "supposed to have defensive properties"
(73). He goes on to locate the function of the "amulet" in primitive cultures
as warding off "the evil eye." In contemporary terms, the amulet (this could
also apply to the lacy "charm," the blinding diamond, and the lustrous pearl)
has psychoanalytic significance: enter the fetish.

Leather

To some extent, fabric always stands for the skin of the person beneath it.[27]

Alison Lurie notes that two features of black leather are slickness and
toughness.[28] Leather lingerie, especially black corsets or brassieres (another pornographic stock-in-trade), connotes toughness, resistance to the elements, a second (impenetrable) skin. Leather may also have a sheen and in these photos is
a glossy leather that invites the look, the touch, the smell: the model is about
to give the reader a "leathering," "a thrashing" (Partridge). Leather, in particular, betrays an erotic theft, producing a fashionable, pornographic ambivalence. Leather gives the appearance of leanness and tautness. It contrasts with
feminine fleshy curves, especially the breasts: with its tight fit, it streamlines
the body. There is here an erotic ambivalence because leather is the (male)
biker's uniform, and because it provides a tough, specular, and odorous sheath,
a second covering to the feminine skin. And leather is the fabric of the shoe,
the staple of the whip (which women brandish):[29] it shares an affinity with
objects that are used as weapons. In this case the ambivalence and theft refer
to the coexistence of taut animal leather and/on the feminine body. Partridge
notes that "leather" is slang for "female pudend." A "leather stretcher" is the
male member. The feminine "leather," impenetrable and used as a thrasher,
moves into the masculine domain as the model articulates her desire through
masculine vocabulary. The reader, at the same time, sees expressions of her desire for his desire and, we may say, sees it in phallic and transgressive terms.

Balint suggests that if a fetish carries an aroma, it may be particularly du-
rable and a dense repository of associations, given its ability to recall repressed
anal-erotic significance.[30] And, as noted by Freud, there is the synthesis of narcissism and defiance which assembles around fetishizing the anal object.[31] The
narcissistic moment is a perverse play on boundaries, objects, possession, and
loss: anal matter is transformative. It becomes an object only upon its transgression of bodily boundaries. It was uncompromisingly and nostalgically once
of the body, and even in its discarded state recalls that original connection to
the body. It thus embodies loss (is fully embodied loss). In sexual terms, and
beyond the materiality of anal eroticism, the anal zone, as mentioned previously, abolishes difference, and is thus another embodied loss.

The color black suggests something slightly wicked; "black," etymologically, is akin to "fire" and "to burn," both fairly incisive associations. Black also suggests that the fetish is most strongly a visual investment, as it is a slick and shiny leather (as least in these photos). The notion of feces-as-fetish-as-phallus (noted in preceding chapters) coalesces with a salience around leather. The leather fetish could be the "phallus as shit," the casting of one's skin, i.e., body refuse.

To sum up, all these symbols are mediators of desire, the artifice(s) of desire within a mimetic and transgressive exchange. The objects themselves, particularly the jewelry, lacy lingerie, and stockings, connote a fragility, in spite of their reproductive potency, thus adding to their doubled role in this play of all "others," in the chimerical performance of seduction. They can so easily be removed ("the fetish is a lifeless thing, which can easily be taken away from its legal owner")[32] and are so obviously a fabrication. This again points to the origin of the fetish, as Baudrillard has noted:

> The term fetish . . . originally signified . . . a *fabrication,* an artifact, a labor of appearances and signs. It appeared in France in the 17th century, coming from the Portuguese *feitico,* meaning "artificial," which itself derives from the Latin *factitius.* The primary sense is "to do" ("to make," *faire*), the sense of "to imitate by signs" ("act as a devotee," etc.; this sense is also found in "makeup" [*maquillage*], which comes from *maken,* related to *machen* and to make). From the same root (*facio, facticius*) as *feitico,* comes the Spanish *afeitar:* "to paint, to adorn, to embellish," and *afeite:* "preparation, ornamentation, cosmetics," as well as the French *feint* and the Spanish *hechar,* "to do, to make" (whence *hechizo:* "artificial, feigned, dummy").[33]

And *hechicero* is "sorcerer" (in Spanish). Any fetish casts a kind of spell (is the sorcerer's apprentice), and induces, as if by magic, the "cut." The fetish re-presents what can only be, and is always, absent, thus showing up the "artificial" nature of desire. Artifice, the jewels and fabrics, is a s(t)imulated moment of both masculine and feminine attributes. This is a safe writing of the masculine— jewels which are hard, which blind; fabrics which are tough or spiked—on the feminine form. In soft-core, the reader relinquishes his phallic attributes in exchange for the "cut." Difference is negotiated at the price of the body doubled (as the other): a small, narcissistic death.

Straight: Hard-Core

Consider first the *soft-core* pornographic uniform. And occasionally there are *precisely* uniforms: e.g., the nurse, the businesswoman in a gray flannel suit, who strip to reveal erotic accouterments, and potential, underneath the ascetic exterior. Like all uniforms, these carry certain designations, notably those of rank and occupation, and one aim within pornographic narratives is to subvert the external picture for a reality of a different kind (i.e., seduce the puritan, the recluse, the abstainer, and unleash the wild, presocial, fully desirous animal restrained by society's uniform: e.g., she had "animal lust," a "wild, untamed look about her").[34] In *hard-core* there is often the uniform; if no formal code, there is still a surfeit of fetish inscriptions in the hard-core regime. Models (both male and female) frequently wear many articles of clothing; men often leave their shirts and socks on. (As well, the settings are busier; the "everyday" is invoked in living rooms complete with crooked paintings on the walls, couches with loud prints, bookshelves, lampshades; fetishes clashing with objects all over the place, fetishizing the normal, the norm.)[35]

Within scenarios attempting to reinstate difference, this is a curious attempt at the disavowal of difference. Why fetishize either body when biological signification establishes a binary opposition? The fetish contributes to the exhaustion of difference by giving women a phallic substitute when the penis is already in the picture. Reality effects are strongest in hard-core, but even the fetish cannot cover up those flaws in the real as the reader is caught up in searching out those blemishes (a microfetish)—the truly everyday body complete with flaws, the completely fallible body.

The straight hard-core ensemble is similar to that of soft-core, with less emphasis perhaps on jewelry. The greatest currency is in the graphic sexual drama and in lingerie-as-fetish. The viciousness of hard-core lies with its simulation of an androgynous sexual union, especially in the context of difference written on the scene. That is, as already discussed in chapter 2, male and female models should, ideologically and according to the discursive production of biology, sustain a balance of difference, and yet fetish inscriptions (along with vocabularies of the bodyscape) implicate an impudent refusal of difference, at least with the female models.

The female model is poised to penetrate with the heel, anally, and through her gaze. The penis of the male model—first flaccid, then erect, penetrating and then deflated—is seldom far from view. The viciousness of hard-core is this play on ambivalence: as it hovers in the nether regions of desire, it plays difference and indifference against each other. Difference is marked out fetishistically through the deployment of the feminine-sexual apparatus (lingerie, etc.), and yet this is at the cutting edge of indifference as it pairs with the anus (the "anal universe" which assigns the same orifice to each sex, "erogenous zones . . . interchangeable and faecalized").[36] The male model's penis (engaging the narcissistic identification of the reader) goes a long way to create a (repressed) homoerotic, selfsame, hence phallic, association. The lingerie, as symbolic of ambisexual potency, is worn by the woman to entice, ensnare, and "leather" the reader, also destabilizing his sexual "fix."

A reading of *Anal Fantasy* should embellish this notion of an economy of loss and ambivalence. This particular magazine involves a visual narrative which *is in some ways* quite at odds with the accompanying written text (this is not uncommon). The linguistic text locates an exchange between a psychiatrist and his female patient: "Gina had gone to a psychiatrist to confess her obsessive sexual fantasies, visions of erotic pleasures that were with her day and night. The head-doctor was no fool! He quickly persuaded her to 'work out' her fantasies, and he had her out of her clothes in no time." Of course, the person quickly out of his clothes is the (male) "doctor," while his "patient" retains both her desire and articles of clothing, those crucial fetishes. "Gina" thus inadvertently seduces the doctor. The photographic account is typical of the genre: of the fifty photographs in the magazine, only eleven depict the male in clothing (a three-piece suit). In ten of them his erect penis sticks out from behind his fly. The female model is wearing a red and black dress; we see the tops of her black stockings, garters, and a veiled glimpse of her vulva. So, in fact, there is nothing in the visual fiction which even remotely suggests a doctor-patient relationship. This contrasts a bit with the descriptive passages which are an eroticization of the injunction to speech. For example, some captions to the photos read: "Erotic confessions"; "Let me tell you about my fantasy." They are her fantasies, her sexual narrative, her desires: "Her hot dreams had them both creaming!"

In *Anal Fantasy*, as is common of the hard-core genre, the fetish inscription of the female body powerfully indicts the discursive other. There are two main scenarios presented, distinguishable by what the female model is wearing. In the first (which includes the front cover) she is wearing a black leather collar with silver and gold studs, gold earrings, darkly painted eyelids, black leather gloves which extend above the elbow, and black silk stockings secured by a red garter belt fringed by black lace and with black garters. On her feet are knee-high leather boots with high heels; in her hands she carries a black leather riding whip. She is a woman dressed to kill; a small death looms ahead.

In the opening photo she holds the end of the riding whip threateningly against the male's neck, while with the other gloved hand she grasps his erect cock and devours it orally. In this photo he is standing on a low settee, pinned against a stark white wall. Her fantasy is explicitly stated as "I ride a man's mouth with my cunt, whipping him, kicking him with my boots," and frames the interpretation of the following photos, which consist of him servicing her (in the manner of her fantasy) orally, vaginally, anally. Her riding crop is in view, as are the collar, stockings, boots, heels, and drops of semen around the anus. In one photo she holds the riding crop pointed at his neck while he partially penetrates her vagina. In another, he administers to her voracious sexual appetite by penetrating her orally. She is lying on a small divan; he stands over her head with his legs apart so that she can perform fellatio (and she is: one sees the penis partially devoured and the testicles), and he inserts a dildo into her vagina. The next five photos are of fellatio (he still in his suit), each one slightly larger than the preceding one, as if to narratively privilege the climax.

In all the photos of fellatio her collar is visible (in three the leather glove is partially there), the testicles are subservient to the penis (they are hidden between his legs), his index and middle finger surround the base of his penis. And the climax comprises two photos in which the visible fetishes are the leather collar and the simulated semen dripping off the nearly detumescent penis. He does look as though he's "died" at his own hands and at the voracious mouth of his partner.

In the second scenario which follows, Gina sits on a black leather couch, this time without her whip, boots, or black leather gloves. Her dress slips up to reveal the tops of her (black) stockings and garters and that she isn't wearing any underwear. However, she coyly covers her crotch with her hand, prohibiting any unadulterated look at her genitals. So both partners are "in uniform" in this exchange: he in his suit, she in her dress and lingerie. Eventually he sheds his apparel to afford a full frontal view of penetration as she sits on his lap and both face the camera (although neither looks at it, suggesting that there is already penetration in excess). They proceed with the usual sexual machinations; however, the subnarrative in this case creates a different twist. The linguistic chronicle, complete with headlines (e.g., "FANTASY NUMBER TWO: He Fucks Me With a Dildo!"), which interact with the visual narrative and attempt to anchor it, is structured around the woman's fantasy desires. Because the male is depicted as her doctor within a psychiatric discourse, the descriptive passages cite as her "cure" the acting out of her sexual obsessions, wildest fantasies, and repressed carnal desires.

But the visual imaginary constructs a different script. Upon the simulated satiation of her desire, she is literally stripped of the fetish(es) heretofore adorning her body. That is, the consummation of her longings is signified through the removal of her garter belt and stockings, her be.longings. The male model pulls off her stockings, for example, until she is finally stripped naked, bereft of the fetish, i.e., no longer needing to signify and project her desires to her partner or the reader: she is sated, she is cured. A small portion of the garter belt and stocking (remnants of her unfulfillable desire and longing) peek in at the edge of the photograph. In the few photos before the logical culmination of desire (according to the code) and the "small death" of the male subject (i.e., signs of his orgasm), her desire is replaced by a dildo. Once, while the male strips off a stocking, he inserts a dildo into her vagina while he, interestingly, sucks on her bare foot. In line with the phallic foot previously slipped into the shoe, is he giving *her* a blow job? At least he is licking her feet, is her manservant ("foot-licker": "A servant; toady," *Historical Slang*).

With the denuding of the body of its fetishes, the sexual scene is then dependent on mere biological distinctions. The question then becomes, since the male in the photo already has a penis, why the dildo? The dildo takes over from the fetish, does its work, is the real phallus, clearly more powerful than the penis. When the fetish is gone, so, obviously, is the phallus; but in this case it is resurrected through the appearance of the dildo. Then, in a seemingly perverse twist, and leading up to its climax, the female model is given back the phallus: she inserts it into *his* anus. His legs are spread apart (one pointed upward toward the ceiling, the other bent at the knee); his hand grasps his penis to reveal a full frontal view of the tip of the penis, but also his testicles and the partially inserted dildo. He is literally penetrated in this instance, feminized by the one who wields the phallus. She brandished the riding whip (held it against his neck), and she wielded the lingerie ("In her imagination, she was naked—except for a sexy garter belt and fine silk stockings—but striding about in riding boots and wielding a wicked leather rider's crop"); and now she manipulates the phallus (or a penis substitute). Her divestment of the lingerie (at his hands) accompanies her satiation of desire (so she loses her desirous be.longings; she surrenders signs of her desire and gives up the fetish after she is fulfilled, as a prelude to *his* fulfillment). But she is then reinvested with the phallus (in the form of a dildo), and a discourse of difference is sustained as her partner is feminized. All of this takes place while the limp reminder of her desire rests at the edge of the bed.

Narrative closure consists of four photographs which begin with depictions of oral sex. In the first there is an extended tongue and her visible teeth, inching toward an erect penis; in the second Gina engulfs the tip of the penis. In both photos the doctor's hand grasps his organ, giving his testicles a prominence as she inserts the dildo in his anus. Finally, we are witness to his orgasm ("Droplets of gooey come [*sic*] clung to her pubic hair") and limp penis: he spends himself on her body.

At first blush, the hard-core regime appears to intensify and aggravate sexual difference: the women and men are identifiable by their body parts, and each sex is elected to its own "performance"—he penetrates and she is penetrated (in the words of Angela Carter: "the probe and the fringed hole, the twin signs of male and female in graffiti").[37] However, the fetish accouterments in hard-core point to an excessive indifference. The female model who appropriates the masculine vocabulary, and who bewitches the reader through her jewelry and lingerie, simulates the androgynous code (and in some scenarios actually holds the dildo/phallus in her hand or mouth). The male model has a penis (and retains articles of clothing), is fetishized in excess though the fetishes cancel out the penis. The sexual choreography in front of the reader is more indifferent than different; and the reader, too, "spends himself" on the bodies beyond the keyhole, lost in the fabrications before him.

"TV": Soft- and Hard-Core

The strongest signifying anchor of the pornographic transsexual body lies with the choreography of the fetish. Otherwise this body would be merely a curiosity, the stuff of medical journals, daytime television, and the tabloids. But

"TV" porn presents the grotesque feminine subject. That is, "she" is elaborately coiffed and made up; wears spikes, stockings, garters, and corsets; she has enormous breasts; s.he has a penis. Without the immodest sartorial exhibition she would be a hermaphrodite, and thus surrender to a discourse of genetics and the anatomically undisciplined, unreproductive body. But dress it up in those culturally feminine sexual signifiers and it enters the nether regions of desire, *refusing* to be disciplined, in fact highlighting the play on indifference, the friction and ambivalence around sexual seduction.

Otherness and difference are restored, however, through the feminine apparel (itself a picture of simulated androgyny on top of the androgynous body). Transgressions are so *clearly* the norm in this genre: transgressions on (of) a body which is in fact prolific, productive. The fetish works hard at investing in difference on a body which appears indifferent to sexual opposition. Difference here is a play on phallic femininity (not a discourse of the body), and with the circulation of the fetish(es), a performative moment of simulation and erotic theft. What appears as the ultimate in transgression (the flouting of the binary biological code) is refashioned as cultural, semiotic, difference. Desire is negotiated in an engagement with the "cut": that is, precisely the borrowing of erotic properties from the other, "embodied" in the lingerie, on a body which doubles as its other.

The invitation to explore the fatal delights of "Sulka" the she-male begins with a "killer" pose. Sulka is sitting on the floor of what appears to be a photographic studio (the photo spread is highly staged, with no pretense to verisimilitude). She is leaning on one hip, resting on one arm, and her legs are extended to the side. The other arm is resting on her right leg (at the knee, which is slightly bent and pulled toward the body). Her arms are attired in vinyl gloves, slick, shiny, and reaching above the elbow. Sulka is wearing a leather corset which leaves her breasts exposed, black garters and stockings, and a black leather neck collar with silver studs. There is also a silver snake bracelet wrapped around her upper left arm, on top of the black glove. Her pubic area, though, is occluded by filmy black gauze. The diegetic space in the photos that immediately follow, however, is given over to the capricious display of the essential signifier. It's that penis that won't go away.

This body fashioned in feminine (i.e., simulated masculine) terms serves to heighten the dangerous allure of the model and also mitigate against the overly close identification of the reader with the penis-bearing woman. In the pictures subsequent to this first one, in which the fetish objects masquerade as the penis, the penis is evident. The model, though still a poseur, abandons the leather for the more sedate satin corset, garters, and stockings. The latter are not so much difference with a vengeance. They accompany instead a body already in possession of the penis, although limp. The lingerie fetishizes, perversely, the body double. The leather and other lingerie (as with straight porn) are the more phallic mediators on a body which, at least in the first photo when the penis isn't visible, appears to recuperate femininity. In other words, the lingerie in "TV" porn fastens difference on a body, fashionably ambivalent about sexual difference.

Sulka is still dressed to kill. She is, through the fetish accouterments, designated as other, but this is otherness with a vengeance. Once again, the fetish/phallus is invoked to adorn the body *already* in possession of the penis. The penis pales in comparison; it is merely a limp rendition on a body which cannot signify without its fetish inscription. The collapse of meaning, difference, on the body is too much to witness (that would be the death of desire). The discursive androgynous moment is written on top of the *already* androgynous body; desire is recuperated through the simulated impulse behind the lingerie. Obviously simulation is the "real" thing; it constructs the indifferent body as different.

This spectacular moment contains a body in excess of normative and pleasurable transgressions. The "body double" in "TV" pornography, in its symbolic, sexual, and feminine masquerade, is a body that doubles as its other. I argue that there is seductive (yet unspeakable) surrender on the part of the (male) reader to the "cut," that incisive moment formed around loss and pleasure. At the moment of reading, the subject is reaffirmed as subject/other, a position originally formed in reflection, opposition, otherness. Also, borrowing from Williams,[38] I suggest that the "freak" in the representation encounters the freakish and mutilated ("cut") body of the viewer. In "TV," model and reader meet the double of the other, through a body which doubles as its other, bearing the marks of a simulated androgynous writing. That is, categories of sexual difference collapse around a law which prescribes transgression of the sexual fix such that there is potency in that "different kind of sexuality" (Williams), but this is a desirable transaction, not totally threatening.

In "TV" porn, potency resides not just in the body double, although signifying nonaligned sexuality, and transgressing the sexual fix. The "apparent" feminine body, read thus through its erotic accouterments, simulates androgyny on top of its biological adornment that flouts sexual binaries. This body must be desirable beyond the fleshy configuration which always threatens to emerge: discursively, psychoanalytically, symbolically, sartorially, and literally, the penis/phallus is never out of sight. That is, the surplus of clothing which marks the masquerade also carries the possessive signs of masculine desire. Thus the "androgyne" bears the simulated traces of erotic theft, a writing of what might never take place. Simulation is incomplete synthesis, which is why the body is written on top of its androgynous properties. In other words, the "androgyne," far from being a unity of opposites (or the desirable, lost, original union), is "jouissance," that which cannot achieve closure, and which plays on the open seam of the "cut" through the simulated properties of masculine and feminine in the fetish clothing.

This seemingly perverse pornographic moment carries more hidden subversive elements which coalesce *not* around a body contemptuous of categories of difference. The spectacular body that "speaks" masculinity through its biological adornment is refashioned as feminine through the fetish. Difference here repairs indifference in the name of desire.

A close reading of all pornographic genres reveals that penetrating exchanges are initiated and carried by the female, feminine model. Masculine projections such as heels, a penetrating gaze, and the fetish objects of lingerie carry the marks of (simulated androgynous) desire and pleasure. These are culture's, the reader's, "be.longings" on the female body. This erotic theft surely speaks to the "flesh of the unconscious," the unsettling body double where the laws of transgression speak the unspeakable, where women in fact are allowed to be men and encounter a reader who, in his fixation on the androgynous model, transgresses his own apparent self-fix. He lends his vision to a she-male—she costumed as female, but only as a masquerade against a surplus of masculine identification.

The freakishness of the "TV" body is this: even when its excessive biological apparatus is revealed, the ultimate, and more desirable, exposure circulates around simulation and loss. The renaissance of desire is not in the excessive biological capacity of the transsexual body. Contrary to appearances, it cannot signify both male and female at the same time, or at least this isn't seductive. What is desirable is the simulated traces and transgressive effects of the lingerie: anything simulated will involve an erotic theft, a borrowing from the other. The freakishness here is the "TV's" signs of loss, not excess.

This is the most *apparent* threat to the sexual fix. This is, in Linda Williams's phrase, the "extreme excitement and surplus danger when the monster and the woman get together" (86). The freakishness of the "TV" display is the "TV" facade always slipping away to reveal the "TS" (transsexual) underneath. To be totally stripped, however, would be the death of language and the death of desire ("Discussions of androgyny . . . come up against a resistance . . . from language itself. . . . Any attempt to *define* androgyny . . . takes us to the limits of language . . . such definitions ask for their own *depassement*").[39] The vestmental code anchors meaning to what appears to be the ultimate transgression, although androgyny is still the longing for loss (not plenitude).

The "TV" *hard-core* story unfolds as one model gradually reveals her hermaphroditic body through the shedding of outerwear (and the male, although surprised by what he sees, is no less desirous at this point). This discourse certainly speaks the unspeakable: the ("she-male") model is dressed up in the possessive marks of masculine desire; the reader is stripped. All of which is not to say that the reader is unremembered in front of the monster/hermaphrodite, but that he surrenders to "la petite mort," the pleasure of his simulated death. He sees himself in the distorting mirror which reflects the unity of voyeur and exhibitionist/narcissist, his own mutilated form repeatedly "cut" in the visual moment. The look which mocks the reader, and the display of the dildo/phallus, enlists him in the partial surrender to the "distorted mirror-reflection of (his) own putative lack in the eyes of. . . . " Linda Williams is talking here of woman's self-recognition in encountering the monster, *her* lack in the "eyes of patriarchy." I would say that in this instance it is *his* loss in the "eyes" of desire. The transvestite's clarity of vision is *precisely* phallic, and s.he gazes at the mutilated body of the viewer who meets himself in the mirror of the (dressed-up) androgynous model adorned with the marks of his desire.

Do clothes make the wo.man? This "cross-dressing inscribed on the body itself"[40] is more than a play on transsexuality or the masquerade. In this case, the "feminine" writing on the body is a parody of difference as it cannot disguise the fleshy masculine extremity. At the same time it parodies the phallus as it is clearly called upon to signify, beyond the biological nomination. This is an erotic theft, a masculinization which points to the textual body as the site to anchor sexual difference. The fetish is that object which restores the lost phallic potential to a body that never had it in the first place.

Pacteau characterizes androgyny as that which eludes a semantic anchor.[41] That is, it is easy enough to identify the androgynous body in physiological terms, but the lines of demarcation between the subject and its object of desire (the androgyne which fascinates) are continually oscillating. True enough. However, in "trying to organize a meaning for androgyny," she argues that the concept represents a repression of desire, that the nature of ambiguous sexual appearance and identity is the specular image of an "uncanny double": nostalgia for the imaginary space during whose reign "desire is unobstructed." This desire, a resurrection of the original plenitude, a merging, and disavowal of otherness, is repressed within the laws of sexual difference. But I would argue that sexual mutations are not simply a "disavowal of sexual difference" upon observation, a "pleasurable perception."[42] Instead, *transgressions are the law* behind the deviations of the sexual fix, and the desire for repression (not the repression of desire) is part of the (simulated) androgynous union.[43] The androgynous textual body is a possessive site of desire, the embodiment of the partial be.longings of the other. In the case of "TV" porn, the body masculinized is in simulated possession of the desirous be.longings of the masculine viewer. Transgressions are the norm, an eroticized "dialogue of lovers," representing desires, in the case of the male reader, for women to be more like men. The "feminine" enunciation may then be a phallicization for the reader, a discursive drama of his desire to be possessed by the powerfully penetrating subject of the photograph.

"The androgynous figure has to do with *seduction* . . . before undressing."[44] It is not so clear that the "fashionable discourse" is the effete prerogative of women, at least within the codes of the dominant representational doxa. Men *are* charged with negotiating the "look," within the contemporary ideological framework, and seeing themselves as "the ones who look at women."[45] But normative transactions within specular economies invite transgression of the boundaries around an apparent fixity of sexual identity and desire. The male spectator lends his eyes to the image, a highly exhibitionist one at that. There are limits, however, to this cultural lawbreaking: misrecognition, suspension, and disbelief (that the reader is looking at a man, himself, "cut" at the moment of his inscription into sexual difference) are anchored on the textual body in the sumptuous (feminine) display of the transsexual/transvestite model.

Because identification involves visual projection, loss, and surrender, and in this case the visual object oscillates between the feminine and the masculine, this represents more than the (repressed) pleasurable wish for a reunion with the original plenitude. That would be the death of the subject (Bataille: "Human beings are only united with each other through rents or wounds"). The pleasurable spectacle is the body which denies difference and yet resurrects it by proxy, through the surplus of (feminine, fetish) signifiers, to create the body textual. Does the fetish disavow difference? In "TV," as with all porn, it bestows virility on the body, making it a body, though still in its feminine writing, poised to penetrate and invade. Desire is not opposed to its correlative threat but may itself be threatening, involving as it does subjection and death ("la petite mort"), the consumptive expenditure of a small death. But why speak of a fetish, a stand-in, when the real thing is so unabashedly visible? It may be that the fascination with looking at the androgyne (the "freak") does not contain the lustful search for a lost "wholeness"; rather, the seductiveness of the image promises a "representation of moments of separation and loss which captivates us more than the promise of plenitude."[46]

Conclusion: Close, Obviously, but No Cigar

WHAT ABOUT GAY pornography? If the semiotic disturbances in the pornographic bodyscape lie with the way it stages not a vicious elaboration of sexual difference (or the appearance of "Eros pitted against Logos" [Chevalier]) but ambivalence and a wishful disregard for difference, then what of institutionalized maneuvers which begin with sameness, which rest on the side of indifferentiation? Here, too, though, the textual narrative of gay pornography (for men) conceals an uneasy resting place for difference. If in straight pornography the discursive limits of the biological corpus are tested, might one say of gay porn that the biological limits of seductive discourses are coded as well? Again, the (gay) body is redrafted: it is a body without alibi.

The Body: Soft-Core

Soft-core consists of various photos of the male pinup. The penis is sometimes depicted in its semi-erect state, but there are no scenarios of penetration or ejaculation. The model touches his genitals with some frequency, thus directing the reader's gaze to the privileged zone. He holds his penis, sometimes with a tight fist, and this has a dual effect (on top of manipulating the look): it makes the penis appear erect and it exposes the testicles, giving them at least equal share in the diegetic framework. When the penis is completely limp, it is routinely placed to the side of the balls, resting against the top of the thigh; this allows for full view of the testicles. Why give diegetic preference, almost, to the balls? As noted, the testicles/balls sustain androgyny on the body. This body's "otherness" is its testicles, its feminine counterpart. The model reveals his pouch/purse.

The partially limp penis endows a biologically supine quality to the model. His partial phallicization, though, is restored in other ways. If the penis appears to be erect, it is presented as disembodied in the sense that the body is fragmented; it is displayed alone and distended from it. Dyer suggests that this represents a kind of phallic achievement, the penis trying to "live up to the mystique implied by the phallus."[1] The erect, phantom, penis "looks awkward, stuck onto the man's body as if it is not a part of him" (72), striving to repre-

135

sent phallic mastery. It is a body which not only betrays an intense investment in itself but reveals its own paradox. The result is beefcake: exaggeratedly pronounced muscles in the legs, arms, and torso. The paradox is that the muscular form creates a roundness on the body. Hard but curvaceous; not fat, but not lean, straight lines, either. These are the signs of intense labor (strenuous workouts: invisible production) but signified in the labor of consumption.

Homosexual desire brings the reader close to both his own likeness and a narcissistic investment in the image. But narcissism is not an object, nor does it, in itself, explain the logic of seduction and desire, nor is it restricted to homoerotic relations. At the same time, there is more going on here "to unbalance the tedious symmetry of the Narcissus image."[2] These gay images rest on the side of indifferentiation, and difference is resurrected in a biological vocabulary, itself composed of androgynous oscillations for both model and reader. This desiring apparatus thus signifies an "otherness" on the body itself.

For example, another common theme in gay soft-core visual imagery is the presentation of the rear end to the camera/reader. The way this is done differs, however, from its stylization in straight soft-core. In those magazines the female model confronts the reader with her buttocks and, to the point of insinuation, her anus. The gay model in soft-core more commonly makes a pass at the reader without the graphic exposure and invasion of the anus; instead he usually offers merely the fleshy buttocks, the more feminine concession in what appears at first blush to be a hyperphallic discourse. Remember, a "buttock" is "a low whore," "a shrew," "a common prostitute . . . also a pickpocket." The soft-core model appears to make a number of sexual overtures, not all of them decidedly phallic. When he deploys his buttocks he is the common harlot, selling his sexual wares. The model's discursive difference is a model constructed "otherwise." As Leo Bersani writes, the gay body that conjoins femininity with machismo is a "*per*version rather than a subversion of real maleness."[3]

A model reclines on a bed, or outside on the grass. He lies on his stomach and presents his rear end but is not perched aggressively, on all fours like his female counterpart in straight porn. Along with this softer bodyscape, however, is a peek from under the buttocks and between the legs, at the testicles and penis. (This presents a sort of bi-sexual masquerade, a reminder that this is still a body with the potential to penetrate.) In this case, the model transgresses the phallic code as he is established as the pinup.

The Body: Hard-Core

Gay hard-core magazines involve two or more models and differ from soft-core in the way the photographs foreground penetration and ejaculation. The most common genital configuration involves oral penetration. The close-up shot fragments the bodies so that the look of pleasure, a key feature of straight hard-core, is difficult to discern. What is given visual preeminence, however, is the penis—although it is partly introjected by the mouth of one of the models. The erect and disembodied penis is the representational equivalent of desire, a stand-in, standing at attention (saluting the reader, as it were), a phallic distension feigning desire. It betrays desire of the same, for the same. But it is also inserted into a discourse of otherness in that it is a sign of desire on the body of one who is at once the other. The visible masquerade of desire is the phallic properties of the other, the other's bodily signification, more powerful than a penetrating gaze, more powerful than a fetish, more powerful than the real thing: desire as the impossible referent.

The embodied map of pornographic significance: how does it work? In hard-core, the model often grasps the bottom of his penis, thus masking the testicles. Moreover, the penis in *Triple Treat* (a magazine containing scenarios of a threesome) is not just disembodied but is an organ destined to be devoured. It is referred to as "meat," "sausage," the reduction of the body to other instrumental functions. Again bodily desire works through its simulations, commuted in phallic terms, in this case carried out *by* the (phantom) phallic term—the penis. This tyrannical and pedantic policing of the body has the body speaking in disembodied terms. "Grinding sausage through the grid" is the text which accompanies photographs of the penis extending through the nylon weaving of a lawn chair, as though straining to be (visually) significant. It is highlighted, subject to clinical measurement, suggesting an intensification of pleasurable identification. The model looks at it poking through.

Another magazine, *Supershaft*, fashions a relationship of otherness by staging interaction between a black and a white model. In this binary, both are one and the other. The black model's penis penetrates the slats of the back of a chair, or the rungs of a ladder. Elsewhere his cock is straining through a chain-link fence. In all three scenarios, his penis is orally introjected by the mouth of the other (white) half of the duo. In both cases—distending from an object, standing on its own with its own ontological status, and the cock's oral intromission—the organ is cut off at one, or both, ends. It appears that the penis itself is fetishized. That is, the other's organ is an ambivalent play on specularity: it's there but only partly there. It appears to circulate on its own but harks back to the other body which (apparently) sustains it. Does it hark back to a phallic referent as well? The fetish is invoked in its "there/not there" status and is powerfully ambivalent. The penis strains to signify phallic desire but is aborted in its attempt. Numerous castrations take place: the penis, as already mentioned, is unincorporated, has taken leave of the body, is a phantom signifier trying to disavow its embodied state. Within this streamlined and self-referential economy it carries the heavy weight of all manner of signification: it is given over to meaning and thus simulates the phallus, the man, desire, the reader. And in its disembodied state it signifies all those absences as well (the phallus, the man, desire, the reader). One ambivalence: it is there (partly), but what does it mean? In straining to signify, it is emptied of all signification. Another ambivalence.

Another castration: the penis is lost within the mouth of the other, the other male performing the blow job. A few frames after the photos of the fragmented body, however, the erect penis is given full view again. It is quickly devoured by the desiring hands of its owner and lies detumescent, surrounded by its milky spendings. The "money shot" is the final loss, the inevitable limpness of desire in the face of its representations (and of representation in the face of desire). Note that "shaft" is from Latin *capon,* a castrated male chicken, and stems from the Greek for "to cut." Ambivalence and castration implicate the cock once again. It symbolizes the power of difference—signs of the desire of the other, the other's sacrifice—and a powerful indifference: it is invested as a narcissistic proxy.

The intense and narcissistic focus on the penis—its length, its turgidity, disembodied or penetrating—appears to heighten phallic identification. As a stand-in for desire, though, the penis is still a limp substitute. Why? If the fetish "is a matter of separation, segregation, isolation . . . of petrification, ossification, glaciation . . . of idealization, mystification, adoration,"[4] and if there is a relative absence of fetish accouterments in the hard-core genre, then there is a surfeit of *presence* here. Desire is represented through its biological stand-in: the penis is the object of (for) desire, and it is the ossified object, that which (if a fetish) tries to paper over absence. But here, in so doing, it serves only to register that absence on the body itself. Desire written on the (gay) body, the penis-as-fetish, points to discursive absence.

This porn (often) without the object-fetish, without the object to signify "separation, segregation, isolation," re-presents a closeness to the reader (the homosexualization of desire). This is perhaps a genre privileging a bodily articulation which offers up too much to see (as opposed to those genres in which absences/castrations are objectified through the fetish and the mutilated genitalia); and it is in this narcissistic fusion—there appears to be nothing lacking in the field of vision—that equivalent exchange between selfsame reader and representation cancels out the phallus, or the reader. If the penis is the fetish, it is merely an inflated substitute for the real thing: close, obviously, but no cigar.

Is the attempt at representing the phallus the decomposed vestige of a lost desire? The black body is fragmented, measured also in the demise of the phallic stand-in, the withering away of the turgid penis with the "little death" of its author. The phallic stand-in can signify only difference: it can't sustain significations of desire; it cancels itself out in exchange with other penises, working ineluctably toward its own detumescence.

In *Triple Treat* there are both anal and testicular imageries. In a photo with two models, one penetrates the other anally with the following exposure: the model on top rests on the buttocks of his partner, legs spread to present a full view of his invulnerable anus and his testicles. The genitals of the model on the bottom are quite visible between his slightly parted legs: his penis is aimed at the reader. In straight pornography, soft- and hard-core, the spike heel penetrates the reader when in the company of anal intrusions (and of course in other scenarios). It has a doubled significance as the phallus, circulating within the same orbit, in exchange with the other. In this genre, however, there is a marked absence of heels, corporal or on the shoe, and the penis takes up the work of the phallus, which puts it in the anal zone: once again it is shit.

In hard-core, the mood is hyperphallic. The phallus thus is affiliated with loss and death upon consumption. And consumed it is: the penis, first of all, in exchange with another is canceled out in the name of sameness. Its oral or anal intromission and its disembodied state orient it toward a phallic referent in decay. The hard-core gay discourse pretends to the fiction of the phallus.

Gay pornography begins with a structure of indifferentiation. But the ambivalence which characterizes the straight genres pertains to these as well. That is, difference is a play on a discursive "other" and is resurrected through strategic genital deployments. These demonstrate the limpness of the penis as a signifier of desire and, in general, the cracks in the phallic code which permit bodily divestment (of the male—both model and reader) in the pathetic striving to represent desire.

The Gaze: Soft-Core

Gay soft-core pornography shares the generic features of "straight" porn: typically, the model is alone in a series of poses which simulate both narrative and sexual closure through the use of small shots which lead up to the climax of the centerfold. The popular look of the models is the one which is incisive and challenging: the men acknowledge the reader. This look takes two forms, either the sidelong glance or the look that is "straight on." The sidelong glance is beady, taking aim at the viewer. It accompanies the head tilted slightly downward or, if the body is not positioned for a full frontal view, the head inclined sideways. This cockeyed look is oblique. The model doesn't smile but participates in the serious business of sex. This look may recognize the closeted sexual response it incites, the popular homosexual expression still being subordinate to the dominant heterosexual motif, or it may bring the look outside the closet.

Another look addresses the reader head-on with the eyes less cunning. It is a look which is frank and self-conscious; the model is a poseur in front of the camera/reader, not caught in the act but ready, waiting, and willing. The eyes are not exactly wide open to the point of innocence, eager to admit anything, but they are a less insinuating variation of the beady-eyed look. The model is on display and looked at, his legs spread but only to reveal a flaccid penis, no turgidity of desire here.

The most remarkable difference in the discursive arrangement of straight and gay genres (along the ocular theme) is in the open/closed pair of ocular possibilities. In gay soft porn the model's eyes (if he is depicted alone) are almost always open: there is an absence of the look of simulated ecstasy at the model's own hands. In some spreads the eyes, while not beady, are shaded, preventing ocular penetration.

A look of pleasure occurs only in conjunction with two men in a scene of flirtatious pursuit. One model will display sexual pleasure, marked on his face, at the hands of the other. The models do not look at each other; however, the model receiving the pleasure (there is clearly one giver and one taker here) will engage the reader in a glance that is sidelong, illicit, knowing: it is the beady-eyed look that takes possession of the reader. Once that is in place (there may be a return to it in a subsequent photo), the signifier of sexual satisfaction dominates, and either the model's eyes are closed or his face is turned downward so that his eyes are blocked from view. His partner, the other who does not visibly display pleasure, avoids looking at the camera.

Another popular look is the "faraway" look, which is cast outside the diegetic framework. Richard Dyer notes, with reference to the male "pinup," that the model disavows the reader by not looking at him. At least this look is directed at a space beyond the view of the reader and either is fixated on an invisible object or person, or strains to look upward, outward, the face tilted and the body contorted to aid ocular projection. The latter look is powerfully endowed: the models are posed in natural settings, for example, in a tree, on a beach, in a field, at one with the elements. The body is part of the panoramic view, communing with nature. It is a leisured body, muscular and bearing the signs of labor, the look fixed on a higher sight, not on a lowly object or the reader. This "look" denotes a bodily posture rather than just ocular possibilities. The whole body is exposed to view; the face/head/eyes do not dominate the photograph, the configuration of the model does not suture the reader's eyes in any penetrating way. Rather, the model's glance is away from the reader, does not acknowledge the reader: the body is on display. This uninviting look is not associated with autoeroticism. These models are not caught unawares; the viewer is not enlisted in voyeuristic complicity. The look is not beady, and neither is the body written in a way that is poised to insinuate; i.e., no erections here.

The specularity which accrues to the models here is not necessarily sexual in its associations. The muscular body and the connotations of "haute" mas-culinity or strength (with the *mise en scène* of the weight room or athletes' clothing) suggest a body perhaps ready for action.[5] However, a contradiction emerges: the model's body (in these scenarios of the "faraway" look) is supine;

there is a marked similarity between the contemporary model of feminine beauty and a masculine picture of muscularity. Female models appropriate the gaze that rivets and are more active in their desire than the male model who wears his muscularity like a second skin. This is a strangely underactive body. Does this point to a phallic redundancy? The penis "can never live up to the mystique implied by the phallus . . . straining after what can hardly ever be achieved."[6] Thus this faraway look is the only projection of/on the body and extends beyond the purview of the model and the reader to the mythic, the unrepresented, the unrepresentable, the phallus.

The Gaze: Hard-Core

The constellation of looks in hard-core slides in and out of view; bodies are severely cropped, often heads are "cut off," leaving only an out-of-focus mouth, for example. Eyes play less of a role in suturing the reader. The predominant look of the models belongs to the one receiving (usually oral) pleasure. It carries open eyes and is fixated on genital union, or genital-oral contact. This downward glance at the other performing fellatio is autovoyeuristic fascination in which the model peeks at himself—and someone else—in copulation. The model is Tom peeping at his own sexual activity. The one performing the blow job does not engage the reader, and does not look at the camera (although the one receiving it will). Most often, the former's concentrated look of fascination is at his own penis, the spectacle, the proletariat of the body politic, in service of bodily desire: in hard-core, it does the body's dirty work.

The one performing oral sex keeps his eyes closed. There are very few instances in which the camera/reader is engaged directly: the penetrating gaze is kept to a minimum as the camera isolates, for the viewer, close-up shots of oral or anal penetration. The penetrating look, the eyes beady and shifting, excludes at the same time as it pierces, but it rarely stands alone and competes with other genital exchanges. It challenges the reader who can offer only his look (he is reduced to observer status) at the same time as the penetrating gaze is paired with the erect penis—being consumed orally.

Still, how is otherness, (sexual) difference, marked? The bodies in gay hard-core are anatomically adorned, and each (physical) body is the same. Fetish objects, articles of clothing, are often downplayed. However, the textual body is embellished through a writing of sexual difference. In straight pornography the witness to "otherness" is borne by biological and discursive femininity. It is "women," that is (in soft-core), who are displayed but whose "gaze" also penetrates, whose eyes permit sexualized transactions between viewer and model. It is women who bear traces of (the other's, his) desire with embodied vocabulary suggestive of "masculine" discourse. It is "women" in straight hard-core porn who engage the reader by looking at the camera, whose gaze is incisive and whose pleasure is sought and signified. In TV porn, sexual difference is partially elided in favor of a feminine "sexual fix." One model in the gay duo is also assigned the space of the other; i.e., one is engaged in ocular penetration, and the same one is weighted with marks of fetish inscription (as we will see below). This calls up the role of the male viewer, and dialectics of reading in a visual exchange, not just as endowed with scopic weight but as in the oscillating position of being the object of the gaze as well.[7]

The Fetish: Soft-Core

The body in the soft-core gay genre is often unadorned, perhaps testimony to the visibility, and potency, of biological embellishment. That is, the body is already male, masculine enough in its dressing, the penis being its most distinctive biological motif. But the penis is represented as a disembodied phallus: the body is often cropped and fragmented so that the head and face are not shown and prominence is given to genital display. And the phallic protrusion is on a body without a discursive array of fetishistic inflations; it circulates among a phallic commerce in which the privileged signifier is the penis. The penis is inserted into a masculine or phallic discourse overdetermined by its association with the world of men. Frequently models are depicted in sport or athletic settings—inside a locker, weight, or gym room, for example, or a soccer or basketball may be nearby. Affiliations with the world of the cultivated physique are also sustained through the donning of sweatshirts, sweatbands, and jockstraps, the latter usually pulled down to reveal the penis or the buttocks. The fetish may, however, be foot-related: often the model wears socks, or athletic shoes are scattered around among the gym equipment. But the foot and shoe are not part of cultural, or fashionable, discourses on masculinity: they are not fetishized to the radical extent that they are for women. Because of the phallic dressing on the body, it doesn't have to be fashioned to penetrate.

When a couple of men appear in a narrative, the arrangement designates positions of difference, in spite of the presence of two biologically male bodies. A close reading of a five-page spread in *Blueboy* may provide entry to the workings of the gay fetish. The diegesis is an erotic encounter between two men, their bodies foregrounded against a plain white background. Their bodies, however, are further differentiated from each other through their adornment. One member of the duo is fully naked, the "other" is dressed. The one dressed is actually always in a state of partial undress, his partner doing the undressing. He sports a tuxedo, complete with suspenders (akin to the garter belt, also sometimes called suspenders). The naked model attends to the other. He, for example, ceremoniously strips off his partner's articles of clothing and, in spite of his own nakedness, presents his partner as the preeminent scopic object. In fact, we are provided with only one vague glimpse of the naked model's flaccid penis: he stands beside and slightly to the back of his friend and pulls a suspender off one shoulder, the end of which dangles at his crotch, occluding most of his cock.

Does clothing make the man here? The clothing is a fetish demarcation of otherness, desire, difference. The model wearing it circulates within a discourse of "other-than" maleness (in its nudity). That is, the model with the fetish inscriptions appropriates the "feminine" vocabulary of straight porn. He is the one who looks at the camera, who engages the reader with ocular penetration, who is the one to-be-looked-at. He is "otherwise." The fetish in straight porn incorporates masculine attributes. The gay fetish is a feminine inscription on the masculine surface. The clothes envelop, the sock covers the whole foot ("sock" is slang for "pocket"); "pocket" is "a small bag . . . a purse"; recall the man with "no money in his purse," the impotent one. And "bag," of course, is slang for "woman" and "milk" (Partridge). And there are the flowers and the athletic balls, like the feminized testicles. Which is to say that the fetish is simulated otherness (in this genre it captures the writing of difference), that it can belong only to the other, it is a "cut" into the referent of otherness. What does the fetish signify in these instances? Both difference and its "ossification."

Scenarios of desire within soft-core are dependent on other fetishized maneuvers as well. There is a dominant motif which suggests a fetishization of a slightly different hue. This motif has to do with the settings in which the pornographic discourses are played out. One is the natural setting, with models located in nature, i.e., outside in the woods, sitting on rocks, standing beside waterfalls. They are almost always totally naked, their bodies at one with the natural world. The models are figuratively aligned with the benign side of Mother Nature: they are, for example, most often supine, limp, indeed a passive display, not, as Dyer suggests, "standing taut ready for action."[8]

However, I think Dyer is right to argue that the location of the male pinup in a natural setting creates the following association: a "generalised physical exertion is conflated with the energies of nature" (68). The photos of the "natural" man render an image of an unconstructed natural, phallic power. The contrast of the lean, muscular, and hard body with the more benevolent aspects of nature sets up a binary. In these nature scenes, for example, models are frequently surrounded by plants and flowers, or hold flowers in their hands or against their penis/testicles, as though implicating their genitals in the fruity bouquet. This is a feminine decoration, and flowers and femininity are twinned with a tenacity: women receive the names of flowers—Rose, Violet—are given flowers as presents, etc., and defloration refers to the feminine induction into sexual practice.[9] The "flower" is that part of a plant "modified for reproduction" ("her snatch overflowed with the thick liquid seed of his balls"). A "flower pot" is the female pudend; a "flower-fancier" is a whoremonger; "flowers": the menstrual flux, "monthly flowers"; "flowers and frolics" is a rhyming scheme for testicles, i.e., "frolics" to rhyme with "ballocks" (all from Partridge). These associations suggest a "feminization" of the male model, but within limits. The limits of this feminization would be reached if the penis were not in view; but it is, thus the biological discourse of masculinity is recruited in the service of otherness. Just as the female model in straight pornography is a play of simulated androgyny, so too are the representations of these men. Transgressions thus enter that side of the "cut" which leaves (apparent) indifference and moves into structures of representational difference.

This benign model, I think, fetishizes the nonphallus (or the nonpresence of the phallus), its presence sustained in its absence. The transcendental fetish would phallicize the model in ways which would hearken closure. It is not there. Rather, to fetishize nature is to fetishize the feminine; by contrast, the fetish in straight porn is partial phallicization.

The Fetish: Hard-Core

The cock ring is a common adornment on the gay hard-core body, a small metal or leather ring which circles the end of the penis behind the testicles. To look at gay hard-core pornographic photographs, and the fetish, is to notice the cock, "jauntily or defiantly" erect, raised in "readiness for firing." The penis is omnipresent but disembodied, threatening to cut away and become a signifier on the loose.

The cock appears otherworldly, a phantom phallus, an awkward addition on the body, standing at full attention, saluting the "other." The "penis as part-object" takes up a lot of the diegetic space, radically fetishized, appearing to detach itself from the body and circulate as the signifier of signifiers. The phallus/fetish is a model of closure, "marked as the object of an erotic gaze."[10] And a narcissistic one. It represents that "satisfying sense of omnipotence"[11] and invites surrender to the mastery of the (complete) image. There appear to be no losses here. Yet the perfection and narcissistic fascination is an exclusion, "in the name of . . . internal logic or perfection . . . perfect closure effected by signs."[12] In this case, the power and omnipotence represented by the erect penis-as-fetish are part of a sign play in which the penis is only an artifact of desire. And castration is effected through the semiotic display of the penis/fetish which is poised to penetrate, either (usually) the mouth of the other model or the gap between text and reader.

There is a sport theme in hard-core as well. A model may be portrayed in a locker room or, more commonly, is simply sporting a sweatband or jockstrap or shorts and shirt. Unlike the spike heel, garters, and lace, these items do not have any independent sexual meaning (none of them could neutrally signify something sexual, erotic, or pornographic), but within the context of these photos they are obviously of some sexual purchase. They are at least metonyms for muscularity and masculinity. Although the former in particular is something more obviously achieved, in the photos we are presented with a view which appears more effortless; i.e., we can see signs of the labor involved, the sweat—labor working through its representations—muscularity as a "*sign* of power—natural, achieved, phallic."[13]

But one must return to the thematics of castration and the fetish to unravel their workings in this genre. The fetish is always a production (whether in Marx, Freud, or Baudrillard), invested with qualities which appear magical or with necro-significance. While masking its production value, however, the fetish circulates as exchange value, works through its representations. It recalls, in this case, the missing phallus, and addresses (again through its representations) that *frisson* around investments and losses. And as with the fetishizing of nature, and the phallus in absentia, this sports universe fetishizes a brute physicality through its presence (the suggested character of the *mise en scène* is one of muscular exertion) and in its absence: i.e., the fetish objects stand in for the (still) missing phallus.

Whither the penis? Its value does appear languished in comparison to the phallus and phallic substitutes (the fetish objects or the fetish for the hard muscles, fabrications themselves). These ritualistic adornments present the male body with the phallus it doesn't, and can't, possess. If the fetish is to allay castration fears and restore the expendable penis to the body (typically, of course, of the woman), what is it doing on the body already so disposed toward a penile projection in the flesh? What does this perverse phenomenon suggest about the castration scenario as it pertains to the fetish and the phallic body? It restores difference to a benignly "other" body.

The masculine bodies traffic with each other (and the reader), and the erotic transformation of one body into the desirable object takes sameness and re-presents it, sartorially, as different. Surely this takes us to the limits of (the possibility of) representing desire. Why difference on a body which presents no threat of castration/difference? Why give a man the phallus when penises are there to signify all they can? Any article of clothing (fetish or otherwise) is in intimate contact with not just the skin of the body but also the flesh of the unconscious. And here we are back not so much to the castrating possibilities of the pornographic moment as to the subsuming of the phallus under the cut. Freud notes that the fetish is a precarious balance between affirmation and denial and suggests that it is that balance (the friction, the ambivalence, the movement, the tension, the s(t)imulation) which ensures its enduring performance. If the fetish is the reliable stand-in called upon as reassurance against the threat, why is it in gay porn? One half of the duo is doubly phallicized, thus the fetish cancels out the penis; that is, the fetish on top of the penis, in a manner of equivalence, voids the penis. The fetish thus moves, again, difference into indifference; it sustains otherness, or symbolic castration, on the body.

The oscillations between fetish/nonfetish are akin to its elusive power: it designates something as "there" in absentia, a fragile double which in the case of the phallus is an investment in something which can't be represented anyway. The gay discursive body, in particular, refuses to be "fixed," is at once "other" to the "same."

A subgenre in gay hard-core consists of leather sadomasochistic paraphernalia. In "A Contribution on Fetishism," Balint makes a number of interpretations regarding the dignified (sexual) status of "worthless object[s]," chosen for their ability to induce, and endure, sexual satisfaction. His hypothesis that fetishes that "smell" (i.e., leather) "surely" signify feces is pertinent here.[14] Given the anal-erotic insinuations of the gay discourse, and the aforementioned kinship between feces and the fetish, Balint's point is particularly well suited to the male body swaddled in leather accouterments. If in soft-core the fetish clothing bears the marks of femininity, in hard-core the leather connotes a hyperphallic extension of the body.

But again, the fetish is invested with properties which take over from biological signification. Leather is more typically masculine. Yet Leo Bersani notes the persistence of the "oxymoronic . . . 'leather queen' " (207). In the case of gay hard-core, then, leather puts the "writing" of the body on the most ascetic side of the "cut," that which involves sacrifices to indifference. The leather phallicizes the model with the penis; thus, when two models are together (one with leather and the other without), otherness is structured around illusory possession/nonpossession of the phallus. If both are in leather, the fetish will again cancel out the penis in favor of the phallic simulacrum. This is an indifference which is close to the "cut."

Gay pornography would appear to efface difference in the name of homoerotic impulses. In soft-core, however, the gay body is written as feminine, thus sustaining "otherness" vis-à-vis both biological signification and the reader. And the reader is returned to a phallic referent. In hard-core, otherness is terrorized as difference collapses on the body: the penis and the phallus meet.

The Logical Phallus

Jean-Joseph Goux demonstrates the historical and mythological alignment of the phallus with the principle of substitution, the abstract universal.[15] That is, it is not possession, not being, not (but the conceit of) "one with." As the original simulacrum, charged with the impossibility of symbolizing the missing penis, it succeeds the materiality of the penis ("the replacement of the loss by an idealizing erection") and enters the realm of "intelligible reason (ideas, model, father)" (43, 46). Not only is the penis subsumed under the phallic principle (an effacement of the flesh), but the phallus looks back to the penis and attempts an alignment. The fusion, though, is unattainable, thus an even greater insistence on the illusion of One. This is the logic of the phallus.

As we have seen from the preceding analyses, the pornographic moment is one of differences, differences transgressed, differences deferred. Cracks in the code reveal, though, that difference per se is not phallic. That is, while "otherness" may be polysemic, difference restores the binary, but binary difference is not necessarily an insistence on a violent hierarchy. Phallic logic instead insists on the rational allegiance to the fixedness of the binary opposition, the naturalness of these categories, and in the (non)schemings of desire, returns its representations to the fictive oneness of/with the self. Phallic logic tries to refuse the "non-dit," the "inter-dit," the boundary/incision; phallic logic tries to unincorporate the other, is indifferent to difference.

Kaja Silverman writes: "Sexual difference, through whose binarisms both homosexuality and heterosexuality are conceptualized, cannot be wished or even written away."[16] The challenge for theorizations of difference is not that they take place within a binary construct—a refusal of the sexual binary is linguistically untenable, undesirable even. The problem—and as I have argued, this is what gives straight pornography its apparent viciousness—is that difference isn't left alone. The grand (phallic) narrative insists on converting difference to its own image. That this grates, i.e., that phallic women are to be feared, is worth investigating. So too is another project, currently gaining a lot of attention, and that is the latent homoerotic, and ascetic, impulses which characterize normative masculine subjectivity.

Notes

Introduction

1. Stephen Heath, *The Sexual Fix* (London: Macmillan, 1982).

2. D. N. Rodowick, *The Difficulty of Difference* (New York and London: Routledge, 1991).

3. See his *Semiotics, Romanticism and the Scriptures* (Berlin: Mouton de Gruyter, 1990).

4. The phrase "published daydream" is from Robert Stoller, *Observing the Erotic Imagination* (New Haven: Yale University Press, 1980). I prefer simply "dream" to underscore the less contrived, less conscious machinations of fantasy and memory.

5. Sigmund Freud, *The Interpretation of Dreams*, ed. and trans. James Strachey (New York: Avon Books, 1965 [1900]).

6. Ibid., p. 313.

7. Ibid., p. 212*n*.

8. See, for example, D. N. Rodowick, "The Difficulty of Difference," *Wide Angle* 5:1 (1982); Rodowick, *The Difficulty of Difference;* Ian Green, "Malefunction," *Screen* 25:4–5 (July–October 1984); Robert Young, "The Same Difference," *Screen* 28:3 (Summer 1987); Kaja Silverman, *Male Subjectivty at the Margins* (New York and London: Routledge, 1992); *Camera Obscura* (special issue on the "spectatrix," 1992).

9. The same could be said of, *inter alia*, ideology, discourse, hegemony, the body.

10. See Rodowick, *The Difficulty of Difference,* for a discussion of the misperception of this radical binary in Freud. For correctives see, among others, Silverman, *Male Subjectivity at the Margins;* Jacques Derrida, *Dissemination*, trans. with an Introduction and Additional Notes by Barbara Johnson (Chicago: University of Chicago Press, 1981); Chevalier, *Semiotics, Romanticism and the Scriptures;* Steve Cohan and Ina Rae Hark, eds., *Screening the Male: Exploring Masculinities in Hollywood Cinema* (New York: Routledge, 1993).

11. "Visual Pleasure and Narrative Cinema," *Screen* 16:3 (Autumn 1975), p. 7.

12. Marjorie Garber uses this adage in the context of an analysis of the uses of transvestism in black American culture "as a device deployed to subvert or disempower that culture." *Vested Interests: Cross-Dressing and Cultural Anxiety* (New York: HarperPerennial, 1993), p. 268.

13. Garber, *Vested Interests.*

14. Gayatri Spivak, in a seminar at the Graduate Program in Communications, McGill University, Montreal, 5 March 1993.

15. John Ellis, "Photography/Pornography/Art/Pornography," *Screen* 21:1 (1980).

16. Ibid., p. 88.

17. One example of this kind of intervention, contained in Ellis's article, is an ad for a Fiat which contains the caption "If this car was a lady, it would get its bottom pinched." The spray-painted graffiti response: "If this lady was a car, she'd run you down." I've found other

examples as well (reproduced in postcard form). (1) An ad for a Volvo reads: "To Volvo, a son. 4,397 pounds." The gorilla response: "Better luck next time." (2) An ad for nylon stockings, called "Pins," with the caption "Where would we be without Pins?" The graffiti intervention: "Free of little pricks. Stop needling us." (3) The written message in an ad for shampoo, accompanied by a picture of a woman standing by a tree with the schoolgirl inscription of a heart with initials inside, reads: "Renew his interest in carpentry." The reply: "Saw his head off."

18. Nancy K. Miller, *Getting Personal* (New York: Routledge, 1991), p. 94.

19. Laura Kipnis, "She-Male Fantasies and the Aesthetics of Pornography," in *Dirty Looks: Women, Pornography, Power,* ed. Pamela Church Gibson and Roma Gibson (London: British Film Institute, 1993), p. 142.

1. Pornography and Desire

1. Rosalind Coward, "Sexual Violence and Sexuality," *Feminist Review* 11 (June 1982).

2. Thomas Laqueur, *Making Sex: Body and Gender from the Greeks to Freud* (Cambridge: Harvard University Press, 1992), p. 19.

3. Gregg Blachford, "Looking at Pornography," *Screen Education* 29 (Winter 1978/79); Beverley Brown, "A Feminist Interest in Pornography—Some Modest Proposals," *m/f* 5/6 (1981); Kathy Myers, "Towards a Feminist Erotica," *Camerawork* 24 (March 1982); Kathy Myers, "Fashion 'n' Passion," *Screen* 23:3–4 (September/October 1982); Coward, "Sexual Violence and Sexuality"; Carole S. Vance and Ann Barr Snitow, "Toward a Conversation about Sex in Feminism," *Signs* 10:11 (Autumn 1984); Annette Kuhn, *The Power of the Image: Essays on Representation and Sexuality* (London: Routledge and Kegan Paul, 1985).

4. Blachford, "Looking at Pornography"; Myers, "Towards a Feminist Erotica"; Myers, "Fashion 'n' Passion"; Brown, "A Feminist Interest in Pornography"; Coward, "Sexual Violence and Sexuality"; Kuhn, *The Power of the Image.*

5. Jean Baudrillard, *For a Critique of the Political Economy of the Sign,* trans. Charles Levin (St. Louis, Mo.: Telos, 1981).

6. Jacques Lacan, *Ecrits: A Selection,* trans. Alan Sheridan (New York: W. W. Norton and Co., 1977); Jacques Lacan, *The Four Fundamental Concepts of Psychoanalysis,* trans. Alan Sheridan (New York: W. W. Norton and Co., 1981); Juliet Mitchell and Jacqueline Rose, eds., *Feminine Sexuality: Jacques Lacan and the Ecole Freudienne* (London: Macmillan, 1982); Toril Moi, *Sexual/Textual Politics: Feminist Literary Theory* (London: Methuen, 1985); Jacqueline Rose, "Femininity and Its Discontents," *Feminist Review* 14 (June 1983); Julien Henriques et al., eds., *Changing the Subject: Psychology, Social Regulation and Subjectivity* (London: Methuen, 1984); Kaja Silverman, *The Subject of Semiotics* (New York: Oxford University Press, 1983); Chris Weedon, *Feminist Practice and Poststructuralist Theory* (Oxford: Basil Blackwell, 1987).

7. Jacques M. Chevalier, *Semiotics, Romanticism and the Scriptures* (Berlin: Mouton de Gruyter, 1990).

8. See Dolf Zillman and Jennings Bryant, "Pornography, Sexual Callousness, and the Trivialization of Rape," *Journal of Communications* 32:4 (Autumn 1982), for an example of this type of research. For critiques of behaviorist assumptions and their pseudoscientific underpinnings, see Augustine Brannigan and Sheldon Goldenberg, "The Study of Aggressive Pornography: The Vicissitudes of Relevance," *Critical Studies in Communication* 4:3 (1987); Thelma McCormack, "Making Sense of the Research on Pornography," in *Women against Censorship,* ed. Varda Burstyn (Vancouver: Douglas and McIntyre, 1985). Beryl Kutchinsky is very much a behaviorist but argues that the activity of viewing pornography produces a ca-

thartic effect, the image acting as a surrogate for repressed emotions. See Beryl Kutchinsky, "The Effects of Easy Availability of Pornography on the Incidence of Sex Crimes: The Danish Experience," *Journal of Social Issues* 29 (1973); and for an argument against Kutchinsky's findings, see Ann Diamond, "Pornography and Repression: A Reconsideration," *Signs* 5:4 (Summer 1980).

9. This is exemplified in Robin Morgan's infamous phrase "Pornography is the theory, and rape the practice," from "Theory and Practice: Pornography and Rape," in *Take Back the Night: Women on Pornography*, ed. Laura Lederer (New York: William Morrow, 1980).

10. Among the classics in this vein are Andrea Dworkin, *Pornography: Men Possessing Women* (New York: Perigree, 1981); Susan Griffin, *Pornography and Silence: Culture's Revenge against Nature* (New York: Harper and Row, 1981); Lederer, *Take Back the Night;* Susanne Kappeler, *The Pornography of Representation* (Minneapolis: The University of Minnesota Press, 1986).

11. Susan Barrowclough, "Not a Love Story," *Screen* 23:5 (November/December 1982).

12. Dworkin, *Pornography*, pp. 13–14.

13. Michel Foucault, *The History of Sexuality, Volume 1* (New York: Vintage, 1980).

14. Ibid.

15. Ibid.; Hubert L. Dreyfus and Paul Rabinow, *Michel Foucault: Beyond Structuralism and Hermeneutics* (Sussex: The Harvester Press, 1982).

16. Michel Foucault, "Introduction," in *Herculine Barbin: Being the Recently Discovered Memoirs of a Nineteenth-Century French Hermaphrodite*, trans. Richard McDougall (New York: Pantheon, 1980).

17. Stephen Heath, *The Sexual Fix* (London: Macmillan, 1982), p. 78.

18. Foucault, "Introduction," p. viii.

19. See also Laqueur, *Making Sex*.

20. Foucault, "Introduction," pp. vii, viii.

21. Frank Mort, "The Domain of the Sexual," *Screen Education* 36 (Autumn 1980).

22. Foucault, *The History of Sexuality*, p. 26.

23. See Dreyfus and Rabinow, *Michel Foucault;* Mark Cousins and Athar Hussain, *Michel Foucault* (New York: St. Martin's Press, 1984); Greg Ostrander, "Foucault's Disappearing Body," *Canadian Journal of Political and Social Theory* 11:1–2 (Spring 1987).

24. See Foucault, *The History of Sexuality*, and Dreyfus and Rabinow, *Michel Foucault*, for an elaboration of the "body" and "sex," determined first by disciplinary technologies (control of productive populations, generalized surveillance, etc.) and then gradually by a proliferation of official "sexualities." See the following for discussions of the utility of Foucault for contemporary feminism: N. P. Ricci, "The End/s of Woman," *Canadian Journal of Political and Social Theory* 11:3 (Autumn 1987); Jana Sawicki, *Disciplining Foucault: Feminism, Power and the Body* (New York: Routledge, 1991); Irene Diamond and Lee Quinby, eds., *Feminism and Foucault: Reflections on Resistance* (Boston: Northeastern University Press, 1988).

25. Linda Williams, *Hard Core: Power, Pleasure and the "Frenzy of the Visible"* (Berkeley: University of California Press, 1989).

26. Luce Irigaray, *Speculum of the Other Woman*, trans. Gillian C. Gill (Ithaca: Cornell University Press, 1986).

27. Ibid.; see Williams, *Hard Core*, pp. 53–55 and 116–17, for a discussion of Irigaray. See also Luce Irigaray, *This Sex Which Is Not One*, trans. Catherine Porter with Carolyn Burke (Ithaca: Cornell University Press, 1985).

28. Laqueur, *Making Sex*, chap. 2, "Destiny Is Anatomy."

29. In Freud's work, of course, the recognition of difference is a visual moment. See, *inter alia*, "Some Psychical Consequences of the Anatomical Distinction between the Sexes,"

in *On Sexuality,* ed. Angela Richards, trans. James Strachey (Harmondsworth: Penguin, 1983 [1925]). Kaja Silverman, via her reworking of Freud and Lacan, argues that scenarios of castration are founded in the induction into linguistic signification. See *The Acoustic Mirror: The Female Voice in Psychoanalysis and Cinema* (Bloomington: Indiana University Press, 1988).

30. See Judith Butler, *Gender Trouble: Feminism and the Subversion of Identity* (New York: Routledge, 1990), for a critique of tropes in the work of Foucault.

31. Linda Williams, "Film Body: An Implantation of Perversions," *Cine-Tracts* 8:4 (Winter 1981), p. 27.

32. Williams, *Hard-Core,* chap. 4. A similar version of this chapter appears in *For Adult Users Only: The Dilemma of Violent Pornography,* ed. Susan Gubar and Joan Hoff (Bloomington: Indiana University Press, 1989).

33. Jean Baudrillard writes of the fetish, too, but his very provocative discussion stresses the fetish for simulation and consequently absence or the "unseen," though this still relies on a metaphor of vision. See *For a Critique of the Political Economy of the Sign,* chap. 3.

34. Karl Marx, *The German Ideology,* ed. C. J. Arthur (New York: International Publishers, 1970 [1846]); Karl Marx, "The Fetishism of Commodities and the Secret Thereof," in *Capital,* vol. 1, ed. Frederick Engels, trans. Samuel Moore and Edward Aveling (New York: International Publishers, 1977 [1887]).

35. Marx, *The German Ideology,* p. 47.

36. Marx, *Capital,* vol. 1, p. 76.

37. Ibid., pp. 71–72.

38. Colin Mercer, "A Poverty of Desire: Pleasure and Popular Politics," in *Formations of Pleasure,* ed. the Formations Collective (London: Routledge, 1983), p. 93.

39. Sigmund Freud, "Fetishism," in *On Sexuality,* ed. Angela Richards, trans. James Strachey (Harmondsworth: Penguin, 1983 [1927]).

40. Baudrillard, *For a Critique of the Political Economy of the Sign,* p. 91.

41. D. N. Rodowick, "Vision, Desire and the Film Text," *Camera Obscura* 6 (1980); D. N. Rodowick, "The Difficulty of Difference," *Wide Angle* 5:1 (1982); D. N. Rodowick, *The Difficulty of Difference: Psychoanalysis, Sexual Difference and Film Theory* (New York: Routledge, 1991). Kaja Silverman, "Fassbinder and Lacan: A Reconsideration of Gaze, Look, and Image," *Camera Obscura* 19 (January 1989), reprinted as chapter 3 in *Male Subjectivity at the Margins* (New York and London: Routledge, 1992).

42. Elizabeth Wilson, *Adorned in Dreams: Fashion and Modernity* (London: Virago, 1985), p. 20.

43. Berkeley Kaite, "Reading the Body Textual: The Shoe and Fetish Relations in Soft and Hard-Core," *The American Journal of Semiotics* 6:4 (1989).

44. Williams, *Hard Core,* p. 108.

45. Gertrud Koch looks at the history of the pornographic film genre in Germany and observes that when pornographic viewing moved from brothel to cinema, the epistemological eye was privileged, involving a reconfiguration of the senses. "The Body's Shadow Realm," in *Dirty Looks: Women, Pornography, Power,* ed. Pamela Church Gibson and Roma Gibson (London: British Film Institute, 1993).

46. Peter Dews, "The 'Nouvelle Philosophie' and Foucault," *Economy and Society* 8:2 (May 1979).

47. I am using the word "perverse" here in the way suggested by Kaja Silverman in her discussion of male masochism. That is to say, "perverse" as "negation of the binarisms." *Male Subjectivity at the Margins,* p. 185.

48. In that sense I am both with and not with Baudrillard on "seduction." See Baudrillard, *Seduction,* trans. Brian Singer (Montreal: New World Perspectives, 1990); Brian Singer, "Baudrillard's Seduction," *Canadian Journal of Political and Social Theory* 15:1–2 and 3 (1991);

Louise Burchill, "Either/Or: Peripeteia of an Alternative in Jean Baudrillard's *de la Seduction*," in *Seduced and Abandoned: The Baudrillard Scene,* ed. André Frankovits (Australia and New York: Stonemoss Services and Semiotext(e), Inc., 1984).

49. See, for example, Annette Kuhn, *Women's Pictures: Feminism and Cinema* (London: Routledge and Kegan Paul, 1982); Kuhn, *The Power of the Image.*

50. Christian Metz, "The Imaginary Signifier," *Screen* 16:2 (Summer 1975).

51. Stuart Hall, "Recent Developments in Theories of Language and Ideology: A Critical Note," in *Culture, Media, Language,* ed. Stuart Hall et al. (London: Hutchinson, 1981); Dave Morley, "Texts, Readers, Subjects," in ibid.

52. Susan Sontag, "The Pornographic Imagination," in *Styles of Radical Will* (New York: Farrar, Strauss and Giroux, 1976); Susan Gubar, "Representing Pornography: Feminism, Criticism and Depictions of Female Violation," *Critical Inquiry* 13 (Summer 1987); Kuhn, *The Power of the Image.*

53. Hall, "Recent Developments in Theories of Language and Ideology," p. 157.

54. Moi, *Sexual/Textual Politics,* p. 8.

55. Williams, *Hard Core;* Linda Williams, "Second Thoughts on *Hard Core:* American Obscenity Law and the Scapegoating of Deviance," in *Dirty Looks: Women, Pornography, Power,* ed. Pamela Church Gibson and Roma Gibson (London: British Film Institute, 1993); Laura Kipnis, "(Male) Desire and (Female) Disgust: Reading *Hustler,*" in *Cultural Studies,* ed. Lawrence Grossberg, Cary Nelson, and Paula Treichler (New York: Routledge, 1991); Chris Straayer, "The She-man: Postmodern Bi-sexed Performance in Film and Video," *Screen* 3 :3 (Autumn 1990); Cindy Patton, "Hegemony and Orgasm—Or the Instability of Heterosexual Pornography," *Screen* 30:1 and 2 (Winter/Spring 1989).

56. Patton, "Hegemony and Orgasm," p. 105.

57. Elsewhere this is referred to as "taking the risk of essence" and is similar to what I mean here. Gayatri Chakravorty Spivak writes, for example, "In that kind of work which is not against essentialism but which completely paralyzes the grid, it is my task as a reader, as it is with deconstruction, to read and run with it somewhere else. It is my task as a reader to see where in that grid there are spaces where, in fact, 'woman' oozes away. Essences, it seems to me, are just a kind of content. All content is not essence. Why be so nervous about it? Why not demote the word 'essence,' because without a minimalizable essence, an essence as *ce qui reste,* as essence as what remains, there is no exchange. Difference articulates these negotiable essences." *Outside in the Teaching Machine* (New York and London: Routledge, 1993), p. 18.

58. See Chevalier, *Semiotics, Romanticism and the Scriptures,* for a discussion of the "logical plotting of sign relations . . . the devious 'schemings of language' " (p. 6).

59. Kathy E. Ferguson, *The Man Question: Visions of Subjectivity in Feminist Theory* (Berkeley: University of California Press, 1993), p. 27. See Jacques Derrida, "Plato's Pharmacy," in *Dissemination,* trans. Barbara Johnson (Chicago: University of Chicago Press, 1981); and Peter Brunette and David Wills, *Screen Play: Derrida and Film Theory* (Princeton: Princeton University Press, 1989).

60. Brown, "A Feminist Interest in Pornography," p. 9. An example of the deployment of the "everyday" is offered in Janice Winship's study of the signifying function of hands in advertisements. Her argument is that the seemingly simple use of the hand relies on certain mythical associations (in the Barthesian sense) of "natural" sexuality, or the "natural" work world of men and the "natural" domesticity of women. In problematizing the "obvious," Winship provides a particularly useful example of a semiotic method. Janice Winship, "Handling Sex," *Media, Culture and Society* 3:1 (January 1981), reprinted in *Looking On: Images of Femininity in the Visual Arts and Media,* ed. Rosemary Betterton (London: Pandora, 1987).

61. See Brown, "A Feminist Interest in Pornography"; Myers, "Fashion 'n' Passion"; Myers, "Towards a Feminist Erotica"; Williams, *Hard Core.*

62. Christian Metz, "Photography and Fetish," *October* 34 (Fall 1985), p. 82.

63. Susan Sontag, *On Photography* (New York: Delta, 1977).

64. Brown, "A Feminist Interest in Pornography."

65. Coward, "Sexual Violence and Sexuality."

66. Roland Barthes, *Camera Lucida,* trans. Richard Howard (New York: Hill and Wang, 1981); Ros Coward, Yve Lomax, and Kathy Myers, "Behind the Fragments: A Conversation with Ros Coward, Yve Lomax and Kathy Myers," *Camerawork* (November 1982).

67. Gloria Steinem, "Erotica and Pornography: A Clear and Present Difference," in Lederer, ed., *Take Back the Night;* Jillian Ridington, "Discussion Paper on Pornography," prepared for the National Action Committee on the Status of Women, March 1983.

68. Brown, "A Feminist Interest in Pornography"; Lesley Stern, "The Body as Evidence," *Screen* 23:5 (November/December 1982).

69. Steinem, "Erotica and Pornography."

70. Ibid., p. 37.

71. Pornography is frequently denounced on the grounds that the (female) models are unwilling participants in the job of creating the photo or film. Linda Lovelace's account of her time as a porn actress (*Ordeal* [New York: Berkley Books, 1981]) and the even more dramatic invocation of fictive "snuff" films, in which women are supposedly murdered (in Lederer, ed., *Take Back the Night*), are examples often used to support the more global definition of pornography as "degrading" and "dehumanizing." This absorption of the labor process into the artifact is another instance of a confusion of the "representation" and the "real." Even if the stories of Lovelace are true, it is a common turn of bourgeois logic to equate the utterance with the author, and vice versa. What is left out of the equation is the recognition that the mass-circulated photograph is, in many ways, distinct from its conditions of production. See Lynne Segal, "Sweet Sorrows, Painful Pleasures: Pornography and the Perils of Heterosexual Desire," in *Sex Exposed: Sexuality and the Pornography Debate,* ed. Lynne Segal and Mary McIntosh (New Brunswick, N.J.: Rutgers University Press, 1993). See also, in *Sex Exposed,* "Gonad the Barbarian and the Venus Flytrap: Portraying the Female and Male Orgasm," by Anne McClintock. McClintock usefully notes that in *Ordeal* Linda Marchiano (Lovelace) explicitly states that she endured "marital battery" at the hands of her husband, *not* the director of *Deep Throat,* "in the 'privacy' of their marital nightmare," and not on the set of *Deep Throat* (p. 129). As well, modern surveillance in most workplaces "insists" on the self-production of a certain "look" to promote the image of the corporation or business. This is not unique to the sex trades. See Sam Ion, *Dear Sam: Advice to the Working Woman* (Toronto: Personal Library Publishers, 1980).

72. Walter Benjamin, "The Work of Art in the Age of Mechanical Reproduction," in *Illuminations,* ed. Hannah Arendt, trans. Harry Zohn (London: Jonathan Cape, 1955).

73. Janet Wolff discusses the concept of the author, artistic value, and art as the production of ideology in *The Social Production of Art* (London: Macmillan, 1981) and *Aesthetics and the Sociology of Art* (London: George Allen and Unwin, 1983). The technique of the photograph has been placed at the center of attention in postmodern analysis to the "death of the author." See, for example, Abigail Solomon-Godeau, "Winning the Game When the Rules Have Been Changed: Art Photography and Postmodernism," *Screen* 25:6 (November/December 1984); Douglas Crimp, "The Photographic Activity of Postmodernism," *October* 15 (Winter 1980); Hal Foster, *Recodings: Art, Spectacle, Cultural Politics* (Port Townsend, Wash.: Bay Press, 1985); Victor Burgin, "Photography, Fantasy, Fiction," in *Thinking Photography* (London: Macmillan, 1982); Victor Burgin, "Seeing Sense," in *Language, Image, Media,* ed. Howard Davis and Paul Walton (Oxford: Basil Blackwell, 1983); Victor Burgin, *The End of Art Theory: Criticism and Postmodernity* (Atlantic Highlands, N.J.: Humanities Press International, 1986).

74. "Fashion 'n' Passion."

75. See Tony Benn, "Perfect Body: Perfect Production. The Nudes of Robert Mapplethorpe and Arthur Tress," *Camerawork* (November 1982); Judith Butler, "The Force of Fantasy: Feminism, Mapplethorpe and Discursive Excess," *differences* 2:2 (1990); Kobena Mercer, "Just Looking for Trouble: Robert Mapplethorpe and Fantasies of Race," in *Sex Exposed: Sexuality and the Pornography Debate,* ed. Lynne Segal and Mary McIntosh (New Brunswick, N.J.: Rutgers University Press, 1993).

76. A clerk in a Hull, Quebec, "boutique" that sells magazines, videos, sex aids, and lingerie told me that customers demand magazines with color photos. In some instances (for example, *TV House Party,* which I purchased there) black and white photos are contained inside, but the magazine itself is covered with a cellophane wrapper, making prepurchase inspection impossible. The clerk indicated that customers, upon returning to the store, complain that there aren't enough color photos inside.

77. Or, in the words of B. Ruby Rich: "If I like it, it's erotica; if you like it, it's pornographic." "Anti-Porn: Soft Issue, Hard World," *Feminist Review* 3 (Spring 1983).

78. Brown, "A Feminist Interest in Pornography."

79. Ridington, "Discussion Paper"; see also, for a critique of this position, Kipnis, "(Male) Desire and (Female) Disgust."

80. Angela Carter, *The Sadeian Woman* (London: Virago, 1979), p. 10.

81. Laura Kipnis, "Reading *Hustler,*" in *Cultural Studies,* ed. Lawrence Grossberg, Paula Treichler, and Cary Nelson (New York: Routledge, 1992).

82. Ibid.

83. Chevalier, *Semiotics, Romanticism and the Scriptures.*

84. See, among others, Jacques Derrida, "Structure, Sign, and Play in the Discourse of the Human Sciences," in *Writing and Difference* (Chicago: University of Chicago Press, 1978).

85. Chevalier, *Semiotics, Romanticism and the Scriptures,* pp. 46–47.

86. Ibid., p. 72.

87. Roland Barthes, *Image-Music-Text,* essays selected and trans. Stephen Heath (Glasgow: Fontana, 1977); Burgin, "Photography, Fantasy, Fiction"; Burgin, "Seeing Sense"; Laura Mulvey, "Visual Pleasure and Narrative Cinema," *Screen* 16:3 (Autumn 1975); Chevalier, *Semiotics, Romanticism and the Scriptures;* Brunette and Wills, *Screen Play.*

88. Burgin, "Seeing Sense," p. 226.

89. Stern, "The Body as Evidence," p. 8.

90. Fredric Jameson, "Postmodernism, or the Cultural Logic of Late Capitalism," *New Left Review* 146 (July–August 1984), p. 66.

91. Jean Baudrillard, "Forgetting Foucault," *Humanities in Society* 3:1 (1980), p. 89n.

92. See, for example, Lisa Henderson, "Lesbian Pornography: Cultural Transgression and Sexual Demystification," in *New Lesbian Criticism: Literary and Cultural Readings,* ed. and introduced by Sally Munt (New York: Columbia University Press, 1992); Terralee Bensinger, "Lesbian Pornography: The Re/Making of (a) Community," *Discourse* 15:1 (Fall 1992); the Samois Collective, eds., *Coming to Power: Writings and Graphics on Lesbian S/M* (Boston: Alyson Publishing Inc., 1982).

93. Andrew Ross, in *No Respect: Intellectuals and Popular Culture* (New York: Routledge, 1989).

94. Linda Williams discusses some of the problems in assuming pornography is a monolith in "Second Thoughts on *Hard Core.*" See also Patton, "Hegemony and Orgasm."

95. See Jean-Joseph Goux, "The Phallus: Masculine Identity and the 'Exchange of Women,'" *differences* 4:1 (1992), for a discussion of the "trials of dismemberment" in the phallic metaphor and the ensuing crisis of authenticity.

96. John Berger, *Ways of Seeing* (Harmondsworth: British Broadcasting Corp. and Penguin, 1972).

97. Heath, *The Sexual Fix.*

98. Claire Pajaczkowska, "The Heterosexual Presumption: A Contribution to the Debate on Pornography," *Screen* 22:1 (1981), p. 83.

99. Freud, "Fetishism"; Mulvey, "Visual Pleasure and Narrative Cinema"; John Ellis, "Photography/Pornography/Art/Pornography," *Screen* 21:1 (Spring 1980); Pajaczkowska, "The Heterosexual Presumption"; Susan Lurie, "The Construction of the Castrated Woman in Psychoanalysis and Cinema," *Discourse* 4 (Winter 1981/82).

100. Elizabeth Wilson, *What Is to Be Done about Violence against Women?* (Harmondsworth: Penguin, 1983), p. 166.

101. Kuhn, *The Power of the Image,* p. 35.

102. Andy Moye, "Pornography," in *The Sexuality of Men,* ed. Andy Metcalfe and Martin Humphries (London: Pluto Press, 1985); Susan Gubar, "Representing Pornography: Feminism, Criticism and Depictions of Female Violation," *Critical Inquiry* 13 (Summer 1987); Lynne Segal, *Is the Future Female? Troubled Thoughts on Contemporary Feminism* (London: Virago, 1987).

103. Pajaczkowska, "The Heterosexual Presumption"; Barrowclough, "Not a Love Story."

104. Gilles Deleuze, *Masochism: Coldness and Cruelty,* trans. Jean McNeil (New York: Zone Books, 1991). Deleuze writes that the fetish "belongs" to masochism, rather than the sadistic impulses to which it is usually assigned. He also insists on the radical separation of sadism and masochism. I emphasize a number of confusions, among them the longing and wishful surrender in any negotiation of subjective differentiation, and the simulation of difference necessary for seduction. Symbolic difference, especially realized in linguistic signification, is subject to phallic, oedipal, law. See Rodowick, *The Difficulty of Difference,* chap. 1; and Williams, *Hard Core,* pp. 211–14.

105. Deleuze, *Masochism,* p. 60.

106. "It is argued, justifiably, that the masochist is not a strange being who finds pleasure in pain, but that he is like everyone else, and finds pleasure where others do, the simple difference being that for him pain, punishment or humiliation are necessary prerequisites to obtaining gratification. However, this mechanism remains incomprehensible if it is not related to the form and in particular to the temporal form that makes it possible. Thus it is a mistake to treat the pleasure-pain complex as a raw material able intrinsically to lend itself to any transformation, beginning with the alleged transformation of sadism into masochism. Formally speaking, masochism is a state of waiting; the masochist experiences waiting in its pure form. Pure waiting divides naturally into two simultaneous currents, the first representing what is awaited, something essentially tardy, always late and always postponed, the second representing something that is expected and on which depends the speeding up of the awaited object. It is inevitable that such a form, such a rhythmic division of time into two streams, would be 'filled' by the particular combinations of pleasure and pain. For at the same time as pain fulfills what is expected, it becomes possible for pleasure to fulfill what is awaited. The masochist waits for pleasure as something that is bound to be late, and expects pain as the condition that will finally ensure (both physically and morally) the advent of pleasure. He therefore postpones pleasure in expectation of the pain which will make gratification possible. The anxiety of the masochist divides therefore into an indefinite awaiting of pleasure and an intense expectation of pain" (ibid., p. 71).

107. Gaylyn Studlar, *In the Realm of Pleasure: von Sternberg, Dietrich, and the Masochistic Aesthetic* (Urbana and Chicago: University of Illinois Press, 1988). Studlar is of course refusing Laura Mulvey's thesis in "Visual Pleasure and Narrative Cinema." See Silverman, *Male*

Subjectivity at the Margins; Williams, *Hard Core;* and Rodowick, *The Difficulty of Difference,* for critical discussions of Studlar.

108. Most important critiques, from a different orientation and with different conclusions, are offered by Kaja Silverman in "Masochism and Subjectivity," *Framework* 12 (Winter 1979); *The Acoustic Mirror;* and *Male Subjectivity at the Margins,* especially chap. 3.

109. Patton, "Hegemony and Orgasm," p. 104.

110. The quote is from Kaja Silverman in a critique of Gaylyn Studlar's Deleuzian-based conception of masochism. Silverman argues that the model privileges "actual" parents over symbolic law. *Male Subjectivity at the Margins,* p. 417n50.

111. Sigmund Freud, "A Child Is Being Beaten," in *The Standard Edition of the Complete Works of Sigmund Freud,* trans. James Strachey, vol. 17 (London: Hogarth Press, 1968 [1919]). Freud writes: "As regards the early and simple phantasies which could not be obviously traced to the influence of school impressions or of scenes taken from books, further information would have been welcome. Who was the child that was being beaten? The one who was himself producing the phantasy or another? Was it always the same child or as often as not a different one? Who was it that was beating the child? A grown-up person? And if so, who? Or did the child imagine that he himself was beating another one? Nothing could be ascertained that threw any light upon all these questions—only the hesitant reply: 'I know nothing more about it: a child is being beaten.'

Enquiries as to the sex of the child that was being beaten met with more success, but none the less brought no enlightenment. Sometimes the answer was: 'I don't know,' or 'It doesn't matter which.' But the point to which the questions were directed, the discovery of some constant relation between the sex of the child producing the phantasy and that of the child that was being beaten, was never established. Now and again another characteristic detail of the content of the phantasy came to light: 'A small child is being beaten on its naked bottom.'

In these circumstances it was impossible at first even to decide whether the pleasure attaching to the beating-phantasy was to be described as sadistic or masochistic" (p. 181).

112. See Rodowick, *The Difficulty of Difference;* Parveen Adams, "Per Os(cillation)," *Camera Obscura* 17 (May 1988); Kaja Silverman, "Masochism and Male Subjectivity," *Camera Obscura* 17 (May 1988); Teresa Brennan, *The Interpretation of the Flesh: Freud and Femininity* (London and New York: Routledge, 1992).

113. Silverman, "Masochism and Male Subjectivity," p. 32. The "cut" is from Silverman, "Masochism and Subjectivity."

114. Silverman, "Masochism and Male Subjectivity," p. 32. I have substituted "transgression" for "perversion" in the original.

115. Chevalier, *Semiotics, Romanticism and the Scriptures.* The book is a "translation" of Longfellow's poem "Evangeline" which considers the explicit, the implicit, and the illicit in the process of symboling, that is, "the fivefold bar, of time, logic, morality, repression and transgression in the act of coding" (p. 67).

116. "Rewards must be offered in compensation for the sufferings endured by virgins, widows, the faithful and all other models of sexual virtue. Logically, promises made to models of chastity must be as alluring as the pleasures renounced, if not more enticing than the joys of sin. The model woman is entitled to live in the hope of receiving all the blessings that the 'harlot' fails to preserve because she never deserved. Blessings of heaven on earth granted at the beginning or at the end of time point the way to what Nietzsche called 'the godly innocence of evil.' Concessions to the flesh must be made if only by way of sublimation—letting signs of Eros be recovered from beneath the language of the ancient Logos." Chevalier, *Semiotics, Romanticism and the Scriptures,* p. 7

117. Ibid., p. 4.

118. Ibid., p. 6.

119. Ibid., pp. 6–7.

120. Lynne Segal makes this point also, in "Sweet Sorrows, Painful Pleasures."

121. Silverman, "Masochism and Subjectivity."

122. Ibid.

123. Stephen Heath, *Questions of Cinema* (Bloomington: Indiana University Press, 1981), pp. 87, 90.

124. Jacques-Alain Miller, "Suture (Elements of the Logic of the Signifier)," *Screen* 18:4 (Winter 1977/78).

125. Silverman, *The Acoustic Mirror*, p. 10.

126. Carol Clover discusses, among other things, spectatorship, gender confusions, and the thrill of horror in the horror film, in *Men, Women, and Chain Saws: Gender in the Modern Horror Film* (Princeton: Princeton University Press, 1992).

127. Jacqueline Rose, "The Imaginary," in *Sexuality in the Field of Vision* (London: Verso, 1986), p. 174.

128. Kaja Silverman is careful to distinguish between the "look" and the "gaze," arguing that a decidedly political consideration of the cultural "pictures" through which we see ourselves would privilege the theoretical separation of these terms, in the way that Lacan insists on the noncoincidence of the penis and phallus. The "gaze" is aligned with cultural spectacle, cultural mirrors, and is characterized by exteriority; the "look" (or the "eye") masquerades for the gaze. See "Fassbinder and Lacan."

129. See Lacan, *Ecrits*.

130. Silverman, *The Subject of Semiotics*, p. 160.

131. Lacan, *The Four Fundamental Concepts of Psychoanalysis*, p. 203ff.

132. Ibid., pp. 204–205.

133. Jane Gallop, *Reading Lacan* (Ithaca: Cornell University Press, 1985), p. 79.

134. Ibid., p. 78.

135. Ibid., p. 80.

136. Ibid., pp. 80–81.

137. Metz, "The Imaginary Signifier," p. 15.

138. Lacan, *Ecrits*, pp. 154, 298; Fredric Jameson, "Imaginary and Symbolic in Lacan: Marxism, Psychoanalytic Criticism and the Problem of the Subject," *Yale French Studies* 55/56 (1977); Chris Weedon, Andrew Tolson, and Frank Mort, "Theories of Language and Subjectivity," in *Culture, Media, Language*, ed. Stuart Hall et al. (London: Hutchinson, 1981).

139. This departs, of course, from Studlar's formulation of masochism. I am more convinced when Silverman writes that the pre-oedipal is "read" only through the filter of symbolic and linguistic meaning.

140. Jameson, "Imaginary and Symbolic in Lacan," p. 326.

141. Ibid., p. 362.

142. Lacan, *Ecrits*, p. 67.

143. Ibid., pp. 150, 152, 153.

144. Jameson, "Imaginary and Symbolic in Lacan."

145. Anika Lemaire, *Jacques Lacan*, trans. David Macey (London: Routledge and Kegan Paul, 1977), p. 929.

146. Jameson, "Imaginary and Symbolic in Lacan," p. 363.

147. Lacan, *Ecrits*, p. 316; Lacan, *The Four Fundamental Concepts of Psychoanalysis*, pp. 207, 236.

148. Lacan, *Ecrits*, p. 299.

149. Lacan, *The Four Fundamental Concepts of Psychoanalysis*, p. 153.

150. Lacan, *Ecrits*, p. 299.

151. Lacan, *The Four Fundamental Concepts of Psychoanalysis*, p. 43.

152. Ibid., p. 206.

153. Ibid., p. 237.

154. Ibid., p. 22.

155. Chevalier, *Semiotics, Romanticism and the Scriptures.*

156. Lacan, *The Four Fundamental Concepts of Psychoanalysis*, p. 237.

157. Jameson, "Imaginary and Symbolic in Lacan," p. 359.

158. Lacan, *The Four Fundamental Concepts of Psychoanalysis*, p. 206.

159. Lacan, *Ecrits*, p. 314.

160. Ibid.

161. Ibid., pp. 314–15.

162. See ibid., p. 154; and Silverman, "Masochism and Subjectivity" and *The Acoustic Mirror.*

163. Sigmund Freud, "Beyond the Pleasure Principle," in *A General Selection from the Works of Sigmund Freud*, ed. John Rickman and Charles Brenner (Garden City, N.Y.: Doubleday Anchor Books, 1957 [1920]); Silverman, "Masochism and Subjectivity" and *The Acoustic Mirror.*

164. Lacan, *The Four Fundamental Concepts of Psychoanalysis*, p. 218.

165. Silverman, "Masochism and Subjectivity," p. 3.

166. Ibid.

167. Rose, "The Imaginary," p. 175.

168. Ibid.

169. Sigmund Freud, "The Dissolution of the Oedipus Complex," in *On Sexuality*, ed. Angela Richards, trans. James Strachey (Harmondsworth: Penguin, 1983 [1924]), p. 318.

170. Lacan, *Ecrits*, pp. 281–91.

171. Ibid., p. 288.

172. Jacqueline Rose, "Introduction II," in Mitchell and Rose, eds., *Feminine Sexuality*, p. 38.

173. See Silverman, *Male Subjectivity at the Margins.*

174. Lacan, *Ecrits*, p. 218.

175. René Girard writes of rivals and the mimetic nature of "triangular desire." His account embellishes the idea of the displacements involved in desire. However, it does not consider anatomy, the body's needs, or the lawful imposition of language. See *To Double Business Bound: Essays on Literature, Mimesis and Anthropology* (Baltimore: Johns Hopkins University Press, 1978).

176. Rose, "Introduction II," p. 38.

177. Lacan, *The Four Fundamental Concepts of Psychoanalysis*, p. 103.

178. Silverman, *The Acoustic Mirror*, p. 1.

179. In Silverman's phrase, the masculine subject "disburdens himself of lack." This is elaborated further in *Male Subjectivity at the Margins.* Her arguments are brilliant and most compelling. Although Lacan seems to use "lack" and "loss" interchangeably, I use "loss" instead of "lack" to retain a commitment to a dialectics of movement and retrieval, in writing and re-presenting, and the strategies of mimesis.

180. See Jane Gallop, *Thinking through the Body* (New York: Columbia University Press, 1988), pp. 124–33, for a useful discussion of the "necessity and impossibility" of this separation.

181. Silverman, *Male Subjectivity at the Margins.*

182. It is both shocking and disturbing to hear this description (by feminists) explicitly used against other "powerful" female academics (i.e., famous for their books and scholarship). Their clothing style is denounced as "phallic," for instance; I have heard one scholar's eyeliner

described as "phallic." These are hurtful yet telling indictments. It is clear, first of all, that they are motivated by (unacknowledged) envy. These statements also suggest an embedded notion of how a woman or feminist "should" look, act, dress. That women who are successful in what is historically and traditionally the domain of men should receive opprobrium by women who wish the same success for themselves is curious. That these scholars' accomplishments and visibility (and, no doubt, their unapologetic confidence: unfeminine!) are defined as "phallic" indicates the extent to which the penis and phallus attempt an alignment. It indicates that the appropriation of signs of maleness, i.e., angularity, straight lines, leanness, firmness (of mind or body), is designated the appropriate place of men. How *should* women dress and act: in soft and round (uterine) terms? Finally, the designation of a powerful woman as "phallic" is an attack on her femininity, particularly its nurturant potential. How could à woman with a penis have a baby? How could you trust a woman with phallic desire? (Do these academic women resemble Madonna's self-description: do they have a "dick in their brain"?) The label is punishment for not being feminine enough. All that for knowing her mind, being focused and unyielding in her beliefs, appropriating language, writing books, and avoiding "natural" eyes and (natural?) frills.

183. Heath, *Questions of Cinema*, p. 83.

184. Mulvey, "Visual Pleasure and Narrative Cinema," p. 13.

185. Ellis, "Photography/Pornography/Art/Pornography," p. 104.

186. Pajaczkowska, "The Heterosexual Presumption," p. 89.

187. Roland Barthes, *The Grain of the Voice*, trans. Linda Coverdale (New York: Hill and Wang, 1985), p. 173.

188. Goux, "The Phallus," p. 43.

189. Ibid., p. 47.

190. See Silverman, *The Acoustic Mirror*.

191. Lemaire, *Jacques Lacan*, p. 85.

192. Chevalier, *Semiotics, Romanticism and the Scriptures*.

2. Sexual Techniques

1. John Berger, in *Ways of Seeing* (Harmondsworth: British Broadcasting Corp. and Penguin Books, 1972), distinguishes between depictions of the "naked" and the "nude" in artistic traditions. To be naked, he writes (paraphrasing Kenneth Clark), "is simply to be without clothes," while nudity is an art form, drawing from conventions which dress it up; it assumes a number of social disguises. I wouldn't use this distinction and wouldn't go so far as to suggest that a body can be depicted "simply" without clothing and thus rendered almost meaningless. As in medical discourses, for example, the body is still problematized around gender identity, and this is a social construction. Affiliation to the law of sexual difference means there is one identity, not a plurality of sexual identities, thus genitalia become a kind of dressing on the body. Also, Berger writes that the "nude" is more reflexively social as it presupposes a spectator, is put together with the ideal viewer in mind. However, I would argue that all texts invoke a reader and all discourses implicate a "speaker" and a "listener."

2. Linda Nochlin, "Courbet's 'L'Origin du Monde': The Origin without an Original," *October* 37 (Summer 1986), p. 77. Andrea Dworkin, as just one example, writes: "In the male system, women are sex; sex is the whore. The whore is *porn*, the lowest whore, the whore who belongs to all male citizens: the slut, the cunt. Buying her is buying pornography. Having her is having pornography. Seeing her is seeing pornography. Seeing her sex, especially her genitals, is seeing pornography"; and in reference to depictions of pregnant women within certain specialized genres: "The women display themselves, display their sex, display their bellies. The

huge belly is fetishized but the whore behind it stays the same: the cunt showing itself." *Pornography: Men Possessing Women* (New York: Perigree, 1981), pp. 202, 222.

3. Lesley Stern, "The Body as Evidence," *Screen* 23:5 (November/December 1982).

4. Margaret R. Miles, "The Virgin's One Bare Breast: Female Nudity and Religious Meaning in Tuscan Early Renaissance Culture," in *The Female Body in Western Culture: Contemporary Perspectives,* ed. Susan Rubin Suleiman (Cambridge: Harvard University Press, 1986).

5. J. C. Flügel, *The Psychology of Clothes* (New York: International Universities Press, 1931), p. 160.

6. Christian Metz, "Photography and Fetish," *October* 34 (Fall 1985), p. 81.

7. Abigail Solomon-Godeau, "The Legs of the Countess," *October* 39 (Winter 1986), pp. 67–68.

8. Metz, "Photography and Fetish," p. 82.

9. Ibid., p. 84.

10. Ibid., p. 86.

11. Robert C. Bak, in "The Phallic Woman," *The Psychoanalytic Study of the Child* 23 (1968), discusses the "breast-penis equation" in a clinical case; and J. C. Flügel also notes the "unconscious equation of breast and penis . . . the breast is also known sometimes to play a part in the formation of the castration complex," "Polyphallic Symbolism and the Castration Complex," *International Journal of Psychoanalysis* 5 (1924), p. 171.

12. Beverley Brown, "A Feminist Interest in Pornography—Some Modest Proposals," *m/f* 5/6 (1981), p. 5.

13. Sigmund Freud, "The Dissolution of the Oedipus Complex," in *On Sexuality,* ed. Angela Richards, trans. James Strachey (Harmondsworth: Penguin, 1983 [1924]), p. 318.

14. Sigmund Freud, "Fetishism," in *On Sexuality,* ed. Angela Richards, trans. James Strachey (Harmondsworth: Penguin, 1983 [1927]), p. 353.

15. Octave Mannoni, *Clefs pour l'imaginaire* (Paris: Seuil, 1969), quoted in Emily Apter, *Feminizing the Fetish: Psychoanalysis and Narrative Obsession in Turn-of-the-Century France* (Ithaca: Cornell University Press, 1991), p. 14.

16. The phrase "the impossible referent" is from Francette Pacteau, "The Impossible Referent: Representations of the Androgyne," in *Formations of Fantasy,* ed. Victor Burgin, James Donald, and Cora Kaplan (London: Methuen, 1986).

17. D. N. Rodowick, "The Difficulty of Difference," *Wide Angle* 5:1 (1982), p. 85.

18. The phrase is from Carol Clover's "Regardless of Sex: Men, Women, and Power in Early Northern Europe," *Representations* 44 (Fall 1993), p. 2. Clover points out that in Early Norse sagas the "insult," prohibited by law, contains linguistic and cultural associations which pair the male anus with the vagina, suggesting that the "category 'man' is, if anything, even more susceptible to mutation than the category 'woman' " (p. 9).

19. Flügel, *The Psychology of Clothes;* Valerie Steele, *Fashion and Eroticism: Ideals of Feminine Beauty from the Victorian Era to the Jazz Age* (New York: Oxford, 1985).

20. Rosalind Krauss, "Corpus Delicti," *October* 33 (Summer 1985), p. 71.

21. Jacques M. Chevalier, *Semiotics, Romanticism and the Scriptures* (Berlin: Mouton de Gruyter, 1990).

22. Bela Grunberger, "Some Reflections on the Rat Man," *International Journal of Psycho-Analysis* 47 (1966).

23. Krauss, "Corpus Delicti," p. 41.

24. Ibid., p. 34.

25. Nochlin, "Courbet's 'L'Origin du Monde,' " p. 77.

26. Angela Carter, *The Sadeian Woman* (London: Virago, 1979), p. 4.

27. The phrase "This woman is her own capital investment" is from a talk by Linda

Hutcheon, "The Post-Modern Erotic," presented at the "Semiotics of Eroticism" conference sponsored by the Toronto Semiotic Circle and the International Summer Institute for Semiotic and Structural Studies, the University of Toronto, 13 June 1987.

28. The phrase is from *TV Tight Ass,* a pornographic publication which depicts transsexuals in feminine drag.

29. Grunberger, "Some Reflections on the Rat Man."

30. Ibid., p. 164.

31. Stephen Heath, *The Sexual Fix* (London: Macmillan, 1982).

32. Carter, *The Sadeian Woman,* p. 5.

33. Heath, *The Sexual Fix,* p. 22.

34. On "Late Night with David Letterman" sometime in 1993, the word "asshole" was repeated a number of times in a conversation. However, part of the word was bleeped out, and that part was "hole." It is indeed the more vicious half of the word.

35. Grunberger, "Some Reflections on the Rat Man."

36. Paul Smith, "Men in Feminism: Men and Feminist Theory," in *Men in Feminism,* ed. Alice Jardine and Paul Smith (New York: Methuen, 1987), p. 34.

37. Janine Chasseguet-Smirgel, "Reflexions on the Connexions between Perversion and Sadism," *International Journal of Psycho-Analysis* 59 (1978), p. 30.

38. Stephen Heath, "Men in Feminism: Men and Feminist Theory," in *Men in Feminism,* ed. Alice Jardine and Paul Smith (New York: Methuen, 1987), p. 42.

39. Kaja Silverman, *The Acoustic Mirror: The Female Voice in Psychoanalysis and Cinema* (Bloomington: Indiana University Press, 1988).

40. Chasseguet-Smirgel, "Reflexions on the Connexions between Perversion and Sadism."

41. This refers to the title of an article by Leo Bersani in *AIDS: Cultural Analysis, Cultural Activism,* ed. Douglas Crimp (Cambridge, Mass.: MIT Press, 1989). In *Written on the Body* (Toronto: Vintage, 1993), Jeanette Winterson evokes the metaphoric twinning of the anus and death/the grave. She writes of the "return to the hole"; "a great leveller the hole"; "rich and poor occupy the same home at last. Air bounded by mud"; "the hole is a frightful place. A dizzy chasm of loss" (p. 177).

42. Carol Clover and Thomas Laqueur write of the conflation of vagina and anus in different historical, medical, ontological, and linguistic contexts. Both note that these follow from the "one-sex" model of the body, prevalent until around the late eighteenth century. Clover writes: "Certainly, Norse words or periphrases for the vagina are typically usable for the anus, and it is indeed with deprecating reference to the male that such terms are conspicuously attested." In contemporary pornography, the situation is reversed. Here the "male" anus is privileged over, or along with, the vagina. Laqueur notes that in Latin, "vagina" has been used "humorously as 'anus.' " Clover, "Regardless of Sex," p. 12; Thomas Laqueur, *Making Sex: Body and Gender from the Greeks to Freud* (Cambridge: Harvard University Press, 1992), p. 270n60.

43. *The Female Eunuch* (London: Paladin, 1970), p. 254.

44. Cf. Kaja Silverman, "Fragments of a Fashionable Discourse," in *Studies in Entertainment: Critical Approaches to Mass Culture,* ed. Tania Modleski (Bloomington: Indiana University Press, 1986).

45. Theodore Thass-Thienemann writes of the Greek myth "when the woman becomes pregnant by the 'tongues' of fire." *Symbolic Behavior* (New York: Washington Square Press, 1968), p. 247. Carol Clover mentions two Old Norse proverbs in which the "equivalence" of old men and women is rendered through the pairing of the tongue and the sword, and thus the homological pairing of tongue and penis. For example: "*Sonatorrek* itself opens with a

complaint about the difficulty of its erection. . . . 'It is very hard for me to stir my tongue or the steel-yard of the song-weigher.' " "Regardless of Sex," pp. 15–16.

46. Sigmund Freud, "Three Essays on the Theory of Sexuality," in *On Sexuality,* ed. Angela Richards, trans. James Strachey (Harmondsworth: Penguin, 1983 [1905]), p. 69.

47. Jean Baudrillard, *Simulations,* trans. Paul Foss, Paul Patton, and Philip Beitchman (New York: Semiotext(e), 1983), p. 144.

48. See Linda Williams, *Hard Core: Power, Pleasure and the "Frenzy of the Visible"* (Berkeley: University of California Press, 1989).

49. Linda Nochlin, "Eroticism and Female Imagery in Nineteenth Century Art," in *Woman as Sex Object: Studies in Erotic Art, 1730–1970,* ed. Thomas B. Hess and Linda Nochlin (London: Allen Lane, 1973), p. 11.

50. Nochlin offers a humorous version of her own design which reverses the sexual imagery. In her own creation Nochlin has photographed a man, naked but for socks and shoes, who holds a tray of bananas at crotch level. What would be more subversive, though, is if the man carried a tray of apples at crotch level, rendering a femininity to his sexuality.

51. Flügel, *The Psychology of Clothes,* p. 186.

52. Laqueur, *Making Sex,* pp. 94, 269n, 159.

53. Marjorie Garber, *Vested Interests: Cross-Dressing and Cultural Anxiety* (New York: HarperPerennial, 1993), p. 125.

54. Henry Lihn provides a case study in which the subject had fantasies of "being kept in a cage or enslaved by dark-skinned Indian or Negro women whom he obediently served by performing cunnilingus"; cf. "Fetishism: A Case Report," *International Journal of Psycho-Analysis* 51 (1970), p. 353.

55. Freud, "Fetishism," pp. 353–54.

56. Linda Williams, "When the Woman Looks," in *Re-Vision: Essays in Feminist Film Criticism,* ed. Mary Ann Doane, Patricia Mellencamp, and Linda Williams (Frederick, Md.: University Publications of America, 1984).

57. Cf. Rodowick, "The Difficulty of Difference"; Kaja Silverman, "Male Masochism and Subjectivity," presented at the "Semiotics of Eroticism" conference sponsored by the Toronto Semiotic Circle and the Summer Institute for Semiotic and Structural Studies, the University of Toronto, 13 June 1987; Silverman, *The Acoustic Mirror.*

58. See Annette Kuhn, *The Power of the Image: Essays on Representation and Sexuality* (London: Routledge and Kegan Paul, 1985); Chris Straayer, "The She-man: Postmodern Bisexed Performance in Film and Video," *Screen* 31:3 (Autumn 1990).

59. Cf. Frank Mort, "The Domain of the Sexual," *Screen Education* 36 (Autumn 1980).

60. Cf. Judith Butler, *Gender Trouble: Feminism and the Subversion of Identity* (New York: Routledge, 1990).

61. Garber, *Vested Interests.*

62. Catherine Millot, *Horsexe* (New York: Autonomedia, 1990).

63. Pacteau, "The Impossible Referent."

64. See Laura Kipnis's discussion of "TV" self-portraiture, "She-Male Fantasies and the Aesthetics of Pornography," in *Dirty Looks: Women, Pornography, Power,* ed. Pamela Church Gibson and Roma Gibson (London: British Film Institute, 1993).

65. Grunberger, "Some Reflections on the Rat Man."

3. The Gaze

1. See Mary Ann Doane, *The Desire to Desire: The Women's Film of the 1940s* (Bloomington: Indiana University Press, 1987).

2. The introduction to Steve Cohan and Ina Rae Hark, eds., *Screening the Male: Exploring Masculinities in Hollywood Cinema* (London: Routledge, 1993), admirably justifies the "renewed" interest in studying masculinity by challenging the premise of the *The Female Gaze* (a book of essays on female spectatorship), captured in its summary statement: "Men act; women are acted upon. This is patriarchy" (p. 2).

3. For a review of "the gaze" in cultural studies, see Craig Saper, "A Nervous Theory: The Troubling Gaze of Psychoanalysis in Media Studies," *Diacritics* 21:4 (Winter 1991).

4. Laura Mulvey, "Visual Pleasure and Narrative Cinema," *Screen* 16:3 (Autumn 1975), p. 11.

5. E. Ann Kaplan, *Women and Film: Both Sides of the Camera* (New York: Methuen, 1983).

6. See Lynda Nead, *The Female Nude: Art, Obscenity and Sexuality* (London: Routledge, 1992); Mary Ann Doane, "Woman's Stake: Filming the Female Body," *October* 17 (Summer 1981).

7. Mulvey, "Visual Pleasure and Narrative Cinema"; Laura Mulvey, "Afterthoughts on 'Visual Pleasure and Narrative Cinema' Inspired by 'Duel in the Sun,' " *Framework* 15/16/17 (Summer 1981).

8. Mulvey, "Afterthoughts on 'Visual Pleasure and Narrative Cinema' Inspired by 'Duel in the Sun.' "

9. Kaja Silverman, "Fassbinder and Lacan: A Reconsideration of Gaze, Look, and Image," *Camera Obscura* 19 (1989); reprinted as chapter 3 in *Male Subjectivity at the Margins* (New York and London: Routledge, 1992).

10. The phrase "dominant fiction" is discussed in full in *Male Subjectivity at the Margins*. Male "lack" is also addressed in "Masochism and Subjectivity," *Framework* 12 (Winter 1979).

11. D. N. Rodowick, "The Difficulty of Difference," *Wide Angle* 5:1 (1982), p. 7.

12. Jacques Lacan, *The Four Fundamental Concepts of Psychoanalysis,* trans. Alan Sheridan (New York: W. W. Norton and Co., 1981), pp. 93, 92.

13. Roland Barthes, *Camera Lucida,* trans. Richard Howard (New York: Hill and Wang, 1981).

14. Jean-Pierre Oudart, "Cinema and Suture," *Screen* 18:4 (1977/78).

15. Ibid., p. 37.

16. Annette Kuhn, *Women's Pictures: Feminism and Cinema* (London: Routledge and Kegan Paul, 1982).

17. Kaplan, *Women and Film.*

18. Mulvey, "Visual Pleasure and Narrative Cinema," p. 11; Kaplan, *Women and Film;* Paul Willemen, "Letter to John," *Screen* 21:2 (Summer 1980).

19. Kaplan, *Women and Film.*

20. Willemen, "Letter to John," p. 56.

21. Stephen Heath, "Difference," *Screen* 19:3 (Autumn 1978), p. 92.

22. Cf. Linda Williams, "When the Woman Looks," in *Re-Vision: Essays in Feminist Film Criticism*, ed. Mary Ann Doane, Patricia Mellencamp, and Linda Williams (Frederick, Md.: University Publications of America, 1984); Mary Ann Doane, "The Clinical Eye: Medical Discourses in the 'Women's Film' of the 1940s," in *The Female Body in Western Culture: Contemporary Perspectives,* ed. Susan Rubin Suleiman (Cambridge: Harvard University Press, 1986).

23. See Richard A. Kallen and Robert D. Brooks, "The Playmate of the Month: Naked but Nice," *Journal of Popular Culture* 8:2 (Fall 1974).

24. Michel Foucault, *The History of Sexuality, Volume 1* (New York: Vintage, 1980), pp. 48, 47.

25. Mary Ann Caws, "Ladies Shot and Painted: Female Embodiment in Surrealist Art,"

in *The Female Body in Western Culture: Contemporary Perspectives*, ed. Susan Rubin Suleiman (Cambridge: Harvard University Press, 1986), p. 270.

26. Theodore Thass-Thienemann discusses the pairing of eye and window. In several languages, for example, eye and window are equated. Thass-Thienemann refers to several of Shakespeare's phrases, such as "eye's window," "window's of thine eye," "her two blue windows faintly she upheaveth," and "crystall window, open, look out." He writes, "People did not dig out the original meaning from an Old English dictionary when they called the 'window shade' *Venetian blind*. The window totally covered by a shade is *blind* indeed." *Symbolic Behavior* (New York: Washington Square Press, 1968), p. 253.

27. Lacan, *The Four Fundamental Concepts of Psychoanalysis*, pp. 105–15.

28. Thass-Thienemann notes that the "downcast" look "does not mean protection against *intro-spection* or *in-sight*, but serves primarily the aggressive looking impulse, the *expectation* into the outside world" (p. 255); and the look askance can be the evil eye with aggressive intention, "if one glances sidewise, obliquely, with suspicion, disdain, disapproval or distrust" (p. 258).

29. For an interesting analysis of precisely this visual circuit and the figure of the look in the movie *The Pirate*, see D. N. Rodowick, "Vision, Desire, and the Film Text," *Camera Obscura* 6 (1980).

30. Silverman, "Fassbinder and Lacan," p. 77.

31. Hal Foster, *Recodings: Art, Spectacle, Cultural Politics* (Port Townsend, Wash.: Bay Press, 1985), p. 90.

32. See Jean-Joseph Goux, "The Phallus: Masculine Identity and the 'Exchange of Women,' " *differences* 4:1 (1992); and Jean Baudrillard, *Simulations*, trans. Paul Foss, Paul Patton, and Philip Beitchman (New York: Semiotext(e), 1983).

33. Jacques M. Chevalier, *Semiotics, Romanticism and the Scriptures* (Berlin: Mouton de Gruyter, 1990).

34. Rodowick, "The Difficulty of Difference," p. 5.

35. Silverman, "Masochism and Subjectivity," p. 5.

36. Ibid., p. 3.

37. Silverman, "Fassbinder and Lacan," p. 78.

38. Silverman, "Fassbinder and Lacan"; Jacques Lacan, *Ecrits: A Selection*, trans. Alan Sheridan (New York: W. W. Norton and Co., 1977). See Jane Gallop, *Reading Lacan* (Ithaca: Cornell University Press, 1985), for a discussion of the mirror image.

39. Silverman, "Fassbinder and Lacan," p. 3.

40. Malcolm Bowie, "Jacques Lacan," in *Structuralism and Since: From Levi-Strauss to Derrida*, ed. John Sturrock (Oxford: Oxford University Press, 1982), p. 134.

41. Silverman, "Fassbinder and Lacan."

42. Stephen Heath, "On Suture," in *Questions of Cinema* (Bloomington: Indiana University Press, 1981), p. 84; Silverman, "Masochism and Subjectivity."

43. Heath, "On Suture," p. 85.

44. Thematics of castration will be explored in other chapters on the fetish, especially with reference to the assumption that fetish elements which adorn the female body disavow knowledge of castration and therefore allay subsequent fears. I will argue that just as there is no pure desire, fear is equally contradictory and rhetorical.

45. Silverman's argument for de-anthropomorphizing the gaze is perhaps the most eloquent to date. She writes: "If feminist theory has reason to lament that system of representation, it is not because woman so frequently functions as the *object* of desire (we all function simultaneously as subject and object), but because the male look both transfers its own lack to the female subject, and attempts to pass itself off as the gaze"; and "The risk implicit in any politics devoted to what might be described as a 'representational contestation' is that

it will give fresh life to the notion that what is needed are 'positive images' of women, blacks, gays, and other disenfranchised groups, images which all too often work to resubstantialize identity, and even at times to essentialize it" ("Fassbinder and Lacan," pp. 71, 79).

46. Beverley Brown, "A Feminist Interest in Pornography—Some Modest Proposals," *m/f* 5/6 (1981), p. 5.

47. The female model in these photos thus appears to be, among other things, a conduit for a suppressed homoeroticism. Similarly, the written text is narrated by a man, from the point of view of his desire, and is addressed to the male viewer. In other words, this is another example of men talking to men, men reaching out and touching men.

48. See Silverman, *The Acoustic Mirror,* for an elaboration of the argument that the masculine subject "disburdens himself of lack" by placing anatomical and discursive inadequacy onto women.

49. John Ellis, "Photography/Pornography/Art/Pornography," *Screen* 21:1 (Spring 1980).

50. Sigmund Freud, "On Narcissism: An Introduction," in *On Sexuality,* ed. Angela Richards, trans. James Strachey (Harmondsworth: Penguin, 1983 [1914]).

51. Steven Neale, "Masculinity as Spectacle," *Screen* 24:6 (November/December 1983), p. 8, reprinted in Cohan and Hark, eds., *Screening the Male.*

52. Janet Bergstrom in Rodowick, "The Difficulty of Difference," p. 10.

53. See Silverman, "Fassbinder and Lacan," for a discussion of the speciousness of arguments which attempt to reproduce the binary of spectator and spectacle, subject and object.

54. Ibid., p. 74.

55. Neale, "Masculinity as Spectacle," p. 14.

56. Bela Grunberger, "Some Reflections on the Rat Man," *International Journal of Psycho-Analysis* 47 (1966).

57. Ibid., p. 160.

58. Theodore Thass-Thienemann reveals the etymological and cultural associations among closed eyes (the "evil" eye), the tightfisted, and anal retentiveness. See *Symbolic Behavior,* pp. 257–59. Freud of course first established the indelible and enduring connections among money, anger, and shit.

59. Sigmund Freud, "Three Essays on the Theory of Sexuality," in *On Sexuality,* ed. Angela Richards, trans. James Strachey (Harmondsworth: Penguin, 1983 [1905]).

60. Kuhn, *Women's Pictures,* p. 82.

61. Sigmund Freud, "Character and Anal Eroticism," in *On Sexuality,* ed. Angela Richards, trans. James Strachey (Harmondsworth: Penguin, 1983 [1908]), p. 213.

62. Ibid., p. 214.

63. Oudart, "Cinema and Suture," p. 36.

4. The Shoe

1. Elizabeth Wilson, *Adorned in Dreams: Fashion and Modernity* (London: Virago, 1985), p. 20.

2. Ibid., p. 23.

3. Valerie Steele, *Fashion and Eroticism: Ideals of Feminine Beauty from the Victorian Era to the Jazz Age* (New York: Oxford, 1985), p. 193.

4. Steele, *Fashion and Eroticism.*

5. Wilson, *Adorned in Dreams,* pp. 29–30.

6. Quoted in Steele, *Fashion and Eroticism,* p. 192.

7. Steven Marcus, *The Other Victorians: A Study of Sexuality and Pornography in Mid-Nineteenth-Century England* (London: Weidenfeld and Nicholson, 1974).

8. Ibid., pp. 252–65.

9. Ibid., p. 257.

10. J. C. Flügel, *The Psychology of Clothes* (New York: International Universities Press, 1931), p. 161.

11. William A. Rossi, *The Sex Life of the Foot and Shoe* (London: Routledge and Kegan Paul, 1977).

12. Alfredo Zenoni, in "Metaphor and Metonymy in Lacanian Theory," *Enclitic* 5:1 (Spring 1981), provides a useful distinction between metaphoric and metonymic transactions in linguistic chains of signification and the rhetorical mechanisms of condensation and displacement. A metaphor affirms "the resemblance . . . the identity between things"; the resemblance does not precede the metaphor (p. 7). Metonymy refers to the pairing of substitutes, brought into contact through their occurrence within a certain discourse. Zenoni writes: "It is only in so far as the signifieds and the referents are articulated in discourse, and thus placed in relationship with one another, that they can function as signifiers. It is only in so far as there is no signification that things can be metonymized mutually, that they can each function as the *name* (nom) of the others. It is because reality is caught in a net of references that an empty space can designate its contrary, that the peripheral can designate the essential. It is thus on the level of signifying contiguities that the accent can be displaced onto details which are stated only to refer to other contextual elements, and even to the context as a whole" (p. 13).

13. Sigmund Freud, "Fetishism," in *On Sexuality*, ed. Angela Richards, trans. James Strachey (Harmondsworth: Penguin, 1983 [1927]), p. 113; Octave Mannoni, *Clefs pour l'imaginaire* (Paris: Seuil, 1969), quoted in Emily Apter, *Feminizing the Fetish: Psychoanalysis and Narrative Obsession in Turn-of-the-Century France* (Ithaca: Cornell University Press, 1991), p. 14.

14. Susan Sontag, *On Photography* (New York: Delta, 1977); Roland Barthes, *Camera Lucida*, trans. Richard Howard (New York: Hill and Wang, 1981).

15. Christian Metz, "Photography and Fetish," *October* 34 (Fall 1985).

16. Ibid., p. 84.

17. Ibid.

18. Ibid.

19. Quoted in ibid., p. 85.

20. Christina Probert, *Shoes in Vogue since 1910* (New York: Abbeville Publishers, 1981), p. 58.

21. Elizabeth Toomey, "Paris Shoes Have Pointed Heel and Toe," *Toronto Globe and Mail* (28 December 1953).

22. Lee Wright, "Objectifying Gender: The Stiletto Heel," in *A View from the Interior: Feminism, Women and Design*, ed. Judy Attfield and Pat Kirkham (London: The Woman's Press, 1989), p. 11.

23. Toomey, "Paris Shoes Have Pointed Heel and Toe," p. 13.

24. Wright, "Objectifying Gender," pp. 10–11.

25. Ibid., pp. 13–14.

26. Probert, *Shoes in Vogue since 1910*, p. 58; Toomey, "Paris Shoes Have Pointed Heel and Toe," p. 13.

27. Wright, "Objectifying Gender," pp. 14, 15, 17.

28. Steele, *Fashion and Eroticism*, p. 25. The connection between the foot and phallic signification is revealed in an advertisement for condoms, as mentioned in a piece in the *New Yorker:* "The most explicit TV spot developed so far by the Federal Centers for Disease Control featured a young man slipping on a sock and telling viewers, 'That wouldn't really save my life, but there's something as simple that could' " (7 August 1989).

29. One exception I have noted occurs in a hard-core narrative involving the "liberating" of a woman's fantasies. In a final photo, after she has been sexually satisfied, her feet are bare, suggesting she no longer needs to s(t)imulate desire.

30. Bela Grunberger, "Some Reflections on the Rat Man," *International Journal of*

Psycho-Analysis 47 (1966); Janine Chasseguet-Smirgel, "Reflexions on the Connexions between Perversion and Sadism," *International Journal of Psycho-Analysis* 59 (1978).

31. Sigmund Freud, "Three Essays on the Theory of Sexuality," in *On Sexuality,* ed. Angela Richards, trans. James Strachey (Harmondsworth: Penguin, 1983 [1905]), p. 155.

32. Grunberger, "Some Reflections on the Rat Man," pp. 161, 160.

33. Ibid., p. 161*n*3.

34. Ibid., p. 161.

35. Freud, "Three Essays on the Theory of Sexuality." For a discussion of perversions and masochism, see Kaja Silverman, "Masochism and Male Subjectivity," *Camera Obscura* 17 (1988), reprinted in *Male Subjectivity at the Margins* (New York and London: Routledge, 1992).

36. Silverman, *Male Subjectivity at the Margins,* p. 185.

37. Ibid., p. 187.

38. Chasseguet-Smirgel, "Reflexions on the Connexions between Perversion and Sadism," p. 30.

39. Ibid., p. 32.

40. Cf. Grunberger, "Some Reflections on the Rat Man," for a discussion of these traits with respect to the case of the "Rat Man."

41. Flügel, *The Psychology of Clothes,* p. 161*n*.

42. Quoted in Havelock Ellis, *Psychology of Sex* (New York: Emerson Books, 1937), pp. 174, 176.

43. Sigmund Freud, "Character and Anal Eroticism," in *On Sexuality,* ed. Angela Richards, trans. James Strachey (Harmondsworth: Penguin, 1983 [1908]).

44. Francette Pacteau, "The Impossible Referent: Representations of the Androgyne," in *Formations of Fantasy,* ed. Victor Burgin, James Donald, and Cora Kaplan (London: Methuen, 1986).

45. Angela Carter, "Japanese Erotica," in *Nothing Sacred* (London: Virago, 1982).

46. Lea Jacobs, " 'Now, Voyageur': Some Problems of Enunciation," *Camera Obscura* 7 (Spring 1981), p. 91.

47. Lea Jacobs uses the distinction between énoncé and enunciation and their overlapping within the terrain of sexual difference, in " 'Now, Voyageur.' "

48. Mary Ann Doane, "The Clinical Eye: Medical Discourses in the 'Women's Film' of the 1940s," in *The Female Body in Western Culture: Contemporary Perspectives,* ed. Susan Rubin Suleiman (Cambridge: Harvard University Press, 1986).

49. Jacobs, " 'Now, Voyageur,' " p. 96. Jacobs writes: "Charlotte's body [is] an image which allows desire to circulate and thus permits a narrative to take shape. The fetishization of a woman's body is valorized as the precondition of the entrance into the story, and therefore romance. Her body-image is read not only as the doctor's work but as the satisfaction of Charlotte's desire itself. . . . This image caps the Walt Whitman poem, the woman's body becoming the final guarantee that this is the definitive discourse."

50. Ibid., p. 99.

51. Cf. ibid. on this point.

52. Linda Nochlin, "Courbet's 'L'Origin du Monde': The Origin without an Original," *October* 37 (Summer 1986), p. 77.

53. See Hal Foster, *Recodings: Art, Spectacle, Cultural Politics* (Port Townsend, Wash.: Bay Press, 1985), pp. 79–96, for a discussion of postmodern simulation and nostalgia.

54. Jacques Lacan, *The Four Fundamental Concepts of Psychoanalysis,* trans. Alan Sheridan (New York: W. W. Norton and Co., 1981), p. 192.

55. Phyllis Greenacre, "Certain Relationships between Fetishism and Faulty Development of the Body Image," *The Psychoanalytic Study of the Child* 8 (1953).

56. Apter, *Feminizing the Fetish*. Apter writes: "On one level the characterization of the maid signals problems of class structure within literary hierarchy itself—questions concerning textual agency, typology, and stereotype, boundaries holding between 'master narratives' and 'servant texts.' On another level, the strangely suppressed power of the *recit de la bonne* allows for a revisionist reading of the role of the female domestic within Freudian theory; for, as we shall see, though the housemaid enters and exits frequently in Freud's case histories, her role within bourgeois neurosis is barely touched upon. One must look to . . . a ramified 'reading' of domestic fetishism, both in the sense of an interiorized, domesticated psychopathology, and in the sense of a servant-inspired erotic economy expressed through specific laws, codes, and semiobscured or scotomized iconographic insignia" (p. 178).

57. Ibid., p. 180*n*.

58. I'm not persuaded by Freud's rationale for the shoe as a preferred fetish. In "Fetishism" he writes that the shoe is "preserved as a fetish" as it was the last, inciteful, thing seen before seizing upon the forbidden desire to glance up a woman's legs, "towards her genitals." But the object itself is much more than a repository of glances avowed and deferred. Furthermore, along with emphasis on the object should be a discussion of fetish *relations* which would privilege the genealogical movement which elects some objects and not others. The shoe in pornography is a symbolic redundancy, after all: genitals are very visibly there.

59. Metz, "Photography and Fetish," p. 86.

60. Beverley Brown, "A Feminist Interest in Pornography—Some Modest Proposals," *m/f* 5/6 (1981), pp. 6, 7.

61. Jean Baudrillard, *For a Critique of the Political Economy of the Sign*, trans. Charles Levin (St. Louis, Mo.: Telos, 1981), p. 94.

62. Nochlin, "Courbet's 'L'Origin du Monde,' " p. 86.

63. Abigail Solomon-Godeau, "The Legs of the Countess," *October* 39 (Winter 1986), p. 103.

64. Apter, *Feminizing the Fetish*, p. 180*n*.

65. Stephen Heath, "Men in Feminism: Men and Feminist Theory," in *Men in Feminism*, ed. Alice Jardine and Paul Smith (New York: Methuen, 1987), p. 42.

66. Metz, "Photography and Fetish," p. 83.

67. Foster, *Recodings*, p. 79.

68. Ibid., p. 90.

69. Jean Baudrillard, *Simulations*, trans. Paul Foss, Paul Patton, and Philip Beitchman (New York: Semiotext(e), 1983), p. 72.

70. Foster, *Recodings*, p. 83.

71. Ibid., p. 82.

72. Freud, "Fetishism," p. 357.

73. Ibid., p. 354.

74. Pacteau, "The Impossible Referent," p. 78.

5. Jewelry and Lingerie

1. The cover of the July 1988 *Penthouse* has the model smoking a cigarette, an item which still signifies in interesting and metonymic ways. For example, a highly typical plot in the daytime soap involves the "double," usually an evil twin resurrected to confound and disrupt the family romance. The audience is introduced to the evil double (and any sexually loose or immoral female character, for that matter) through a thumbnail sketch; i.e., the camera first focuses on her cigarette (sometimes the spike heel), and we see the character smoking before we know she is actually the evil double. In Walt Disney animated films, the evil stepmother is often found smoking, an image powerful enough to signify to very young children.

In *American Beauty* (New York: Knopf, 1981) Lois Banner notes that by the mid-1850s in New York, prostitutes distinguished themselves from other women by smoking cigarettes because "fashionable women themselves were wearing make-up as well as gaudy attire." The associations between smoking and the slut are, it appears, strong and transcend many media and cultural texts. See also Marjorie Garber, *Vested Interests: Cross-Dressing and Cultural Anxiety* (New York: HarperPerennial, 1993), pp. 156–57, for a discussion of the cigarette and its associations with "virile females" and sexuality.

2. J. C. Flügel, *The Psychology of Clothes* (New York: International Universities Press, 1931), pp. 21, 20.

3. Of course men wear jewelry as well, and have done so across history. The variables of class, age, and sexual orientation figure in the exhibition of the male body. The latter two in particular challenge the strict assignment of femininity to the spectacle. For work on youth cultures and the manipulation of signs, see Dick Hebdige, *Subculture: The Meaning of Style* (London: Routledge, 1985). The point to be emphasized, though, is the specific selection of items for circulation in the pornographic photo. For example, the pearl is a favored jewel and is most certainly worn only by women these days. But it used to be worn by men, and this is one example of its (repressed) ambisexuality.

4. Doris Langley Moore, *The Woman in Fashion* (London: B. T. Batsford, 1949).

5. Blanche Payne, *History of Costume: From the Ancient Egyptians to the Twentieth Century* (New York: Harper and Row, 1965), p. 128.

6. Helen Benton Minnich, *Japanese Costume and the Makers of Its Elegant Tradition* (Rutland, Vt.: Charles E. Tuttle Co., 1963), p. 72.

7. Stella Mary Newton, *The Dress of the Venetians, 1495–1525* (Brookfield, Vt.: Scholar Press, 1988), p. 134.

8. Lois Sherr Dubin, *The History of Beads* (New York: Harry N. Abrams, 1987).

9. Mary Evans, *Costume throughout the Ages* (Philadelphia: J. B. Lippincott, 1930), p. 144; Mab Wilson, *Gems* (New York: The Viking Press, 1967), p. 127. Wilson also notes that "to this day" men in India don necklaces of "manly sized pearls."

10. Elizabeth Burris-Meyer, *This Is Fashion* (New York: Harper and Brothers, 1943), p. 259.

11. Wilson, *Gems*, p. 127.

12. Ibid.

13. In *Vested Interests*, Marjorie Garber notes the sign of the Jew with an earring, by "sartorial fiat," during the Italian Renaissance, complete, as with the prostitute, with rhetorics of pollution. This accompanies the idea of the Jewish male grounded sartorially, "scientifically," and "theoretically" as effeminate (p. 224).

14. In advertisements for birth control pills, a string of pearls is frequently shown.

15. Germaine Greer, *The Female Eunuch* (London: Paladin, 1970).

16. Roland Barthes, "The Striptease," in *Mythologies*, selected and trans. Annette Lavers (New York: Hill and Wang, 1980), p. 86.

17. Ibid.

18. Flügel, *The Psychology of Clothes*, p. 74.

19. See n. 13.

20. The phrase is from the title of Kaja Silverman's 1986 article.

21. Theodore Thass-Thienemann notes that in most languages the hand is feminine while fingers are masculine (pp. 266–74).

22. Janice Winship, "Handling Sex," *Media, Culture and Society* 3:1 (January 1981), reprinted in *Looking On: Images of Femininity in the Visual Arts and Media,* ed. Rosemary Betterton (London: Pandora, 1987).

23. Cf. n. 28 in chap. 4.

24. David Kunzle, *Fashion and Fetishism: A Social History of the Corset, Tight-Lacing and Other Forms of Body-Sculpture in the West* (Totowa, N.J.: Rowman and Littlefield, 1982). See Anne Hollander, "A Tight Squeeze," *The New York Review of Books* (4 March 1982), for a review of Kunzle.

25. Hollander, "A Tight Squeeze," p. 21; Elizabeth Wilson, *Adorned in Dreams: Fashion and Modernity* (London: Virago, 1985).

26. Flügel, *The Psychology of Clothes,* p. 72.

27. Alison Lurie, "Sex and Fashion," *The New York Review of Books* (22 October 1981), p. 38.

28. Ibid.

29. Cf. Thais E. Morgan, "A Whip of One's Own: Dominatrix Pornography and the Construction of a Post-Modern (Female) Subjectivity," *The American Journal of Semiotics* 6:4 (1989).

30. Michael Balint, "A Contribution on Fetishism," *International Journal of Psycho-Analysis* 16 (1935).

31. Sigmund Freud, "On Transformations of Instinct as Exemplified in Anal Eroticism," in *On Sexuality,* ed. Angela Richards, trans. James Strachey (Harmondsworth: Penguin, 1983 [1917]).

32. Balint, "A Contribution on Fetishism," p. 482.

33. Jean Baudrillard, *For a Critique of the Political Economy of the Sign,* trans. Charles Levin (St. Louis, Mo.: Telos, 1981), p. 91.

34. See Laura Kipnis, "(Male) Desire and (Female) Disgust: Reading *Hustler,*" in *Cultural Studies,* ed. Lawrence Grossberg, Cary Nelson, and Paula Treichler (New York: Routledge, 1991).

35. One of the most cunning distinctions among soft-core genres themselves involves the way women are signified, via a formal elaboration of the pornographic technique. For example, *Hustler* often receives more opprobrium from the humanist feminist and conservative contingents than do *Penthouse* and *Playboy.* The subtext of this contempt relates, I believe, to Beverley Brown's contention that within the "more violent protest . . . it is the everyday which is perhaps more galling than the exotic." "A Feminist Interest in Pornography—Some Modest Proposals," *m/f* 5/6 (1981), p. 6. And, *Hustler* is incessantly "everyday": the models are photographed without the benefit of soft lighting, gauzed lenses, or even the airbrushed body. The effect is a harshness, i.e., a greater fidelity to "reality" (the same is true of hard-core, and that genre elicits the greatest outrage.) These women have zits on their asses, greasy hair, runs in their stockings, chipped fingernail polish. They look, in other words, like the "girl next door." By conventional standards they are ordinary, and not at all different. Their more exotic, fantasy-like sisters in *Penthouse* and *Playboy,* whose bodies are airbrushed to near-perfection, are deemed less offensive, more erotic (as opposed to pornographic), more artistic or aesthetic.

36. Janine Chasseguet-Smirgel, "Reflexions on the Connexions between Perversion and Sadism," *International Journal of Psycho-Analysis* 59 (1978).

37. Angela Carter, *The Sadeian Woman* (London: Virago, 1979), p. 4.

38. Linda Williams, "When the Woman Looks," in *Re-Vision: Essays in Feminist Film Criticism,* ed. Mary Ann Doane, Patricia Mellencamp, and Linda Williams (Frederick, Md.: University Publications of America, 1984).

39. Francette Pacteau, "The Impossible Referent: Representations of the Androgyne," in *Formations of Fantasy,* ed. Victor Burgin, James Donald, and Cora Kaplan (London: Methuen, 1986).

40. Rosetta Brooks, "The Body of the Image," *ZG* 10 (Spring 1984), p. 1.

41. Pacteau, "The Impossible Referent."

42. Ibid., p. 78.

43. Jacques M. Chevalier, *Semiotics, Romanticism and the Scriptures* (Berlin: Mouton de Gruyter, 1990).

44. Pacteau, "The Impossible Referent," p. 78.

45. Kaja Silverman, "Fragments of a Fashionable Discourse," in *Studies in Entertainment: Critical Approaches to Mass Culture,* ed. Tania Modleski (Bloomington: Indiana University Press, 1986).

46. Mary Kelly, "Woman-Desire-Image," in *Desire,* ed. Lisa Appighanesi (London: Institute for Contemporary Art, 1984), p. 31.

Conclusion

1. Richard Dyer, "Don't Look Now," *Screen* 23:3–4 (September/October 1982), p. 71.

2. Tom Waugh, "The Third Body: Patterns in the Construction of the Subject in Gay Male Narrative Film," in *Queer Looks: Perspectives on Lesbian and Gay Film and Video,* ed. Martha Gever, John Greyson, and Pratibha Parmar (Toronto: Between the Lines, 1993), p. 142.

3. Leo Bersani, "Is the Rectum a Grave?" In *AIDS: Cultural Analysis, Cultural Activism,* ed. Douglas Crimp (Cambridge: MIT Press, 1989), p. 208.

4. Victor Burgin, *The End of Art Theory: Criticism and Postmodernity* (Atlantic Highlands, N.J.: Humanities Press International, 1986), p. 106.

5. Dyer, "Don't Look Now."

6. Ibid., p. 71.

7. Tom Waugh writes of gay cinema, "Subject and object within the diegesis are often fused, and these roles are dispersed interchangeably among all the bodies within the frame," and "the separation of subject and object is no longer a given, nor is the fixity of observer status, the immutability of difference" ("The Third Body," pp. 153, 157).

8. Dyer, "Don't Look Now," p. 67.

9. J. C. Flügel, *The Psychology of Clothes* (New York: International Universities Press, 1931), pp. 124–25.

10. Stephen Neale, "Masculinity as Spectacle," *Screen* 24:6 (November/December 1983), p. 8.

11. Laura Mulvey, "Visual Pleasure and Narrative Cinema," *Screen* 16:3 (Autumn 1975), p. 12.

12. Jean Baudrillard, *For a Critique of the Political Economy of the Sign,* trans. Charles Levin (St. Louis, Mo.: Telos, 1981), p. 96.

13. Dyer, "Don't Look Now," p. 68.

14. Michael Balint, "A Contribution on Fetishism," *International Journal of Psycho-Analysis* 16 (1935), p. 482.

15. Jean-Joseph Goux, "The Phallus: Masculine Identity and the 'Exchange of Women,' " *differences* 4:1 (1992). See Alice Jardine's brief discussion of Goux in *Gynesis* (Ithaca: Cornell University Press, 1985).

16. *Male Subjectivity at the Margins* (New York and London: Routledge, 1992), p. 346.

Bibliography

Adams, Parveen. "Per Os(cillation)." *m/f* 1 (1978).

———. "Representation and Sexuality." *Camera Obscura* 17 (May 1988).

Althusser, Louis. "Ideology and Ideological State Apparatuses." In Althusser, *Lenin and Philosophy and Other Essays.* New York: New Left Books, 1971.

Anderson, Perry. "Structure and Subject." In Anderson, *In the Tracts of Historical Materialism.* London: Verso, 1983.

Apter, Emily. *Feminizing the Fetish: Psychoanalysis and Narrative Obsession in Turn-of-the-Century France.* Ithaca: Cornell University Press, 1991.

Bak, Robert C. "The Phallic Woman." *The Psychoanalytic Study of the Child* 23 (1968).

Balint, Michael. "A Contribution on Fetishism." *International Journal of Psycho-Analysis* 16 (1935).

Banner, Lois. *American Beauty.* New York: Knopf, 1981.

Barrowclough, Susan. "Not a Love Story." *Screen* 23:5 (November/December 1982).

Barthes, Roland. *Camera Lucida.* Translated by Richard Howard. New York: Hill and Wang, 1981.

———. *The Grain of the Voice.* Translated by Linda Coverdale. New York: Hill and Wang, 1985.

———. *Image-Music-Text.* Essays selected and translated by Stephen Heath. Glasgow: Fontana, 1977.

———. "The Striptease." In Barthes, *Mythologies,* selected and translated by Annette Lavers. New York: Hill and Wang, 1980.

Bataille, Georges. *Visions of Excess: Selected Writings, 1927–1939.* Edited and with an Introduction by Allan Stoekl. Minneapolis: University of Minnesota Press, 1985.

Baudrillard, Jean. "The Ecstasy of Communication." In *The Anti-Aesthetic: Essays on Postmodern Culture,* edited by Hal Foster. Port Townsend, Washington: Bay Press, 1983.

———. *For a Critique of the Political Economy of the Sign.* Translated by Charles Levin. St. Louis, Missouri: Telos, 1981.

———. "Forgetting Foucault." *Humanities in Society* 3:1 (1980).

———. *In the Shadow of the Silent Majorities; or The End of the Social and Other Essays.* New York: Semiotext(e), 1983.

———. *Seduction.* Translated by Brian Singer. Montreal: New World Perspectives, 1990.

———. *Simulations.* Translated by Paul Foss, Paul Patton, and Philip Beitchman. New York: Semiotext(e), 1983.

Benjamin, Walter. "The Work of Art in the Age of Mechanical Reproduction." In *Illu-*

minations, edited by Hannah Arendt, translated by Harry Zohn. London: Jonathan Cape, 1955. Reprinted in *Mass Communication and Society,* edited by James Curran et al. London: Edward Arnold, 1977.

Benn, Tony. "Perfect Body: Perfect Production. The Nudes of Robert Mapplethorpe and Arthur Tress." *Camerawork* (November 1982).

Bensinger, Terralee. "Lesbian Pornography: The Re/Making of (a) Community." *Discourse* 15:1 (Fall 1992).

Berger, John. *Ways of Seeing.* Harmondsworth: British Broadcasting Corporation and Penguin, 1972.

Bergstrom, Janet. "Enunciation and Sexual Difference." *Camera Obscura* 3–4 (Summer 1979).

Bersani, Leo. "Is the Rectum a Grave?" In *AIDS: Cultural Analysis, Cultural Activism,* edited by Douglas Crimp. Cambridge, Massachusetts: MIT Press, 1989.

Betterton, Rosemary, ed. *Looking On: Images of Femininity in the Visual Arts and Media.* London: Pandora, 1987.

Blachford, Gregg. "Looking at Pornography." *Screen Education* 29 (Winter 1978/79).

Bowie, Malcolm. "Jacques Lacan." In *Structuralism and Since: From Levi-Strauss to Derrida,* edited by John Sturrock. Oxford: Oxford University Press, 1982.

Brannigan, Augustine, and Sheldon Goldenberg. "The Study of Aggressive Pornography: The Vicissitudes of Relevance." *Critical Studies in Communication* 4:3 (1987).

Brennan, Teresa. *The Interpretation of the Flesh: Freud and Femininity.* London and New York: Routledge, 1992.

Brooks, Rosetta. "The Body of the Image." *ZG* 10 (Spring 1984).

Brown, Beverley. "A Feminist Interest in Pornography—Some Modest Proposals." *m/f* 5/6 (1981).

Brown, Beverley, and Parveen Adams. "The Feminine Body and Feminist Politics." *m/f* 3 (1979).

Brownmiller, Susan. "Excerpt on Pornography from *Against Our Will: Men, Women and Rape.*" In *Take Back the Night: Women on Pornography,* edited by Laura Lederer. New York: William Morrow and Company, Inc., 1980.

Brunette, Peter, and David Wills. *Screen Play: Derrida and Film Theory.* Princeton, New Jersey: Princeton University Press, 1989.

Burchill, Louise. "Either/Or: Peripeteia of an Alternative in Jean Baudrillard's *de la Seduction.*" In *Seduced and Abandoned: The Baudrillard Scene,* edited by Andre Frankovits. Australia and New York: Stonemoss Services and Semiotext(e), Inc., 1984.

Burgin, Victor. *The End of Art Theory: Criticism and Postmodernity.* Atlantic Highlands, New Jersey: Humanities Press International, 1986.

———. "Photography, Fantasy, Fiction." In Burgin, *Thinking Photography.* London: Macmillan, 1982.

———. "Seeing Sense." In *Language, Image, Media,* edited by Howard Davis and Paul Walton. Oxford: Basil Blackwell, 1983.

Burris-Meyer, Elizabeth. *This Is Fashion.* New York: Harper and Brothers, 1943.

Burstyn, Varda. "Political Precedents and Moral Crusades: Women, Sex and the State" and "Beyond Despair: Positive Strategies." In *Women against Censorship,* edited by Varda Burstyn. Vancouver and Toronto: Douglas and McIntyre, 1985.

Butler, Judith. "The Force of Fantasy: Feminism, Mapplethorpe and Discursive Excess." *differences* 2:2 (1990).

———. *Gender Trouble: Feminism and the Subversion of Identity.* New York: Routledge, 1990.

Cameron, Deborah. *Feminism and Linguistic Theory.* London: Macmillan, 1985.

Carter, Angela. "Japanese Erotica." In Carter, *Nothing Sacred.* London: Virago, 1982.

———. *The Sadeian Woman.* London: Virago, 1979.

Caws, Mary Ann. "Ladies Shot and Painted: Female Embodiment in Surrealist Art." In
The Female Body in Western Culture: Contemporary Perspectives, edited by Susan Rubin Suleiman. Cambridge, Massachusetts: Harvard University Press, 1986.

Chambers, Iain. *Popular Culture: The Metropolitan Experience.* London: Methuen, 1986.

Chasseguet-Smirgel, Janine. "Reflexions on the Connexions between Perversion and Sadism." *International Journal of Psycho-Analysis* 59 (1978).

Chevalier, Jacques M. *Semiotics, Romanticism and the Scriptures.* Berlin: Mouton de
Gruyter, 1990.

Clover, Carol. *Men, Women, and Chain Saws: Gender in the Modern Horror Film.* Princeton, New Jersey: Princeton University Press, 1992.

———. "Regardless of Sex: Men, Women, and Power in Early Northern Europe." *Representations* 44 (Fall 1993).

Cohan, Steve, and Ina Rae Hark, eds. *Screening the Male: Exploring Masculinities in
Hollywood Cinema.* London: Routledge, 1993.

Cousins, Mark, and Athar Hussain. *Michel Foucault.* New York: St. Martin's Press, 1984.

Coward, Rosalind. *Female Desires: How They Are Sought, Bought and Packaged.* New
York: Grove Press, 1985.

———. "Sexual Violence and Sexuality." *Feminist Review* 11 (June 1982).

Coward, Rosalind, and John Ellis. *Language and Materialism: Developments in Semiology
and the Theory of the Subject.* London: Routledge and Kegan Paul, 1977.

Coward, Ros; Yve Lomax; and Kathy Myers. "Behind the Fragments: A Conversation
with Ros Coward, Yve Lomax and Kathy Myers." *Camerawork* (November 1982).

Crimp, Douglas. "The Photographic Activity of Postmodernism." *October* 15 (Winter
1980).

Debord, Guy. *Society of the Spectacle.* Detroit: Black and Red, 1983.

de Lauretis, Teresa. *Alice Doesn't: Feminism, Semiotics, Cinema.* Bloomington: Indiana
University Press, 1984.

———. *Technologies of Gender: Essays on Theory, Film, and Fiction.* Bloomington: Indiana University Press, 1987.

Deleuze, Gilles. *Masochism: Coldness and Cruelty.* Translated by Jean McNeil. New York:
Zone Books, 1991.

Derrida, Jacques. "Plato's Pharmacy." In Derrida, *Dissemination,* translated by Barbara
Johnson. Chicago: University of Chicago Press, 1981.

———. "Structure, Sign, and Play in the Discourse of the Human Sciences." In Derrida, *Writing and Difference.* Chicago: University of Chicago Press, 1978.

Dews, Peter. "The 'Nouvelle Philosophie' and Foucault." *Economy and Society* 8:2 (May
1979).

Diamond, Irene. "Pornography and Repression: A Reconsideration." *Signs* 5:4 (Summer
1980).

Diamond, Irene, and Lee Quinby, eds. *Feminism and Foucault: Reflections on Resistance.*
Boston: Northeastern University Press, 1988.

Doane, Mary Ann. "The Clinical Eye: Medical Discourses in the 'Women's Film' of the
1940s." In *The Female Body in Western Culture: Contemporary Perspectives,* edited

by Susan Rubin Suleiman. Cambridge, Massachusetts: Harvard University Press, 1986.

———. *The Desire to Desire: The Women's Film of the 1940s.* Bloomington: Indiana University Press, 1987.

———. "The 'Woman's Film': Possession and Address." In *Re-Vision: Essays in Feminist Film Criticism,* edited by Mary Ann Doane, Patricia Mellencamp, and Linda Williams. Frederick, Maryland: University Publications of America, 1984.

———. "Woman's Stake: Filming the Female Body." *October* 17 (Summer 1981).

Donnerstein, Edward. "Pornography and Violence against Women." In *Pornography and Censorship,* edited by David Copp and Susan Wendell. New York: Prometheus, 1983.

Dreyfus, Hubert L., and Paul Rabinow. *Michel Foucault: Beyond Structuralism and Hermeneutics.* Sussex: The Harvester Press, 1982.

Dubin, Lois Sherr. *The History of Beads.* New York: Harry N. Abrams, 1987.

Dworkin, Andrea. *Pornography: Men Possessing Women.* New York: Perigree, 1981.

Dyer, Richard. "Don't Look Now." *Screen* 23:3–4 (September/October 1982).

Ehrenreich, Barbara. *The Hearts of Men: American Dreams and the Flight from Commitment.* Garden City, New York: Anchor, 1984.

Ellis, Havelock. *Psychology of Sex.* New York: Emerson Books, 1937.

Ellis, John. "Photography/Pornography/Art/Pornography." *Screen* 21:1 (Spring 1980).

———. *Visible Fictions.* London: Routledge and Kegan Paul, 1981.

Ellis, Kate, et al., eds. *Caught Looking: Feminism, Pornography and Censorship.* New York: Caught Looking, Inc., 1986.

English, Deirdre; Amber Hollibaugh; and Gayle Rubin. "Talking Sex: A Conversation on Sexuality and Feminism." *Socialist Review* 11:4 (July/August 1981).

Evans, Mary. *Costume throughout the Ages.* Philadelphia: J. B. Lippincott, 1930.

Ferguson, Kathy E. *The Man Question: Visions of Subjectivity in Feminist Theory.* Berkeley: University of California Press, 1993.

Flügel, J. C. "Polyphallic Symbolism and the Castration Complex." *International Journal of Psycho-Analysis* 5 (1924).

———. *The Psychology of Clothes.* New York: International Universities Press, 1931.

Formations Collective. *Formations of Pleasure.* London: Routledge and Kegan Paul, 1983.

Foster, Hal. *Recodings: Art, Spectacle, Cultural Politics.* Port Townsend, Washington: Bay Press, 1985.

Foucault, Michel. *The History of Sexuality, Volume 1.* New York: Vintage, 1980.

———. "Introduction." In *Herculine Barbin: Being the Recently Discovered Memoirs of a Nineteenth-Century French Hermaphrodite,* translated by Richard McDougall. New York: Pantheon, 1980.

———. "Michel Foucault, An Interview: Sex, Power and the Politics of Identity." With Bob Gallagher and Alexander Wilson. *The Advocate* (7 August 1984).

———. "The Subject and Power." Afterword in Hubert L. Dreyfus and Paul Rabinow, *Michel Foucault: Beyond Structuralism and Hermeneutics.* Sussex: Harvester, 1982.

Freud, Sigmund. "Beyond the Pleasure Principle." In *A General Selection from the Works of Sigmund Freud,* edited by John Rickman and Charles Brenner. Garden City, New York: Doubleday Anchor Books, 1957 (1920).

———. "Character and Anal Eroticism." In *On Sexuality,* edited by Angela Richards, translated by James Strachey. Harmondsworth: Penguin, 1983 (1908).

———. "A Child Is Being Beaten." In *The Standard Edition of the Complete Psychologi-*

cal Works of Sigmund Freud, vol. 17, translated by James Strachey. London: Hogarth Press, 1968 (1919).

———. "The Dissolution of the Oedipus Complex." In *On Sexuality,* edited by Angela Richards, translated by James Strachey. Harmondsworth: Penguin, 1983 (1924).

———. "Fetishism." In *On Sexuality,* edited by Angela Richards, translated by James Strachey. Harmondsworth: Penguin, 1983 (1927).

———. *The Interpretation of Dreams.* Edited and translated by James Strachey. New York: Avon Books, 1965 (1900).

———. "On Narcissism: An Introduction." In *On Sexuality,* edited by Angela Richards, translated by James Strachey. Harmondsworth: Penguin, 1983 [1914].

———. "On the Sexual Theories of Children." In *On Sexuality,* edited by Angela Richards, translated by James Strachey. Harmondsworth: Penguin, 1983 (1908).

———. "On Transformations of Instinct as Exemplified in Anal Eroticism." In *On Sexuality,* edited by Angela Richards, translated by James Strachey. Harmondsworth: Penguin, 1983 (1917).

———. "Some Psychical Consequences of the Anatomical Distinction between the Sexes." In *On Sexuality,* edited by Angela Richards, translated by James Strachey. Harmondsworth: Penguin, 1983 (1925).

———. "Three Essays on the Theory of Sexuality." In *On Sexuality,* edited by Angela Richards, translated by James Strachey. Harmondsworth: Penguin, 1983 (1905).

Gallop, Jane. *Reading Lacan.* Ithaca: Cornell University Press, 1985.

———. *Thinking through the Body.* New York: Columbia University Press, 1988.

Garber, Marjorie. *Vested Interests: Cross-Dressing and Cultural Anxiety.* New York: HarperPerennial, 1993.

Gilbert, Sandra M. "Costumes of the Mind: Transvestism as Metaphor in Modern Literature." In *Writing and Sexual Difference,* edited by Sandra M. Gilbert. Chicago: University of Chicago Press, 1982.

Girard, René. *To Double Business Bound: Essays on Literature, Mimesis and Anthropology.* Baltimore: Johns Hopkins University Press, 1978.

Goux, Jean-Joseph. "The Phallus: Masculine Identity and the 'Exchange of Women.' " *differences* 4:1 (1992).

Green, Ian. "Malefunction." *Screen* 25:4–5 (July–October 1984).

Greenacre, Phyllis. "Certain Relationships between Fetishism and Faulty Development of the Body Image." *The Psychoanalytic Study of the Child* 8 (1953).

Greer, Germaine. *The Female Eunuch.* London: Paladin, 1970.

Griffin, Susan. *Pornography and Silence: Culture's Revenge against Nature.* New York: Harper and Row, 1981.

Grunberger, Bela. "Some Reflections on the Rat Man." *International Journal of Psycho-Analysis* 47 (1966).

Gubar, Susan. "Representing Pornography: Feminism, Criticism and Depictions of Female Violation." *Critical Inquiry* 13 (Summer 1987).

Gubar, Susan, and Joan Hoff, eds. *For Adult Users Only: The Dilemma of Violent Pornography.* Bloomington: Indiana University Press, 1989.

Hall, Stuart. "Recent Developments in Theories of Language and Ideology: A Critical Note." In *Culture, Media, Language,* edited by Stuart Hall et al. London: Hutchinson, 1981.

Heath, Stephen. "Difference." *Screen* 19:3 (Autumn 1978).

———. "Men in Feminism: Men and Feminist Theory." In *Men in Feminism,* edited by Alice Jardine and Paul Smith. New York: Methuen, 1987.

———. "On Suture." In Heath, *Questions of Cinema.* Bloomington: Indiana University Press, 1981.

———. *The Sexual Fix.* London: Macmillan, 1982.

Hebdige, Dick. *Subculture: The Meaning of Style.* London: Routledge, 1985.

Heidegger, Martin. "The Age of the World Picture." In Heidegger, *The Question concerning Technology and Other Essays.* New York: Harper Colophon Books, 1977 (1955).

Henderson, Lisa. "Lesbian Pornography: Cultural Transgression and Sexual Demystification." In *New Lesbian Criticism: Literary and Cultural Readings,* edited and introduced by Sally Munt. New York: Columbia University Press, 1992.

Henriques, Julien, et al., eds. *Changing the Subject: Psychology, Social Regulation and Subjectivity.* London: Methuen, 1984.

Hollander, Anne. "A Tight Squeeze." *The New York Review of Books* (4 March 1982).

Hutcheon, Linda. "The Post-Modern Erotic." Presented at the "Semiotics of Eroticism" conference sponsored by the Toronto Semiotic Circle and the International Summer Institute for Semiotic and Structural Studies, 13 June 1987.

Ion, Sam. *Dear Sam: Advice to the Working Woman.* Toronto: Personal Library Publishers, 1980.

Irigaray, Luce. *Speculum of the Other Woman.* Translated by Gillian C. Gill. Ithaca: Cornell University Press, 1986.

———. *This Sex Which Is Not One.* Translated by Catherine C. Porter with Carolyn Burke. Ithaca: Cornell University Press, 1985.

Jacobs, Lea. " 'Now, Voyageur': Some Problems of Enunciation." *Camera Obscura* 7 (Spring 1981).

Jameson, Fredric. "Imaginary and Symbolic in Lacan: Marxism, Psychoanalytic Criticism and the Problem of the Subject." *Yale French Studies* 55/56 (1977).

———. "Postmodernism, or The Cultural Logic of Late Capitalism." *New Left Review* 146 (July–August 1984).

Jardine, Alice A. *Gynesis: Configurations of Woman and Modernity.* Ithaca: Cornell University Press, 1985.

Kaite, Berkeley. "Reading the Body Textual: The Shoe and Fetish Relations in Soft and Hard-Core." *American Journal of Semiotics* 6:4 (1989).

Kallen, Richard A., and Robert D. Brooks. "The Playmate of the Month: Naked but Nice." *Journal of Popular Culture* 8:2 (Fall 1974).

Kaplan, E. Ann. *Women and Film: Both Sides of the Camera.* New York: Methuen, 1983.

Kappeler, Susanne. *The Pornography of Representation.* Minneapolis: The University of Minnesota Press, 1986.

Kelly, Mary. "Woman-Desire-Image." In *Desire,* edited by Lisa Appighanesi. London: Institute for Contemporary Art, 1984.

Kipnis, Laura. "(Male) Desire and (Female) Disgust: Reading *Hustler.*" In *Cultural Studies,* edited by Lawrence Grossberg, Cary Nelson, and Paula Treichler. New York: Routledge, 1991.

———. "She-Male Fantasies and the Aesthetics of Pornography." In *Dirty Looks: Women, Pornography, Power,* edited by Pamela Church Gibson and Roma Gibson. London: British Film Institute, 1993.

Koch, Gertrud. "The Body's Shadow Realm." In *Dirty Looks: Women, Pornography, Power,* edited by Pamela Church Gibson and Roma Gibson. London: British Film Institute, 1993.

Krauss, Rosalind. "Corpus Delicti." *October* 33 (Summer 1985).

Kuhn, Annette. *The Power of the Image: Essays on Representation and Sexuality.* London: Routledge and Kegan Paul, 1985.

———. *Women's Pictures: Feminism and Cinema.* London: Routledge and Kegan Paul, 1982.

Kunzle, David. *Fashion and Fetishism: A Social History of the Corset, Tight-Lacing and Other Forms of Body-Sculpture in the West.* Totowa, New Jersey: Rowman and Littlefield, 1982.

Kutchinsky, Beryl. "The Effects of Easy Availability of Pornography on the Incidence of Sex Crimes: The Danish Experience." *Journal of Social Issues* 29 (1973).

Lacan, Jacques. *Ecrits: A Selection.* Translated by Alan Sheridan. New York: W. W. Norton and Company, 1977.

———. *The Four Fundamental Concepts of Psychoanalysis.* Translated by Alan Sheridan. New York: W. W. Norton and Company, 1981.

Laqueur, Thomas. *Making Sex: Body and Gender From the Greeks to Freud.* Cambridge: Harvard University Press, 1992.

Lederer, Laura, ed. *Take Back the Night: Women on Pornography.* New York: William Morrow and Company, 1980.

Lemaire, Anika. *Jacques Lacan.* Translated by David Macey. London: Routledge and Kegan Paul, 1977.

Lihn, Henry. "Fetishism: A Case Report." *International Journal of Psycho-Analysis* 51 (1970).

Linker, Kate. "From Imitation to the Copy to Just Effect: On Reading Jean Baudrillard." *Art Forum* 22:8 (April 1984).

———. "Representation and Sexuality." In *Art after Modernism,* edited by Brian Wallis. New York: New Museum of Contemporary Art, 1984.

Lovelace, Linda. *Ordeal.* New York: Berkley Books, 1981.

Lurie, Alison. *The Language of Clothes.* New York: Random House, 1982.

———. "Sex and Fashion." *The New York Review of Books* (22 October 1981).

Lurie, Susan. "The Construction of the Castrated Woman in Psychoanalysis and Cinema." *Discourse* 4 (Winter 1981/82).

Marcus, Steven. *The Other Victorians: A Study of Sexuality and Pornography in Mid-Nineteenth-Century England.* London: Weidenfeld and Nicholson, 1974.

Marx, Karl. *Capital,* vol. 1. Edited by Frederick Engels. New York: International Publishers, 1977 (1887).

———. *The German Ideology.* Edited by C. J. Arthur. Translated by Samuel Moore and Edward Aveling. New York: International Publishers, 1970 (1846).

McClintock, Ann. "Gonad the Barbarian and the Venus Flytrap: Portraying the Female and Male Orgasm." In *Sex Exposed: Sexuality and the Pornography Debate,* edited by Lynne Segal and Mary McIntosh. New Brunswick, New Jersey: Rutgers University Press, 1993.

McCormack, Thelma. "Making Sense of the Research on Pornography." In *Women against Censorship,* edited by Varda Burstyn. Vancouver: Douglas and McIntyre, 1985.

Mercer, Colin. "A Poverty of Desire: Pleasure and Popular Politics." In *Formations of Pleasure,* edited by the Formations Collective. London: Routledge, 1983.

Mercer, Kobena. "Just Looking for Trouble: Robert Mapplethorpe and Fantasies of Race." In *Sex Exposed: Sexuality and the Pornography Debate,* edited by Lynne Segal and Mary McIntosh. New Brunswick, New Jersey: Rutgers University Press, 1993.

Metz, Christian. "The Imaginary Signifier." *Screen* 16:2 (Summer 1975).

———. "Photography and Fetish." *October* 34 (Fall 1985).

Miles, Margaret R. "The Virgin's One Bare Breast: Female Nudity and Religious Meaning in Tuscan Early Renaissance Culture." In *The Female Body in Western Culture: Contemporary Perspectives,* edited by Susan Rubin Suleiman. Cambridge, Massachusetts: Harvard University Press, 1986.

Miller, Jacques-Alain. "Suture (Elements of the Logic of the Signifier)." *Screen* 18:4 (Winter 1977/78).

Miller, Nancy K. *Getting Personal.* New York: Routledge, 1991.

Millot, Catherine. *Horsexe.* New York: Autonomedia, 1990.

Minnich, Helen Benton. *Japanese Costume and the Makers of Its Elegant Tradition.* Rutland, Vermont: Charles E. Tuttle Company, 1963.

Mitchell, Juliet, and Jacqueline Rose, eds. *Feminine Sexuality: Jacques Lacan and the École Freudienne.* London: Macmillan, 1982.

Moi, Toril. *Sexual/Textual Politics: Feminist Literary Theory.* London: Methuen, 1985.

Moore, Doris Langley. *The Woman in Fashion.* London: B. T. Batsford, 1949.

Morgan, Robin. "Theory and Practice: Pornography and Rape." In *Take Back The Night: Women on Pornography,* edited by Laura Lederer. New York: William Morrow, 1980.

Morgan, Thais E. "A Whip of One's Own: Dominatrix Pornography and the Construction of a Post-Modern (Female) Subjectivity." *The American Journal of Semiotics* 6:4 (1989).

Morley, Dave. "Texts, Readers, Subjects." In *Culture, Media, Language,* edited by Stuart Hall et al. London: Hutchinson, 1981.

Mort, Frank. "The Domain of the Sexual." *Screen Education* 36 (Autumn 1980).

———. "Sex, Signification and Pleasure." In *Formations of Pleasure,* edited by the Formations Collective. London: Routledge and Kegan Paul, 1983.

Moye, Andy. "Pornography." In *The Sexuality of Men,* edited by Andy Metcalfe and Martin Humphries. London: Pluto Press, 1985.

Mulvey, Laura. "Afterthoughts on 'Visual Pleasure and Narrative Cinema' Inspired by 'Duel in the Sun.' " *Framework* 15–17 (1981).

———. "Visual Pleasure and Narrative Cinema." *Screen* 16:3 (Autumn 1975).

Myers, Kathy. "Fashion 'n' Passion." *Screen* 23:3–4 (September/October 1982).

———. "Towards a Feminist Erotica." *Camerawork* 24 (March 1982). Reprinted in *Looking On: Images of Femininity in the Visual Arts and Media,* edited by Rosemary Betterton. London: Pandora, 1987.

Nead, Lynda. *The Female Nude: Art, Obscenity and Sexuality.* London: Routledge, 1992.

Neale, Steve. "Masculinity as Spectacle." *Screen* 24:6 (November/December 1983).

Newton, Stella Mary. *The Dress of the Venetians, 1495–1525.* Brookfield, Vermont: Scholar Press, 1988.

Nochlin, Linda. "Courbet's 'L'Origin du Monde': The Origin without an Original." *October* 37 (Summer 1986).

———. "Eroticism and Female Imagery in Nineteenth Century Art." In *Woman as Sex*

Object: Studies in Erotic Art, 1730–1970, edited by Thomas B. Hess and Linda
   Nochlin. London: Allen Lane, 1973.
Norris, Christopher. *Deconstruction: Theory and Practice.* London: Methuen, 1982.
Ostrander, Greg. "Foucault's Disappearing Body." *Canadian Journal of Political and
   Social Theory* 11:1–2 (Spring 1987).
Oudart, Jean-Pierre. "Cinema and Suture." *Screen* 18:4 (1977/78).
Pacteau, Francette. "The Impossible Referent: Representations of the Androgyne." In
   Formations of Fantasy, edited by Victor Burgin, James Donald, and Cora Kaplan.
   London: Methuen, 1986.
Paden, Roger. "On the Discourse of Pornography." *Philosophy and Social Criticism* 1:10
   (Summer 1984).
Pajaczkowska, Claire. "The Heterosexual Presumption: A Contribution to the Debate
   on Pornography." *Screen* 22:1 (1981).
Partridge, Eric. *The Dictionary of Historical Slang.* Harmondsworth: Penguin, 1972.
Patton, Cindy. "Hegemony and Orgasm—Or the Instability of Heterosexual Pornogra-
   phy." *Screen* 30:1 and 2 (Winter/Spring 1989).
Payne, Blanche. *History of Costume: From the Ancient Egyptians to the Twentieth Century.*
   New York: Harper and Row, 1965.
Penley, Constance. " 'A Certain Refusal of Difference': Feminism and Film Theory." In
   Art after Modernism, edited by Brian Wallis. New York: New Museum of Contem-
   porary Art, 1984.
Probert, Christina. *Shoes in Vogue since 1910.* New York: Abbeville Publishers, 1981.
Renov, Michael. "From Fetish to Subject: The Containment of Sexual Difference in
   Hollywood's Wartime Cinema." *Wide Angle* 5:1 (1982).
Ricci, N. P. "The End/s of Woman." *Canadian Journal of Political and Social Theory*
   11:3 (Autumn 1987).
Rich, B. Ruby. "Anti-Porn: Soft Issue, Hard World." *Feminist Review* 3 (Spring 1983).
Ridington, Jillian. "Discussion Paper on Pornography." Prepared for the National Ac-
   tion Committee on the Status of Women, March 1983.
Rodowick, D. N. "The Difficulty of Difference." *Wide Angle* 5:1 (1982).
———. *The Difficulty of Difference: Psychoanalysis, Sexual Difference and Film Theory.*
   New York and London: Routledge, 1991.
———. "Vision, Desire and the Film Text." *Camera Obscura* 6 (1980).
Rose, Jacqueline. "Femininity and Its Discontents." *Feminist Review* 14 (June 1983).
———. "The Imaginary." In Rose, *Sexuality in the Field of Vision.* London: Verso, 1986.
———. "Introduction II." In *Feminine Sexuality: Jacques Lacan and the Ecole Freudi-
   enne,* edited by Juliet Mitchell and Jacqueline Rose. London: Macmillan, 1982.
Ross, Andrew. *No Respect: Intellectuals and Popular Culture.* New York: Routledge,
   1989.
Rossi, William A. *The Sex Life of the Foot and Shoe.* London: Routledge and Kegan Paul,
   1977.
Samois Collective. *Coming to Power: Writings and Graphics on Lesbian S/M.* Boston:
   Alyson Publishing, Inc., 1982.
Saper, Craig. "A Nervous Theory: The Troubling Gaze of Psychoanalysis in Media Stud-
   ies." *Diacritics* 21:4 (Winter 1991).
Saussure, Ferdinand de. *Course in General Linguistics.* London: Fontana, 1974.
Sawicki, Jana. *Disciplining Foucault: Feminism, Power and the Body.* New York: Rout-
   ledge, 1991.

Segal, Lynne. *Is the Future Female? Troubled Thoughts on Contemporary Feminism*. London: Virago, 1987.

———. "Sweet Sorrows, Painful Pleasures: Pornography and the Perils of Heterosexual Desire." In *Sex Exposed: Sexuality and the Pornography Debate*, edited by Lynne Segal and Mary McIntosh. New Brunswick, New Jersey: Rutgers University Press, 1993.

Silverman, Kaja. *The Acoustic Mirror: The Female Voice in Psychoanalysis and Cinema*. Bloomington: Indiana University Press, 1988.

———. "Fassbinder and Lacan: A Reconsideration of Gaze, Look, and Image." *Camera Obscura* 19 (1989).

———. "Fragments of a Fashionable Discourse." In *Studies in Entertainment: Critical Approaches to Mass Culture*, edited by Tania Modleski. Bloomington: Indiana University Press, 1986.

———. "Male Masochism and Subjectivity." Presented at the "Semiotics of Eroticism" conference sponsored by the Toronto Semiotic Circle and the Summer Institute for Semiotic and Structural Studies, 13 June 1987.

———. *Male Subjectivity at the Margins*. New York and London: Routledge, 1992.

———. "Masochism and Male Subjectivity." *Camera Obscura* 17 (May 1988).

———. "Masochism and Subjectivity." *Framework* 12 (Winter 1979).

———. *The Subject of Semiotics*. New York: Oxford University Press, 1983.

Singer, Brian. "Baudrillard's Seduction." *Canadian Journal of Political and Social Theory* 15:1–2 and 3 (1991).

Smith, Paul. "Men in Feminism: Men and Feminist Theory." In *Men in Feminism*, edited by Alice Jardine and Paul Smith. New York: Methuen, 1987.

Solomon-Godeau, Abigail. "The Legs of the Countess." *October* 39 (Winter 1986).

———. "Winning the Game When the Rules Have Been Changed: Art Photography and Postmodernism." *Screen* 25:6 (November/December 1984).

Sontag, Susan. *On Photography*. New York: Delta, 1977.

———. "The Pornographic Imagination." In Sontag, *Styles of Radical Will*. New York: Farrar, Strauss and Giroux, 1976.

Spivak, Gayatri. *Outside in the Teaching Machine*. New York and London: Routledge, 1993.

Steele, Valerie. *Fashion and Eroticism: Ideals of Feminine Beauty from the Victorian Era to the Jazz Age*. New York: Oxford, 1985.

Steinem, Gloria. "Erotica and Pornography: A Clear and Present Difference." In *Take Back the Night: Women on Pornography*, edited by Laura Lederer. New York: William Morrow, 1980.

Stern, Lesley. "The Body as Evidence." *Screen* 23:5 (November/December 1982).

Stoller, Robert J. *Observing the Erotic Imagination*. New Haven: Yale University Press, 1980.

Straayer, Chris. "The She-man: Postmodern Bi-sexed Performance in Film and Video." *Screen* 31:3 (Autumn 1990).

Studlar, Gaylyn. *In the Realm of Pleasure: von Sternberg, Dietrich, and the Masochistic Aesthetic*. Urbana and Chicago: University of Illinois Press, 1988.

Sturrock, John. "Introduction." In Sturrock, ed., *Structuralism and Since: From Levi-Strauss to Derrida*. New York: Oxford University Press, 1979.

Suleiman, Susan Rubin. "(Re)Writing the Body: The Politics and Poetics of Female Eroticism." In *The Female Body in Western Culture: Contemporary Perspectives*, edited by Susan Rubin Suleiman. Cambridge, Massachusetts: Harvard University Press, 1986.

Thass-Thienemann, Theodore. *Symbolic Behavior.* New York: Washington Square Press, 1968.

Toomey, Elizabeth. "Paris Shoes Have Pointed Heel and Toe." *Toronto Globe and Mail* (28 December 1953).

Vance, Carole S. "Pleasure and Danger: Toward a Politics of Sexuality." In *Pleasure and Danger: Exploring Female Sexuality,* edited by Carole S. Vance. Boston: Routledge and Kegan Paul, 1984.

Vance, Carole S., and Ann Barr Snitow. "Toward a Conversation about Sex in Feminism: A Modest Proposal." *Signs* 10:11 (Autumn 1984).

Waugh, Tom. "The Third Body: Patterns in the Construction of the Subject in Gay Male Narrative Film." In *Queer Looks: Perspectives on Lesbian and Gay Film and Video,* edited by Martha Gever, John Greyson, and Pratibha Parmar. Toronto: Between the Lines, 1993.

Weedon, Chris. *Feminist Practice and Poststructuralist Theory.* Oxford: Basil Blackwell, 1987.

Weedon, Chris; Andrew Tolson; and Frank Mort. "Theories of Language and Subjectivity." In *Culture, Media, Language,* edited by Stuart Hall et al. London: Hutchinson, 1981.

Willemen, Paul. "Letter to John." *Screen* 21:2 (Summer 1980).

Williams, Linda. "Film Body: An Implantation of Perversions." *Cinétracts* 8:4 (Winter 1981).

———. *Hard Core: Power, Pleasure and the "Frenzy of the Visible."* Berkeley: University of California Press, 1989.

———. "Hard Core Pornographic Films." Paper presented to the Society of Cinema Studies, 1986.

———. "Pre-history, Power, Pleasure and the Feminine Film Body." Unpublished manuscript, 1986.

———. "Second Thoughts on *Hard Core:* American Obscenity Law and the Scapegoating of Deviance." In *Dirty Looks: Women, Pornography, Power,* edited by Pamela Church Gibson and Roma Gibson. London: British Film Institute, 1993.

———. "When the Woman Looks." In *Re-Vision: Essays in Feminist Film Criticism,* edited by Mary Ann Doane, Patricia Mellencamp, and Linda Williams. Frederick, Maryland: University Publications of America, 1984.

Williamson, Judith. *Consuming Passions: The Dynamics of Popular Culture.* London: Marion Boyars, 1986.

———. "Woman Is an Island: Femininity and Colonization." In *Studies in Entertainment: Critical Approaches to Mass Culture,* edited by Tania Modleski. Bloomington: Indiana University Press, 1986.

Wilson, Elizabeth. *Adorned in Dreams: Fashion and Modernity.* London: Virago, 1985.

———. *What Is to Be Done about Violence against Women?* Harmondsworth: Penguin, 1983.

Wilson, Mab. *Gems.* New York: The Viking Press, 1967.

Winship, Janice. "Handling Sex." *Media, Culture and Society* 3:1 (January 1981).

Winterson, Jeanette. *Written on the Body.* Toronto: Vintage, 1993.

Wolff, Janet. *Aesthetics and the Sociology of Art.* London: George Allen and Unwin, 1983.

———. *The Social Production of Art.* London: Macmillan, 1981.

Wright, Lee. "Objectifying Gender: The Stiletto Heel." In *A View from the Interior: Feminism, Women and Design,* edited by Judy Attfield and Pat Kirkham. London: The Woman's Press, 1989.

Young, Robert. "The Same Difference." *Screen* 28:3 (Summer 1987).

Zenoni, Alfredo. "Metaphor and Metonymy in Lacanian Theory." *Enclitic* 5:1 (Spring 1981).

Zillman, Dolf, and Jennings Bryant. "Pornography, Sexual Callousness, and the Trivialization of Rape." *Journal of Communication* 32:4 (Autumn 1982).

Index

BERKELEY KAITE is Assistant Professor in the Graduate Program in Communications at McGill University, Montreal, Canada.

Lightning Source UK Ltd.
Milton Keynes UK
UKOW041149251012

201158UK00001BA/70/A